WHY CAN'T THEY GET ALONG?

A conversation between a Muslim, a Jew and a Christian

Dawoud El-Alami
Dan Cohn-Sherbok
George D. Chryssides

LION

The right of George D. Chryssides, Dan Cohn-Sherbok, and Dawoud El-Alami to be identified as the author of this work has been asserted by them in accordance with the Copyright, Designs and Patents Act 1988.

Published by Lion Books
an imprint of
Lion Hudson plc
Wilkinson House, Jordan Hill Road,
Oxford OX2 8DR, England
www.lionhudson.com/lion

ISBN 978 0 7459 5605 3
e-ISBN 978 0 7459 5756 2

First edition 2014

Acknowledgments
Extracts from the Qur'an: Saheeh International, *The Qur'an: English Meanings and Notes*, Riyadh: Al-Muntada Al-Islami Trust, 2001-2011; Jeddah: Dar Abul-Qasim 1997-2001.

Extract pp. 156–57 taken from Peter Vardy, Good and Bad Religion, SCM Press 2010 © Peter Vardy. Used by permission of Hymns Ancient & Modern Ltd.

Cover image © Sebastien Desarmaux / GODONG/Godong/Corbis

A catalogue record for this book is available from the British Library

Printed and bound in the UK

The contributors' candid and critical trialogue about their respective religious beliefs and traditions shows that whether they agree or disagree, and they do both, they can indeed get along.

HRH Princess Badiya of Jordan

This is a profoundly helpful and timely book. It offers a model of what respectful dialogue between the Abrahamic faiths can reveal and in so doing removes popular misunderstandings and confusions and lifts the conversation onto an honest evaluation of difference and complementarity. The practical focus on how believers from all three faiths address life questions and make moral decisions and judgments is also really useful. The authors' faith commitments give the book a key ingredient: lived expertise and humility in the face of what they try to present to us. This is a book that every leader of a faith community ought to read and be able to commend.

The Very Reverend Adrian Dorber, Dean of Lichfield

This absorbing book… is a model of a new type of interfaith dialogue no longer afraid to confront where and why the three Abrahamic faiths part company. It could well prove humanity's best, if not only, hope of peacefully resolving some of its oldest and most intractable conflicts.

Professor David Conway, Visiting Senior Research Fellow at Civitas, Institute for the Study of Civil Society

This open and honest book confirms my conviction developed over many years that humane and responsive practitioners of different religions have more in common with each other than they do with the rigid literalists of their own religion. A Jew, a Christian and a Muslim, each learned in their own faith, eloquently outline the beliefs of their tradition, illustrate how much they share, and where they differ point out those differences with the courtesy and respect that has to be the precondition of any serious interfaith dialogue.

Rabbi Dr David J. Goldberg OBE, Emeritus Rabbi, The Liberal Jewish Synagogue, London

A most illuminating and unparalleled introduction to the complexities and rewards of genuine interfaith dialogue. The richness and uniqueness of this book lies in how the authors – from their vastly different and distinctive c~~_____~~ _____ ____ ___ ____ _____ of personal and mature reflection – ~~__~~ ct that must surely persuade the reader of the need for understanding and tolerance towards the beliefs and sensitivities of all those who share the heritage of Abraham. An authoritative, yet most accessible, distillation of what can unite but also what can separate the "peoples of the book".

Professor Martin O'Kane, University of Wales Trinity Saint David

El-Alami, Cohn-Sherbok, and Chryssides have produced a genuine inter-religious conversation, providing the reader with a delightful Abrahamic encounter. This book consists of a series of honest dialogues between a Jew, Christian, and Muslim, which result in an engaging narrative of co-existence.

Dr Edward Kessler MBE, Founder Director, Woolf Institute, Cambridge

In the twenty-first century, religious conflict and extremism continues to result in violence and destruction despite all three of the Abrahamic faiths calling for peace, pluralism, and co-existence. This timely book is essential reading in emphasising the importance of honest and constructive dialogue between Jews, Muslims, and Christians and in highlighting that as human beings, there is far more that unites us than divides us.

Sara Khan, Director, Inspire

Why Can't They Get Along is an invaluable text for undergraduate religious studies. It is generally valuable in providing students with the example of interfaith dialogue, demonstrating how one can discuss controversial issues in a respectful manner whilst maintaining the integrity of one's faith position.

It is specifically valuable for undergraduate students as an exploration of the methodology of interfaith dialogue, and as an insight to the details of the position of each faith on featured topics.

Rather than just going over the old ground of controversy, there are attempts by these experienced scholars, who have some understanding of each other's traditions, to offer solutions to the historical impasse.

Dr Deirdre Burke, Religious Studies, University of Wolverhampton

This is a model of what dialogue should be: spelling out overlaps and differences, while taking both seriously. Best of all, the authors attend to detail. We are not "all going the same way", yet we have much to love and much to grapple with in what seem to be roughly equal proportions. Both the loving and the grappling must continue in this vein.

The Very Reverend Christopher Lewis, Dean of Christ Church, Oxford

CONTENTS

FOREWORD

Ignorance of other people's religious beliefs and practices is a cause of much misunderstanding and dangerous prejudice and may embitter communal tensions. This timely book gives a clear summary of the teachings of Judaism, Christianity, and Islam and of the way of life that is expected of their respective followers; by juxtaposing them it makes it easy to see where they agree and where they disagree.

Each of the three authors – Professor Dan Cohn-Sherbok, Dr George D. Chryssides, and Dr Dawoud Sudqi El-Alami – has long experience of teaching and writing about his own religion and has studied other religions. They are, therefore, very well qualified to show where the three religions converge and diverge.

Sometimes, when members of different faiths meet and converse, out of politeness and fear of offence, they avoid contentious subjects. Where, however, there is genuine friendship and trust, asking difficult questions helps one to learn more about what another person really believes. At the same time, answering the other's questions encourages one to reflect more carefully on one's own religious path and to see more clearly what is essential to it and what is culturally conditioned – and the contributors to this book are not afraid to question their own religion as well as the religions of their colleagues.

The authors are all aware of the challenges that modern attitudes pose to the traditional teaching of each religion – for example, in terms of sexual behaviour, the ritual slaughter of animals, or blasphemy laws. They also grapple with the bitter memories of past antagonism, for example of Christian anti-Semitism, and the contemporary hostility of many Israelis and Palestinians. At the same time, they emphasize the importance of people of faith working together for peace and justice, relief for the poor, and respect for the environment, but recognize that effective cooperation requires both honesty and trust.

Individual readers will be both informed and challenged by this book and interfaith groups stimulated to explore sensitive topics that they have so far avoided.

Marcus Braybrooke (Revd Dr)
President of the World Congress of Faiths,
Co-Founder of the Three Faiths Forum

PREFACE

Jews, Christians, and Muslims have often been in conflict in human history. In what follows we attempt to bring out some of the sources of conflict and disagreement, and to discuss them frankly.

The book is divided into four broad sections – theology, religious practice, ethics and lifestyle, and societal issues. Within these divisions there are a further four sub-themes, reflecting issues on which the three religions are often divided. We have taken turns to start the ball rolling, trying to make sure that it is not the same person who always has the last word. The various issues are interrelated, and it is inevitable that some of the discussion at times spills over into other topics. We have tried to keep the discussion as focused as possible, however. Sometimes it may seem that we are ignoring each other's points where someone went beyond the set theme. However, we have endeavoured to ensure that points don't get lost, and readers should find that, if something does not get taken up immediately, the response can be found further on in the book. We have tried to ensure that our criticisms of each other's religions have been taken seriously, and not simply ignored them when the discussion gets difficult.

One of the problems in writing a book like this is that each follower of a religion has his or her own distinctive stance on the kinds of issues that we are discussing here. It would be wrong of us to write as if we were all truly perfect and traditional believers in our respective faiths. To be honest, everyone is to some degree a bad practitioner of their religion and holds views that are not always endorsed by one's fellow believers. We have therefore tried to indicate that there are different viewpoints within our faiths, while at the same time revealing our own views on these topics, and trying to make clear which are which. At times individual believers can hold idiosyncratic views that might raise eyebrows within their communities. Where we have felt that we may be out on a limb, we have refrained from putting forward views that might be misleading as representations of our faiths – but this has happened only rarely.

A WORD FROM THE AUTHORS

In engaging in the ensuing discussion, we are aware that there are many forms of Judaism, Christianity, and Islam. In the case of Christianity, one estimate suggests that there are 44,000 different Christian denominations; the World Council of Churches embraces around 350 of them. Clearly, we cannot speak on behalf of every believer, or even for our own traditions or denominations.

In what follows, we speak with our own voices although, where appropriate, we have indicated that a range of opinion exists within our respective faiths. We appreciate that there will be readers in our various traditions who would defend their faiths differently in a dialogue like this. We respect their views, but we hope at least that they will find it interesting to hear how different members of their faith traditions offer different insights and perspectives.

On a number of issues it has simply not been possible to discuss ranges of opinion in much depth. Even seemingly simple questions such as what makes someone a Christian, a Jew, or a Muslim, which books are in the Bible, or what prophecy is, can generate enormously varied answers. For readers who wish to explore matters in more depth, we have set out a short list of books for possible further reading at the end.

ABOUT THE AUTHORS

DAN COHN-SHERBOK

My great grandfathers were immigrants to the United States from Hungary at the end of the nineteenth century. Initially the family lived on the East Side of New York City; one of my grandfathers was a kosher butcher, and I have a photograph of him standing in front of his shop. After my maternal grandmother married my grandfather, who worked initially as a cigar-roller, they moved to Denver, Colorado. He worked there as a clothing salesman, and the family belonged to a modern Orthodox synagogue. My father, an orthopaedic surgeon, came to do medical research at the National Jewish Hospital in Denver, and met and married my mother. They joined a large Reform Jewish temple where I had a *bar mitzvah* and was confirmed. I went to a typical American high school, and then studied philosophy at a small, all-male, liberal arts college, Williams College, in Massachusetts.

From a young age I wanted to be a Reform rabbi, and I subsequently was a student at the Hebrew Union College-Jewish Institute of Religion, the largest Reform seminary in the world. During the five years I was there I studied biblical and rabbinic Hebrew, Aramaic, Hebrew Bible, Midrash, Mishnah, Talmud as well as other related subjects. I also served small congregations as a student rabbi in Jasper, Alabama; Galesburg, Illinois; Harrisburg, Pennsylvania; Boulder, Colorado; and Denver, Colorado. After ordination I was a rabbi in Melbourne, Australia before embarking on a PhD at Cambridge University. During these years I also served as a rabbi at West London Synagogue, and in Johannesburg, South Africa. These rabbinic experiences, however, convinced me that I am more suitable to academic life, and in 1975 I became a lecturer in theology at the University of Kent; subsequently I became Professor of Judaism at the University of Wales where I am now an Emeritus Professor. Over the years I became increasingly interested in interfaith encounter and dialogue, and I have written a number of books dealing with this subject, including *Judaism and Other Faiths*. I also edited several books concerned with world religions, including *Islam in a World of Diverse Faiths*, and *World Religions and Human Liberation*.

Judaism has always been central in my life. In this connection I should say something about the notion of Jewish identity. Unlike Christianity and Islam, Jewishness is determined not primarily by belief but by ethnic descent (although it is also possible to convert to the Jewish faith). According to tradition, a person is Jewish if that individual's mother is Jewish – in other words, Jewish identity is based on maternal descent. In modern times, various branches of non-Orthodox Judaism have redefined this criterion to include patrilineal descent as well. Yet, even with such flexibility, Jewishness is perceived as a form of inherited ethnic identification. Ever since I was a child, I have seen myself as Jewish in this sense. In addition, I am loyal to Reform Judaism. From its origins in the nineteenth century, this branch of the faith – which is the largest worldwide – has championed prophetic ideals as found in scripture and is also open to change and development based on modern knowledge. It is, I believe, the most reasonable and sensible form of Judaism – ideally suited to the modern world. As far as Christianity and Islam are concerned, although I admire Jesus' and Muhammad's moral teachings, I reject the theology of both religions. I do not believe that Jesus is God incarnate, nor that the Qur'an is God's revelation to Muhammad.

GEORGE D. CHRYSSIDES

I was baptized as a baby in the Church of Scotland, and attended Sunday school and, later, youth organizations in a somewhat conservative evangelical church in Glasgow. Although I later came to reject Christian fundamentalism, I came to know my Bible really well, and decided to train for the ministry in the Church of Scotland. In order to do this, I studied philosophy at the University of Glasgow, and then "divinity", as it was called: this included the various "churchy" subjects such as Old Testament, New Testament, Church History, and Theology. Having gained first-class honours degrees in both subjects, I decided to embark on an academic instead of a church career, and went to Oxford to complete a doctoral thesis.

My first teaching job was in Plymouth Polytechnic (as it was then called), later to be renamed the University of Plymouth. At that time – the early 1970s – the Open University was starting up, and launched a new course in world religions. When I was asked to consider becoming one of its part-time tutors, I replied that I knew little about religions other than Christianity. I was told that this was no obstacle, since most of us would be in the same position. This put me on a huge learning curve, and also brought me into contact with the adherents of many faith traditions, including rabbis and *imams*, since the course involved encouraging students to meet people, and not just learn from books.

Plymouth was mainly white and Christian, so I was glad in 1992 to be able to move to the University of Wolverhampton, in the English Midlands, where there is wealth of religious communities. Having moved here, I decided to join the Church of England, for a variety of reasons. I have been an amateur church organist since my youth, and the local parish church called upon my services. My wife has always belonged to the Church of England and it seemed natural that we should want to worship together. I also like the more elaborate liturgy that is found in many Anglican churches, in contrast to the Church of Scotland and the English Free Churches.

I took early retirement from the University of Wolverhampton in 2008, and am currently Honorary Research Fellow at the University of Birmingham.

Would I ever consider becoming a Jew or Muslim? While I have every respect for both faiths, I don't think I would fit in, either culturally or theologically. I can't see myself accepting any body of scriptures, whether it's the Torah or the Qur'an, as infallible. Apart from its fundamentalist sector, the Christian faith has encouraged critical scholarship, and most scholars accept that the Bible's first five books had a variety of sources, and were not simply written by Moses. I don't think it would be appropriate for me to accept a whole set of ritual obligations, such as one finds in the Jewish Torah: that makes sense if one is keeping up one's faith tradition, but not for an outsider like me. As far as Islam is concerned, I can accept that the Bible went through various stages of compilation, but not that God's message became corrupted and needed correction centuries later.

No doubt these are matters that we shall discuss within this book, and I look forward to this dialogue.

DAWOUD SUDQI EL-ALAMI

I was born in the mountains of Lebanon, although my birth was registered in Jerusalem. My eight siblings were born in Palestine before 1948, and the older ones who have memories of life before the Catastrophe own their own personal sense of Palestinian identity. I had no direct experience of Palestine so all of my sense of being Palestinian has been mediated through my family.

My maternal grandfather was a religious scholar and teacher, and my paternal grandfather was a landowner. My father studied law in France but did not practise as a lawyer, devoting himself to managing his property, while my mother devoted herself to managing everything else. My parents were keen, however, that I should follow my father's profession.

My brothers went to the St George School (an Anglican school) in Jerusalem, which my father had attended, and some went to the Friends School in Ramallah. Two of my three sisters, like my mother, went to the Schmidt School for girls (a German Catholic school run by nuns), and one went to the Friends. This was completely normal among their peers.

I attended the St Joseph Catholic primary school in Cairo and later a state secondary school. Growing up in secular post-Revolution Egypt under Nasser, religion was just there; we went to Friday prayer and celebrated feasts just as part of normal life. It wasn't something we discussed much – we were too busy studying and enjoying life like any other young people – going to the cinema, the Gezira Club, or the Officers' Club.

My mother was devout but in a moderate and personal way; she prayed and read the Qur'an and books of prayer privately, and taught us as children through stories and examples. My parents had friends of all faiths and many nationalities and maintained a close relationship and regular correspondence with some of the Jesuit priests who taught three of my brothers at Gonzaga University in Washington State and who called my mother "Mother", so difference of religion was never an issue.

My first degree was the Licence en Droit from the University of Cairo in 1978 and I started my career as a lawyer in Egypt. I worked briefly as a legal adviser for a company in Saudi Arabia in the early eighties but that environment was not for me. My particular interest was in family law, and in 1986 I commenced my doctoral studies at the University of Glasgow on the marriage contract in the *Shari'a* and the Personal Status laws of Egypt and Morocco. Over the next few years I worked at the University of Kent on a project analysing marriage and divorce records from a Libyan civil archive, and then in the early nineties at Oxford University on a project investigating the way in which Arab Muslim communities in the UK apply Islamic family law within the framework of UK law. I was Chair of the Higher Studies Institute during the inaugural year of Al al-Bayt University in Jordan and then moved to Wales in 1995, where for sixteen years or so I taught Islamic Studies at the University of Wales Lampeter. This was a unique community of staff and students of all faiths which was a model of interfaith cooperation and respect, and it is where I met Dan Cohn-Sherbok.

I briefly took early retirement in 2012 but I have since taken up a post as part-time Senior Teaching Fellow at the University of Aberdeen.

I am a believing Sunni Muslim and could not envisage being anything else, but my faith is personal and I am not a member of any specific group, denomination, or congregation.

PART I

TEACHINGS

CHAPTER 1

PREDICAMENT AND HOPE

Religions are seldom complimentary about human nature. They typically identify a very serious condition from which escape seems difficult, even impossible. For Christians the predicament is sin – a condition inherited even before birth. Why can't they lighten up and look at humanity's good side? Why couldn't God simply forgive Adam for his disobedience, as Muslims claim? And why did God, as Jews believe, create human beings with a good and evil inclination? Is there a way out and, if so, where to? Is it a heavenly paradise, a messianic age, or a world of love and justice?

1(A) DAN:

For Jews, the human predicament is rooted in human nature itself. Rabbinic literature teaches that there are two tendencies in every person: the good inclination (*yetzer ha-tov*), and the evil inclination (*yetzer ha-ra*). The good inclination urges each person to do what is right, whereas the evil inclination encourages sinful acts. At all times, a person is to be on guard against assaults of the *yetzer ha-ra*. It is not possible to hide one's sins from God since God knows all things. In the words of the Mishnah (the earliest code of rabbinic law), "Know what is above thee – an eye that sees, an ear that hears, and all the deeds are written in a book" (Mishnah Avot 2:1). Thus God is aware of all sinful deeds, yet through repentance and prayer it is possible to achieve reconciliation with Him.

In rabbinic sources the *yetzer ha-ra* is often identified with the sex drive, which embraces human physical appetites in general as well as aggressive desires. Frequently it is portrayed as the force that impels human beings to satisfy their longings. To some degree, it resembles the Id in Freudian psychology. Human beings are thus engaged in a constant struggle with the evil within. For the Jew, there is only one cure to this universal malady: obedience to God's will. The Talmud (a later code of rabbinic law) declares that the Torah is the antidote to the poison of the evil inclination. The implication is that when human beings submit to the discipline provided by the Torah, they are liberated from its influence. In this regard, the rabbis tell a story about a king who struck his son and subsequently urged him to keep a plaster on his wound. When the wound was protected in this way the prince could eat and drink without coming to harm. But if he removed the plaster, the wound would grow worse. For the rabbis the Torah is the plaster that protects human beings from their own sinful nature.

Rabbinic literature also teaches that this struggle is unending. All that one can do is to subdue it through self-control: no person can destroy it. Arguably such a view parallels the Christian concept of original sin, yet unlike Christian scholars, the rabbis interpreted Genesis 2–3 as simply indicating how death became part of human destiny. According to the rabbis death was the direct result of Adam's disobedience. Although they did not teach a doctrine of original sin on this basis, they did accept "how great the wickedness of the human race had become on the earth, and that every inclination of the thoughts of the human heart was only evil all the time" (Genesis 6:5). They explain this by positing the existence of the evil inclination within every person.

In this context, the concept of repentance is of fundamental importance. Throughout the prophetic books sinners are admonished to give up their evil ways and return to God. According to traditional Judaism, atonement can only be attained after a process of repentance involving the recognition of sin. It requires remorse, restitution, and a determination not to commit a similar offence. Both the Bible and rabbinic sources stress that God does not want the death of the sinner, but desires that he return from his evil ways. Unlike Christianity, God does not instigate this process through grace; rather, atonement depends on the sinner's sincere act of repentance. Only at this stage does God grant forgiveness and pardon.

This account of sin, law, and redemption would not be complete without saying something about the coming of the messiah. Traditional Judaism teaches that at the end of time, the king messiah will bring about the resurrection of the dead, the ingathering of all those Jews outside Israel to the Promised Land, and a golden age of human history. Clouds of glory will then spread over these returning exiles, and all humankind will be united in peace. This is the Jewish view of a hopeful future. I should stress in this connection that from the first century until the present, the Jewish community has rejected Christian claims about Jesus' messiahship. Instead, strictly observant Jews pray for the coming of God's anointed, a human king who will bring about the redemption of the world.

So far I have briefly outlined the central tenets of traditional Judaism as it evolved over the centuries. Yet, I should stress that non-Orthodox Jews do not fully subscribe to these doctrines about the human predicament and hope for the future. As I will explain later in much more detail, only the strictly Orthodox believe that all the Law in scripture and in rabbinic codes is binding. Further, the belief in messianic redemption has for many Jews seemed implausible in the light of scientific and secular knowledge. Nonetheless across the Jewish religious spectrum, the belief in humankind's sinful nature and the need for redemption continues to play a central role in Jewish life.

1(B) GEORGE:

When the interfaith dialogue movement began, it tended to focus on points of similarity, probably because dialogue partners wanted to get to know each other, and because they felt that differences between religions were not quite as great as they had supposed. The time has come to move forward.

There is much in Dan's exposition that strikes a chord. I agree that many Christians, if asked about such matters, would express a variety of views, while others would profess ignorance. We can also acknowledge important points in common: Jews and Christians share common scriptures, and both religions acknowledge sin and repentance as key concepts. Although the Bible does not explicitly mention sex in the Adam and Eve story, Saint Augustine and others have taught that humankind's fall was bound up with sexual desire.

Some Christians, particularly Protestant fundamentalists, regard the story of Adam and Eve as a piece of literal history, explaining how sin entered the world. Others regard the story as symbolic and look to its spiritual meaning, namely that sin is endemic in human nature. Such a message may seem to paint an unduly black picture of humanity, reminiscent of the street preachers we still see occasionally with their sandwich boards proclaiming, "The wages of sin is death." Such people no doubt give Christianity a bad name, and perhaps Christians could afford to emphasize the good side of human nature a bit more. Matthew Fox, in his *Creation Spirituality*, refers to "original virtue", emphasizing the fact that God saw that his creation was "very good" (Genesis 1:31). However, Christian teaching draws attention to the way in which humans have marred God's creation, and the Adam and Eve story highlights sin's seriousness and its inescapability. One only has to glance at our daily news reports to be reminded of the prevalence of war, violence, crime, and poverty – all the results of sin.

So what is the remedy for sin? Dan suggests that it is obedience to the Jewish law. I think that Christians have at least two problems with this. First, most Christians do not see the point of obeying long lists of regulations about not boiling kids in their mother's milk (Deuteronomy 14:21), not wearing garments that mix linen and wool (Deuteronomy 22:11), being circumcised, or avoiding pork and shellfish. The Gospels portray the Pharisees as being obsessed with this kind of detail, rather than with the spirit of the Law.

Second, Christians have long recognized the impossibility of fulfilling the Law. Early apostles like Peter wanted to retain the Jewish law, but the Bible recounts an acrimonious argument about this with Paul, in which Paul's views prevailed (Galatians 2). Particularly in the Protestant tradition, Christianity has preached grace rather than works. This does not mean that one's deeds are unimportant, as our subsequent discussion will make clear. What it does mean is that more than human effort is required to make one's life acceptable to God.

Sin is the bad news. However, the word "gospel" means the opposite ("good news"), which is the assurance that sin and death can be – and have been – overcome. Regarding the Christian hope, Christians are less specific than Dan. The phrase "kingdom of God" occurs frequently in Jesus' teaching. Its exact meaning has been much debated. Some Christians look forward to life in a supernatural realm, while others expect a renewed earth. The word "kingdom" is better translated as "rule", and the concept therefore connotes a state in which human beings are subject to God's sovereignty. According to Jesus' teaching, acceptance of God's rule can begin here and now within one's heart (Luke 17:21), although the vast majority of Christians expect it to extend beyond death, after the resurrection.

I have to take issue with Dan on two important points concerning his "golden age". First, I find it somewhat worrying that he should identify Jerusalem as its focus. If it involves repatriating Jews to this "Promised Land", what is to become of the Palestinians? Has not this Jewish sense of entitlement to the land of Israel contributed to so much of the conflict in the Middle East and beyond? Second, Christians would agree that the messiah has an essential role in their final hope, but of course we would claim that he has already come in Jesus Christ – a topic we shall discuss more fully in subsequent chapters.

1(C) DAWOUD:

In the Qur'an God says, "O mankind, indeed We have created you from male and female and made you peoples and tribes that you may know one another" (49:13). In this there is both an acknowledgment of diversity and emphasis on the importance of knowledge of each other. As Dan and George have both emphasized, knowledge means not only identifying the things we agree on, of which there will no doubt be many, but also the areas where we must accept that we will always disagree.

On the whole it is probably true to say that the majority of Muslims have a general grasp of the key tenets of Islamic theology and law because they are familiar with the Qur'an and because the theology is so deeply entwined in the culture. I have a sense that while Western culture is permeated and patterned by its Judeo-Christian heritage in ways of which people are not always aware, Islamic theology is much closer to the surface of everyday life.

Muslims believe the Qur'an to be the literal and infallible word of God as revealed to the Prophet Muhammad and the duty of human beings is to obey its commands and injunctions and avoid those things that it prohibits. The core message of Islam is belief in one God, and the greatest offence is the ascription of any partners to God.

In the Qur'an, Adam is the first man and God commands the angels to bow down before His creation. The angels are created to obey God and have no free will, unlike mankind and the *jinn*. Iblis, described as one of the *jinn* whom God created from smokeless fire, defies God and refuses to prostrate himself before Adam, who is created from clay. Iblis is condemned to hell for all eternity, but persuades God to postpone his punishment until the Day of Judgment. Iblis makes it his purpose during this time to tempt mankind into sin, to whisper evil into the hearts of human beings; he is therefore identified with al-Shaytan or Satan.

In the Qur'an Adam and Eve are both tempted by Iblis to eat the forbidden fruit and they bear the responsibility equally. Having repented they are then forgiven by God and sent out of the garden to go forth and populate the earth. There is then no concept of original sin in Islam. The slate has been wiped and it is the responsibility of each individual to avoid sin in his or her own life.

Muslims believe that God sent His message to mankind through prophets of the past starting with Adam and including Abraham, Moses, Jesus, and many more of the biblical prophets. Islam is then the continuation and perfection of Judaism and Christianity. Muslims revere the prophets of the Bible, including Jesus, although they do not recognize him as divine and they deny his crucifixion and resurrection, claiming that God replaced him on the cross with a substitute. Muhammad is, however, the Seal of the Prophets, the last ever to be sent by God.

Muslims refer to the pre-Islamic period, particularly with the regard to life in the Arabian Peninsula at the time of the revelation of the Qur'an, as *Al-Jahiliyya*, the age of ignorance. Although the historical evidence does not entirely support the received view of this period, this is popularly understood to mean an age of idolatry and barbarity in which gambling, drunkenness, and sexual immorality were rife. Muslim belief is that Islam came to sweep all of this away and bring in a new era of peace and justice, although there is an alternative interpretation of the age of ignorance simply as a time of not knowing, that is, before mankind was made aware of the One God and His purpose for humanity.

For Muslims the purpose of creation is to worship God and obey His will. This begins with the profession of faith: "There is no God but God and Muhammad is the Prophet of God", which is all that is required to be acknowledged as a Muslim. The word "Islam" itself means submission, specifically submission to the will of God. This does not mean the submission of the broken or oppressed but the act of faith in entrusting one's life and destiny to God through following His law. Obedience to God's law will bring eternal reward in the hereafter, while disobedience will result in eternal punishment. Both of these are graphically described in the Qur'an, although there is disagreement whether this is literal or metaphorical. There is no suggestion that Muhammad will return, but there is a popular belief based on an interpretation of a Qur'anic verse that 'Isa or Jesus will return immediately before the Day of Judgment. There are also verses that refer to a gathering of the Children of Israel in the Promised Land in the Last Days, and some Muslims believe that the *Ka'aba* will be transported to Jerusalem for the gathering of the dead on the Day of Judgment. I am sure, however, that we will talk in greater depth about eschatology later on as well as our respective attachments to the Holy Land.

1(D) DAN:

In my last exchange, I stressed that modern Judaism in its various forms is very different from Judaism in previous centuries. The vast majority of Jews no longer feel obliged to accept the central tenets of the faith nor observe the manifold commandments in the Bible and rabbinic legal sources. Instead, most Jews feel free to select from the tradition those elements that they find spiritually meaningful. It should be remembered too that many Jews in Israel and in the diaspora (countries outside Israel) are totally secularized. Thus, in responding to the various points you both make about the human predicament and hope, I need to distinguish between the traditional Jewish view and modern theological interpretations of the Jewish heritage.

It is true as you both point out that Jews, Christians, and Muslims share the same scriptures. In the past Jews viewed the Torah (Genesis, Exodus, Leviticus, Numbers, and Deuteronomy) as divinely revealed to Moses on Mount Sinai. In this light, the account of Adam and Eve in Genesis was regarded as a true story about the origin of human beings (although it should be noted that some rabbinic exegetes rejected such fundamentalism). Today most Jews believe that the Torah (and the rest of scripture) is a mosaic composed of elements written by ancient Israelites over centuries of development. In this light the story of Adam and Eve is perceived as a myth – rather than a factual account.

This of course has important consequences for what you both say about human nature. George referred to the Christian belief in humankind's fall as a result of Adam and Eve's disobedience. Protestant fundamentalists, he points out, regard this narrative as literal history. Certainly most Jews today would reject such an idea, and view the notion of original sin as mistaken. As I pointed out in my previous exchange, it is not because of Adam and Eve's rejection of God's command that human beings are subject to sin, but because of human psychology: the inner struggle between the good and evil inclination is unending. For this reason, Jews would similarly reject the Islamic belief that Adam is the first man. Further, Dawoud's description of Iblis tempting Adam and Eve to eat forbidden fruit in the garden (which parallels the account of the snake tempting Adam in Genesis) would be perceived as myth rather than historical fact.

Let me turn next to what George has said about Jesus. At the end of his exchange he notes that Christians believe that Jesus as messiah has a crucial role to play in humanity's final hope. Here the paths between Judaism and Christianity diverge fundamentally. As I noted in my previous exchange, through the centuries Jews have anticipated the arrival of a messiah-king who will redeem the world. As a human descendant of King David, he will come in glory and bring about peace and harmony. From the first century to the present day Jews have rejected the Christian identification of Jesus with this figure. The strictly Orthodox continue to pray for his coming; within Reform Judaism the idea of messianic deliverance has been largely rejected. But despite their differences, Jews are united in their rejection of Christian claims about Jesus' messiahship. (In this connection, George, you have questioned the Jewish view of the exiles' return to the Promised Land at the end of time – I will hold off responding until later when we discuss the Palestine-Israeli crisis.)

Distancing themselves from Muslims, Jews reject Islamic claims about Muhammad. In his last exchange Dawoud cites the Islamic profession of faith: "There is no God but God and Muhammad is the Prophet of God." No Jew believes that Muhammad is God's final prophet, or that the Qur'an is God's perfect revelation. On the contrary, most Jews would view the Qur'an in the same way as the sacred books of the world's faiths – it should be conceived as a record of Muhammad's spiritual life and testimony of his religious quest. Thus the Qur'an should be perceived in much the same way as the New Testament, the Bhagavad Gita, and the Vedas. For Muslims it has special significance, but it should not be regarded as possessing truth for all humankind.

Finally, I should say something about George's comments regarding Jewish law. He notes that there are a number of reasons why Christians do not feel obliged to keep biblical law. Most Christians, he writes, do not see the point of obeying long lists of regulations about food, clothing, and other matters. He might be surprised to learn that most Jews (excluding the strictly Orthodox) feel the same. As I said previously, the vast majority of Jews today select from the tradition those biblical and rabbinic laws which they find spiritually relevant. They, too, think that the task of fulfilling all the Law is unnecessarily difficult. Here then, despite our differences, modern Jews and liberal Christians surprisingly appear to share similar attitudes.

1(E) GEORGE:

We entitled this book *Why Can't They Get Along?*, but I can get along quite well with much of what Dan says. Although there are Christians who go along with the traditional view of original sin, liberal Christians such as me would be more inclined to view the doctrine as "myth". That is not to say that it is false, but rather that the idea of a first man and woman transmitting sin to all subsequent generations bears important meaning. I would agree with Dan that it makes a statement about human psychology: all of us are faced with agonizing choices between good and evil, and have the marked propensity to choose evil much of the time.

I have less in common with Dawoud's account, which sees Iblis as a real figure who whispers in people's ears. I don't need anyone whispering to remind me to do evil – it comes quite naturally! The idea of Satan in fact develops over time. He is mentioned very little in the Old Testament, and he is not named in the Adam and Eve story at all, where it is a serpent that tempts the first two humans (Genesis 3:1–20). Satan is only mentioned in later Hebrew scriptures, notably Chronicles and Job (1 Chronicles 21:1; Job 1 and 2). In the latter, he is a member of God's heavenly court rather than a declared enemy. It is only in the last book of the Christian Bible – the book of Revelation – that the author explicitly states that the Dragon, the serpent, the devil, and Satan are one and the same, predicting that he will be bound for a thousand years and subsequently thrown into a lake of burning sulphur, to be eternally tormented (Revelation 20:7–10). Most twenty-first-century Christians would take this with a pinch of salt, rather than sulphur! It is strong imagery, pointing to the final triumph of good over evil, for which all of our three religions hope. Many Christians would regard Satan as a personification of all that is evil, rather than a real spirit being.

I have to disagree with both Dan and Dawoud regarding the means of escape from sin. Christians have portrayed Jesus as the "Second Adam", meaning that, just as Adam introduced sin to the world, Jesus Christ brings redemption. He is the messiah and the Redeemer, as well as the world's greatest spiritual teacher, and we see no need for any further revelation from God to deal with sin. If only I could put all of

Jesus' teachings into practice, I would be a much better person, and if all humankind were to do so, the vast majority of the world's problems would be instantly solved.

However, Dan is right in suggesting that Jews and Christians are irreconcilably divided on the messiah's role in humanity's fundamental hope. We don't believe that it is simply enough to observe God's law, even if (as Dan says) this doesn't involve all the onerous requirements that are associated with traditional Judaism. In my youth our minister used to say, "You don't need to turn over a new leaf; you need to turn over a new life." Christianity teaches newness of life. The Christian story is a recapitulation of the Garden of Eden: Jesus came to earth, was subjected to the devil's temptations, yet overcame (Matthew 4:1–11). His crucifixion recapitulated the death that resulted from sin. As a consequence, Jesus Christ offers life, and Christians symbolize this new life by the rite of baptism, in which water is used to demonstrate cleansing from sin.

I know all this raises a number of difficult questions. How can a man dying on a cross 2,000 years ago cancel out the world's sin? How do we explain Christ's atonement? Are we talking about supernatural reality here, or are we still in the realm of myth? These are not easy questions, but the Christian faith affirms a number of important points. First, reconciliation with God is a real possibility: we need not fear eternal punishment – whether it is fire and brimstone, or some other sanction – as a consequence of sin. Second, being made right with God does not demand the impossible: while, as Dawoud says, submission to God's law is important, failing to live up to God's standards is not a barrier to salvation. Third, it is not only Israel who is God's people: all who believe in Jesus Christ come under God's covenant relationship. Ultimately it is God who saves, not ourselves. As a famous Christian hymn puts it: "All for sin could not atone; / Thou must save, and thou alone."

1(F) DAWOUD:

I can see that we have already started to touch on all kinds of topics that I know we are going to go on to explore: the founding stories of our respective faiths, the prophets, and the scriptures and their literal or metaphorical interpretation. But before getting too far ahead of ourselves, for now I should turn back to the human predicament.

As I mentioned, for Muslims the key to salvation is belief in and obedience to God and the avoidance of sin, and this is entirely our own individual responsibility. The Qur'an and the *Sunna* (the example of the Prophet), provide us with guidance, but human beings are endowed with free will to choose the right or the wrong path. There is no saviour either past or future to atone for us or intercede. The *Shari'a* is God's law. God is the law-giver and man's duty is to seek to understand it and obey its divine provisions. The *Shari'a* governs all aspects of life, including belief and worship and every field of law – constitutional, international, criminal, civil and commercial, marriage and the family. Islam has its own dietary laws which, although perhaps not as complex as Jewish law, correspond with it in some aspects such as the prohibition of pork and the manner of slaughter. No doubt we will come to discuss whether these have innate value as religious duties for which we will be rewarded or punished, or whether they were prescribed at particular times in history on health grounds.

For Muslims Islam and Islamic law are not two separate entities. Islam should be a complete way of life in which mindfulness of God in all daily activity is the essence. Human nature of course means that this is not always achieved, and like Christianity and Judaism, Islam comprises the notion of forgiveness. People will err through sin or through weakness, and this is understood. God is merciful and forgiving and accepts true repentance. No ritual is required for this. A Muslim's relationship with God is direct through prayer. "In the name of God the Compassionate the Merciful" is the invocation of God's name used by Muslims numerous times a day before commencing any action, whether it be reading a book, preparing or eating food, or starting the engine of the car. The "Compassionate" and the "Merciful" are just two of the "ninety-nine most beautiful names of God", many of which refer to God's mercy towards those who repent, such as the "All-Forgiving", the "Accepter of Repentance", the "Pardoner".

God will forgive all who turn to Him in repentance. The only sin that cannot be forgiven is *shirk*, or the ascription of partners to God. It is on this basis that Muslims find the notion of the Trinity difficult as they understand it to be a contradiction with the belief in the absolute oneness of God as expressed in the profession of faith.

The profession of faith is the first of the Five Pillars of Islam, which also include prayer at five appointed times in the day, fasting during the month of Ramadan, the giving of alms in a prescribed proportion of one's wealth, and pilgrimage to Mecca at least once in a lifetime. The Qur'an is clear, however, that no soul is charged with a burden greater than it can bear and so there are exemptions for specific circumstances such as illness and infirmity or poverty and debt.

For Muslims the life of the Prophet and the early years of Islam are not just stories in which to seek guidance but a real part of their shared history. They look to an idealized past as the model for the creation of a perfect society in which people live as God intended. Dan has mentioned that many Jews feel free to select those elements that they find spiritually meaningful. I think this is very much less the case with Muslims as, where the texts are explicit, they do not feel that they can be selective about what they believe and accept, and no one will challenge the infallibility of the Qur'an as the literal word of God as to do so would be tantamount to apostasy. This does not mean that there is no scope for interpretation where the text allows this. It does not mean either that Muslims do not fail in the practice of their faith and many Muslims, particularly in non-Muslim societies, live with a sense that they are not completely fulfilling their duty to God and the intention of reforming their lives in the future.

CHAPTER 2

GOD

Christians hold that God sent His son – the messiah – to save the world, which he accomplished by his saving death on the cross. Such a claim is unacceptable to Jews and Muslims. Jews do not accept his messianic status, and the Qur'an states that Allah never had a son. Christianity has maintained the doctrine of the Trinity, which Jews and Muslims believe compromises its professed monotheism.

2(A) DAWOUD:

We all worship the same God, don't we? We call Him different names in different languages, but He is the God of Abraham, Moses, and Jesus. Do we see Him so very differently?

The most important article of faith in Islam is *tawhid*, the doctrine of the oneness of God, a pure and absolute monotheism.

The city of Mecca at the time of the revelation of the Qur'an to the Prophet Muhammad was a commercial centre on the crossroads of trade routes and a centre of annual pilgrimage for the surrounding pagan tribes. There were also Jewish and Christian tribes in the region, as well as Hanifs, who Muslims believe were people who had preserved the monotheism of Abraham but were neither Christians nor Jews as such. At the heart of Mecca was the *Ka'aba*, which Muslims believe was built by Ibrahim (Abraham) and his son Isma'il (Ishmael) for the worship of the One God. The Qur'an refers to Ibrahim's recrimination to his father Azar, saying, "How could you worship statues as gods? I see that you and your people have gone astray."

By the time of Muhammad, however, according to Muslim belief the pagan Arab tribes had filled the *Ka'aba* with idols. During the early period of the Revelation of the Qur'an in Mecca, the emphasis was on absolute belief in the One God and rejection of idolatry. Throughout the Qur'an the idolators, *al-Mushrikin* (those who commit *shirk* or the ascription of partners to God) are the gravest sinners and the enemies of the Muslims. This absolute prohibition of idolatry is the reason why figurative art is generally forbidden in Islam and Islamic art tends to be restricted to geometric, calligraphic, or abstract botanical forms. It is uncommon to find images of people or animals in traditional Muslim homes. The notion is that if such images are created then over time it is human nature for people to begin to revere or worship them. It is, moreover, forbidden to create any image of God or of His prophets. The Ten Commandments prohibit the making of graven images or the likeness of anything in heaven, on the earth, or in the waters under the earth. It appears, however, that iconography and figurative imagery in paintings, frescoes, stained glass, and in other forms are of particular importance in some churches and I am interested to know how this is understood by Christians.

The name Allah means "The God", with the sense of the one and only. The Qur'an is insistent on this – *Sura* (chapter) 112 contains the imperative: "Say, 'He is Allah, [who is] One, Allah, the Eternal Refuge. He neither begets nor is born, nor is there to Him any Equivalent'" (112:1–4). This highlights one of the most important differences that Muslims raise with regard to Christianity. They revere 'Isa (Jesus) as a prophet and the story of his birth to the virgin Maryam is narrated in the Qur'an, but they do not accept that God could have a son. To Muslims this looks suspiciously like polytheism. When it comes to the concept of the Trinity, Muslims do not understand how Christians claim to worship one God yet appear to believe in three distinct entities.

I alluded earlier to the most beautiful or the most excellent names of God. These ninety-nine names, which are all sourced from the Qur'an, are in addition to the "greatest name", Allah, and describe the attributes of God – the All-Powerful, the All-Knowing, the Compassionate, the Giver of Life, the Taker of Life, the Just, the First, the Last, to name but a few. They are often found in decorative objects – on ceramics, inlay work, engravings, and calligraphic works of art. These names, some more commonly than others, are used in combination with the noun *Abd* (servant or worshipper) to form personal names such as Abd al-Rahman (Worshipper of the Compassionate), Abdallah (Worshipper of God), Abd al-Malik (Worshipper of the Absolute Ruler), Abd al-Aziz (Worshipper of the Victorious). Contrary to popular perception in non-Muslim countries, there is no such name as Abdul, this being the noun *Abd* plus the definite article which would just mean "worshipper of the" and is therefore meaningless without one of the names of God attached.

Muslims will write the name of God above the doors of their houses, in invocation at the top of their correspondence or any written work and on all kinds of decorative artefacts. I am interested to know, then, why it is that many Jews avoid the writing of the name of God.

2(B) DAN:

Rabbinic sages interpreted Deuteronomy 12:3 as prohibiting erasing or defacing the name of God. For this reason observant Jews often do not write the name of God, fearing that it could be erased or defaced in some way.

I think both Dawoud and I are puzzled by much the same thing: how could otherwise reasonable and sensible people (like George) subscribe to belief in the divinity of Christ and the doctrine of the incarnation? Through the ages Jews have regarded Jesus as nothing more than a first-century Jewish teacher and preacher. At times he was described with antipathy by Jewish scholars (as in the Talmud, which was condemned and burned by Christians for this reason). More recently a number of Jewish thinkers have viewed Jesus as a great moral teacher. In a book I wrote some years ago, *On Earth as it is in Heaven: Jews, Christians and Liberation Theology*, I placed Jesus in the line of the prophets of ancient Israel such as Amos, Hosea, and Isaiah and encouraged Jews to regard him as a great moral teacher. But the Son of God – never.

I remember that when I first attended a Eucharist service in Canterbury Cathedral (we used to live in Canterbury and my wife taught at King's School there), I was disturbed to hear the priest refer to the consecrated wine as "Christ's blood" and the bread as his body. This, I thought, is a form of religious cannibalism (though of course Christians who are used to this ritual would never see it this way). Equally strange, I think, is the idea that somehow this first-century Jew's death brings atonement for the sins of all humanity. To my mind this is a complete misconception, as is the notion that in some mysterious way Jesus' death on the cross illustrates that God suffers when we suffer. God is not three-in-one. This is bad mathematics. It is bad theology. In the minds of some Jewish thinkers such as the twelfth-century philosopher Moses Maimonides, it is nothing less than idolatry.

For the Jew (as for the Muslim) God is one. He is the transcendent creator of all things, immanent in human history. For some Jewish thinkers He is ultimately unknowable. His nature is beyond human understanding. For the Kabbalists (Jewish mystics), He is the *En Sof* (Infinite), beyond comprehension. Maimonides in his *Guide for the Perplexed* argues that the only thing we can know about God is that He is one, and that He exists. It is a mistake, he continues, to ascribe positive attributes to God. We can only say what God is not, not what He is.

In a post-Holocaust world there are a number of Jewish thinkers who have grappled with the question how God could have allowed 6 million innocent Jewish victims to die at the hands of the Nazis. Some writers assert that God has given humans free will – hence it is inevitable that moral evil is possible. Others maintain that God was in the death camps suffering with His people. There are some theologians who believe that although God created the universe, He does not act in human history. And of course there are some pious thinkers who contend that God's ways are not our ways and thus we cannot understand His will. In their view we must be like Job at the end of the book of Job, silent in the face of His presence.

Because of the theological chasm that exists between Jews and Christians that I have briefly described, our two faiths do not really get along. Today organizations such as the Council of Christians and Jews foster positive encounter. This is certainly to be encouraged. But at a fundamental level Jews and Christians are deeply divided. The doctrine of God separates us from one another in the most radical way. In this connection it must be remembered that severe wounds have been inflicted on Jews because of crucial differences in belief. For 2,000 years Christians have hated us and murdered us because we have refused to accept Jesus as Lord and Saviour. We are traumatized by such history. Make no mistake about it. Paradoxically it is our Muslim brothers and sisters with whom we join ranks in proclaiming that God is one. In the liturgy we say: "Hear O Israel, The Lord our God, The Lord is One." Dawoud's response says just this.

2(C) GEORGE:

I was expecting a forceful attack on the doctrine of the Trinity, but let me deal with some easier points first. Dawoud comments on the Christian use of images in architecture and worship. Although God is invisible, many Christians believe that physical aids can be helpful. Christians hold that God has come among us in human form, and hence it seems appropriate to express one's faith in a physical way. We would not consider this idolatry, since we do not worship the image itself, and no Christian would confuse a physical image with the maker of heaven and earth. Christians would take the second Commandment to prohibit worshipping idols, and in Protestant circles "graven images" is taken to mean three-dimensional, rather than two-dimensional, art. So Protestants dislike statues and crucifixes, preferring stained glass and the symbol of the empty cross. In Orthodoxy, a church is typically designed to be a microcosm. Humans enter at ground level; Christ the "Pantocrator" (the judge of all) is depicted on the roof; and saints and the Virgin Mary occupy an intermediary position on the walls, since Orthodox (as well as Catholic) Christians regard them as having a mediatory role.

Now on to the Trinity! To be candid, I have known several vicars to become quite worried when Trinity Sunday came round, since they were expected to preach on the subject. It is certainly not easy to understand, and many Christians would appeal to the notion of mystery in connection with the idea.

Dawoud said earlier that he thought the doctrine militated against the absolute oneness of God, but Christians are not polytheistic: there is only one God, shared by all of our three faiths. Islam has produced excellent mathematicians, but Christians are not innumerate, as Dan suggests! We know that $1 + 1 + 1 = 3$, but of course if you multiply three ones instead of add them, $1 \times 1 \times 1 = 1$!

The doctrine affirms that God has appeared in the world in three different ways: first as creator and sustainer of the universe, second through Jesus Christ who is God come among us, and third as the Holy Spirit, who is the inner source of inspiration for the believer, and for the church.

"Three persons" does not mean three different people. The word "person" can be somewhat misleading. I once worked at a university which had a small elevator with the instruction, "Only three persons allowed in this lift". I often used this example to highlight the difference between the popular sense of "person", and the theological sense. God is not three different people, or some kind of three-headed monster.

The Latin word *persona* had its origins, not in theology, but in the ancient theatre. The word meant "mask", and it referred to the practice of one actor assuming several different roles. To make role changes obvious, he would wear a mask appropriate to the part he was playing. On changing role, he would put on a different mask, and come back on stage, thus adopting several *personae*. In modern-day acting, it is not so common to play several parts in the same performance, but many actors have had multiple roles during their careers. Helen Mirren, for example, was detective Jane Tennison in the television series *Prime Suspect*, and Queen Elizabeth I and Queen Elizabeth II in the TV series and film respectively. In a sense, Mirren was each of these characters, but each character was not the other, since Queen Elizabeth II is not a detective, and Queen Elizabeth I is not Queen Elizabeth II.

Like most analogies, this example has its weaknesses. God was not merely acting the part of Jesus, or the Holy Spirit, nor was He performing different roles sequentially. Christian teaching has insisted that all three persons are co-eternally God – but more about this when we discuss Jesus.

I don't think the notion of sharing sovereign power is confined to Christianity, however, and I'd like to put a couple of points to Dan and Dawoud about their absolute monotheism. In the book of Daniel, a being "like a son of man" came on the clouds of heaven, approached the "Ancient of Days", and was given sovereign power over the world (Daniel 7:13–14). It's a difficult passage for Jews and Christians, but I wonder whether it doesn't indicate some sharing of divinity in Jewish thought?

I'd be interested to hear what Dawoud has to say about angels, who have an important role in Islam. Obviously they are not Allah's equal partners, but are they not divine messengers who assist Allah with his work? Might we all at least agree that God uses – maybe even needs – helpers and intermediaries in order to work in the world?

2(D) DAWOUD:

We do not really disagree then about the oneness of God. For Muslims God is omnipotent: "When He decrees a matter, He only says to it, 'Be,' and it is" (Qur'an 2:117). This does not mean, however, that He controls all human actions. Human beings make their own choices to take the path of right or wrong but at the same time Muslims believe that an individual's destiny is already written, including the day and the hour of his or her birth and death. This is not a contradiction; it is not because God has decided a person's destiny in advance but just that He already knows what is going to happen. He is omniscient; more than a hundred verses in the Qur'an describe Him as all-knowing. He knows everything that happens in the universe, including each individual's thoughts: "… and fear Allah. Indeed, Allah is Knowing of that within the breasts" (5:7).

Despite His many names, however, He is unknowable. The ninety-nine names describe His power but they do not describe Him in an anthropomorphic sense. He cannot be imagined physically or visually. The Qur'an refers to God's face and His hand, but it is universally agreed that this is metaphorical and that God has no physical form. Although He is always referred to in the masculine, He is neither male nor female but above such description. It would be unthinkable, however, to use the feminine form of pronouns, verbs, or adjectives to refer to Him as this would imply a specifically female entity. I have noticed that some of my Jesuit friends refer in their newsletters to "our Mother-Father God". This concept is something that many Muslims would have difficulty with although I suspect most Muslims never even think about the implications of ascribing the masculine form to God. I wonder if George and Dan have a similar impression with regard to the way Christians and Jews conceive of God.

I should mention that I am using the word "God" here rather than "Allah" to avoid confusion, because Allah means God. Using the name Allah in English may give the wrong impression that it is a specific name. It is the same word that Arab Christians use to refer to God.

God exists before everything and is the creator of everything. He created human beings from clay, the *jinn* from smokeless fire, and the angels from light, all with the main purpose of worshipping Him. Unlike humans and the *jinn*, however, the angels have no free will; they have no gender and no desire. They were created before human beings. In response to George's question, they do not share in the divinity of God. It is one of the articles of faith that Muslims should believe in the angels, but they are not intercessors and do not carry people's prayers to God. Some of them have specific roles in the world such as Jibril, who conveyed messages to the prophets, Uzra'il (the angel of death), Munkar and Nakir (who test the faith of Muslims in the grave), and various other individuals and cohorts who accompany Muslims in battle or seek out gatherings where God is remembered.

In several places, the Qur'an refers to God's throne and I am interested to know how this compares with the representation of the throne in Judaism and Christianity. Two distinct words are used to refer to it: *al-Kursi* and *al-'Arsh*, and scholars distinguish between them. Some classical scholars describe *al-'Arsh* in graphic terms as the almighty throne over the entire universe carried by angels of enormous size, although in general it is interpreted metaphorically to mean His absolute transcendent power. *Al-Kursi* is usually interpreted as God's dominion over the earth and the heavens. There is a section of the long second *sura* of the Qur'an which sums up Muslim belief about God. Known as the "Throne Verse" or *Ayat al-Kursi,* it is one of the verses most commonly recited and used in writing to bring protection to the person:

> *God – there is no deity except Him, the Ever-Living, the Sustainer of [all] existence. Neither drowsiness overtakes Him nor sleep. To Him belongs whatever is in the heavens and whatever is on the earth. Who is it that can intercede with Him except by His permission? He knows what is [presently] before them and what will be after them, and they encompass not a thing of His knowledge except for what He wills. His Kursi extends over the heavens and the earth, and their preservation tires Him not. And He is the Most High, the Most Great. (2:255)*

2(E) DAN:

There are two points I should mention first with regard to Dawoud's questions. First, Judaism maintains that God is beyond gender. However, within the mystical tradition, feminine terms are used to refer to various aspects of the Godhead. Dawoud has also asked about terminology such as "throne", which is used in relation to God. I should stress that within the Jewish tradition, God is understood as omnipresent; however, terms such as "throne" are used figuratively to denote God's presence.

George has presented a plausible case for the doctrine of the Trinity. He contends that in fact Christians are not bad mathematicians and that the concept of three in one as a theological notion is entirely reasonable. He uses the example of an actress taking on three different roles; this is an analogy, he believes, of the way in which God has manifested Himself. Now, I should say at the outset that Jews are not disturbed by the idea that God has made Himself known in various manifestations as George has described. It is a fundamental belief that God acts in human history: He chose the Jewish nation as His people, revealed His law, liberated them from bondage, led them to the Promised Land, and will guide them to their ultimate destiny. Indeed, in the Midrash (commentary on scripture), Jewish sages explained that the reason why God has so many names in scripture is because they refer to His manifold roles. In kabbalistic texts, God is described as the *En Sof* (Infinite) who has emanated into the world. These divine emanations (*sefirot*) constitute a hierarchal structure of divine realms.

However, George's explanation of the Trinity is, I believe, too simplistic and arguably comes close to a heresy condemned by the early church: Sabellianism. The Sabellianists taught that the Father, Son, and Holy Ghost are aspects of how humanity has interacted with or experienced God. In the role of the Father, God is the provider and creator of all; in the role of the Son, God is manifested in the flesh as a human being to bring about the salvation of humankind; in the role of the Holy Spirit, God manifested Himself from heaven through His actions on earth and within the lives of Christians. Yet, in contrast to such a heretical notion, the traditional doctrine of the Trinity defines God as three divine persons or hypostates: the Father, the Son (Jesus Christ), and the Holy Spirit. These three persons are distinct, yet are one substance, essence, or nature. According to this doctrine, there is only one God in three persons, yet each person is God, whole and entire. They are distinct from one another in their relations of origin, as the Fourth Lateran Council declared: "It is the Father, who generates, the Son who is begotten, and the Holy Spirit who proceeds." These three persons are co-equal, co-eternal and consubstantial.

For Jews and Muslims, the most difficult aspect of such a doctrine is the belief that Jesus, a Jew living in Judaea in the first century BCE, is God on earth. The concept of the incarnation asserts that God became flesh, assumed a human nature, and became man in the form of Jesus Christ. This foundational Christian position holds that the divine nature of the Son of God was perfectly united with human nature in one divine Person, Jesus, making him both truly God and truly man. The theological term for this is the hypostatic union: the Second Person of the Holy Trinity, God the Son, became flesh when he was miraculously conceived in the womb of the Virgin Mary. Both Judaism and Islam completely reject the doctrine of the incarnation of God in any form. For Muslims, the concept is *shirk*. In mainstream Islam God is one and "neither begets nor is begotten". In Judaism, the idea of an incarnation of God is regarded as impossible.

As I noted previously, in the Hebrew scriptures the Israelites experienced God as the Lord of history. The most uncompromising expression of His unity is the *Shema* prayer: "Hear, O Israel, The Lord, our God, The Lord is One." In contrast to Christian exegetes who interpreted the *Shema* with its three references to God as denoting the Trinity, Jewish scholars maintained that the *Shema* implies that there is only one God, rather than three persons of the Godhead. For such medieval scholars as the tenth-century theologian Saadiah Gaon, the Divine should be understood as a single incorporeal Being who created the universe out of nothing. In the twelfth century, the Jewish philosopher Abraham Ibn Daud derived God's absolute unity from His necessary existence. In this view, the concept of divine oneness precludes the possibility of any divine attributes of God. Similarly, Moses Maimonides in the same century argued that no positive attributes can be predicated of God since the Divine is an absolute unity.

Such philosophical theories have little impact on contemporary Jewish thought, yet Jewry is united in rejecting any form of trinitarianism. George has made a compelling case for the doctrine of the Trinity and by implication the incarnation. But in simplifying these complex ideas through the use of a theatrical analogy (and the elevator carrying three persons), he has not given full expression to the complexity and, in my view, implausibility of the Christian concept of God. For the Jew, it makes no sense to believe that Jesus was "God of God, Light of Light, Very God of Very God, Begotten not Made."

2(F) GEORGE:

Dan says I've been simplistic, but it's difficult to fit God into a few hundred words! I think we would all agree that God, being the greatest conceivable being, is greater than the universe itself – and scientists certainly don't claim to understand the entire universe. In fact, they've recently acknowledged that they can't even find nine-tenths of it! That's why I agree with Dawoud that we need to resort to metaphor, and even anthropomorphic language, when we describe God.

I'm happy to share the same metaphors as Dawoud, and I don't think that any Christian could quarrel with any of the Islamic ninety-nine names. We talk about God's hands and face, but the Church of England's "Thirty-Nine Articles" appropriately says that He is "without body, parts or passions" (Article I). Dan mentions Maimonides' view that we can't describe any positive aspects to God, and in Christianity Thomas Aquinas paralleled this notion with his *via negativa* (negative way). Christianity also uses the metaphors of God's throne and kingship: He is not an elected president, who carries out humankind's agenda, but has laws that stand above human desires.

It is interesting that Dawoud raises the question of gender. Although Christians tend to use the word "He" when referring to God, some present-day believers find this inappropriate and want to avoid gender-specific language. Those feminists who want to refer to God as "She" are, I think, trying to redress the balance and jolt us into recognizing some unwarranted implications of overemphasizing the masculine – power and might, rather than nurturing and compassion. All our three faiths have tended to be male-dominated, with male thinkers and theologians, and hence we have tended to project masculinity on to God.

But back to the Trinity – Dan says that my position is close to Sabellianism: he understands Christian heresies well! Sabellianism – sometimes called Modalism – can be traced back to the third-century priest Sabellius, who taught that the three persons of the Trinity are simply more modes or manifestations of God, rather than that each person is wholly and fully divine. Although Sabellianism draws on the analogy of using theatrical masks, I hope I made it clear that the analogy had its weaknesses, and that it incorrectly suggested that God was merely playing different roles. Actors can only perform one role at a time; hence the analogy, if pressed too hard, leads to absurd conclusions. If God had merely taken time out to become Jesus, what was happening to the rest of the world during these thirty years? Was He unable to govern the universe for this period? Were prayers unheard except by those who were with Jesus in ancient Palestine? Clearly any sound doctrine of the Trinity cannot place limitations on God, or diminish His attributes in any way.

One way of explaining the Trinity is a pictorial triangular diagram that is sometimes found in churches, often on the altar cloth. More often than not, it is written in Latin, being the ancient language of the church:

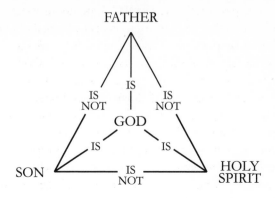

The diagram makes the point that each member of the Trinity is fully God, yet distinct from each of the others. Each member of the Trinity is wholly God at all times: God does not become a different person on different occasions.

Dan refers to Hebrew scripture affirming the oneness of God. We can certainly agree that there is one and only one God, and although the Bible does not explicitly mention the doctrine of the Trinity, Christians see hints of it in various parts of scripture. For example, the second verse of Genesis mentions God's Spirit moving over the primordial watery chaos, and being God's creative agency. The book of Proverbs talks about Wisdom – the divine Word – affirming its existence from eternity, emanating from God as the agent of creation (8:22–23). It is God's Word that effects the creative process: God speaks and the various aspects of creation come into being (Genesis 1:3–29). Saint John, in his Gospel, brings these ideas together in his opening statement: "In the beginning was the Word, and the Word was with God, and the Word was God" (1:1). Just as the divine Word speaks through His creation, Christians believe that He has also spoken in Jesus Christ, and Christ's words are God's words.

Dawoud suggests this is *shirk* – associating the physical with God. While Christians would agree that the worship of physical things, such as wealth, power, or fame is inappropriate, even idolatrous, Christianity teaches the involvement of God in the physical world in His plan to redeem it. But more of this in the next section.

CHAPTER 3

JESUS

All three faiths are agreed in their acceptance of ancient Hebrew prophets. Christianity often appears to teach that Jesus set himself up as a greater teacher than Moses, and the Bible sets Jesus in opposition to the scribes and Pharisees. Islam regards Muhammad as the "Seal of the Prophets", and Jesus as no more than a prophet. What happened to Jesus after his crucifixion? Are the Jews "Christ-killers"?

3(A) GEORGE:

One of the titles given to Jesus is Immanuel – "God with us". God is not only the being who stands above the world. God became involved in the human predicament, sharing and understanding humanity. Jesus is also the messiah – the fulfilment of Jewish expectations, even though his status is largely unacknowledged by Jews. In the previous section I mentioned Jesus Christ as the divine Word, or Wisdom. Jesus' words are God's words, and through him God has decisively spoken: there is no need for any further prophet to provide any new revelation or any further key to salvation. The Christian tradition has had its subsequent saints and theologians, but these are people who have lived out Christ's teachings, or have endeavoured to interpret them; they have not delivered any additional divine message.

The title "Immanuel" relates to Isaiah's prophecy, "The virgin will conceive and give birth to a son, and will call him Immanuel" (Isaiah 7:14). At a popular level, Christians believe that Isaiah was predicting the coming of Christ, but most scholars would agree that this is a mistranslation, and that "virgin" is more properly rendered "young woman". Dan mentions the virgin birth in a previous section (2e). Again, most Christians probably take the conservative view that Jesus' birth was miraculous. However, I recall William Barclay, under whom I studied many years ago, saying provocatively that the world's salvation can hardly depend on the state of one woman's hymen! Matthew and Luke trace Jesus' ancestry through his paternal lineage, which some scholars suggest would make little sense if he had no human father. It is not uncommon for the birth and infancy of great religious leaders to be surrounded by stories that emphasize their status. The Buddha is said to have had a miraculous birth, Muhammad reputedly recited the *shahada* as a baby, and the story of Moses being found in the bulrushes is another remarkable infancy story.

There can be little doubt that Jesus of Nazareth was a real historical figure, although there are widely different views about precisely who he was and how much can truly be known about him. Was he a revolutionary, a mystic, an end-time prophet or a peasant-turned-sage? In recent times the "quest for the historical Jesus" has been greatly helped by Jewish scholars like Geza Vermes and Donald Hagner, who have provided important insights into Jewish life and practice.

Jesus is referred to as "rabbi", and he interpreted the Torah. He appears to be very critical of the Pharisees, who are portrayed as over-meticulous interpreters of the Jewish law. Jesus teaches that Jewish ritual requirements must come second to the prime duties of loving God and loving one's neighbour (Matthew 22:36–39). His identification of the "greatest commandment" was not an innovation, but was perfectly in line with contemporary rabbinical ideas. Jesus' more distinctive teaching was what the scholar Rudolf Bultmann calls "radical obedience to the Law". In his Sermon on the Mount, Jesus says that the prohibition on murder also requires restraining one's anger and refusing to insult an enemy (Matthew 5:21–22) – the Law of Moses applies to one's thoughts as well as one's deeds.

There can be little doubt that Jesus was crucified. The Christians would hardly have spread a story that was so much to their disadvantage, and the Roman governor – Pontius Pilate – who authorized the sentence is clearly identified. The event is corroborated by non-Christian sources, such as Josephus, Tacitus, and – centuries later – the Talmud. I therefore have problems with the Muslim view that Jesus was not crucified, since this seems to fly in the face of all the historical evidence and to be based merely on implicit faith in the Qur'an's infallibility.

Central to the Christian faith is the belief in Christ's resurrection. As Saint Paul said, "If Christ has not been raised, our preaching is useless" (1 Corinthians 15:14). However, the Gospel accounts of Jesus' resurrection are ambiguous. He is sometimes portrayed as a physical being, who can eat breakfast with his disciples on the seashore; at other times he appears to be able to walk through closed doors. Paul talked about a "spiritual body", perhaps indicating that the resurrection is not to be understood merely as the resuscitation of a corpse. Whatever the nature of Jesus' resurrection body, something remarkable certainly happened to change the first disciples from unconfident despondent people to confident proclaimers that Jesus was God's messiah, who offers new life to the believer. As Paul said, "We were therefore buried with him through baptism into death in order that… we too may live a new life" (Romans 6:4).

Why is it that Jews have confidently taught that the messiah will come, but yet are reluctant to acknowledge that this may have happened?

3(B) DAN:

Through the centuries Jesus has been understood as the risen Christ who sits at the right hand of God. The doctrines of the incarnation and the Trinity have been and remain central tenets of the Christian faith, and this perhaps more than anything else has made fruitful Jewish–Christian dialogue difficult if not impossible. In the past Jews have consistently repudiated the kinds of claims that George has made about Jesus, and as a result Christians have denounced Jews for their unwillingness to accept Christ as their Saviour and Lord. In the last chapter I highlighted why Jews find these theological doctrines objectionable; I want to turn now to the concept of messiahship.

George asks why, given the traditional Jewish expectation of messianic redemption, Jews have through the centuries refused to acknowledge Jesus as their long-awaited redeemer. The term "messiah" comes from the Hebrew root *mashiah* and means "the anointed one". In the Bible this term originally referred to any person anointed with sacred oil for the purpose of holding high office such as a king or priest. In certain contexts it was applied to any person for whom God had a special purpose. Eventually these biblical ideas were elaborated in the Apocrypha and Pseudepigrapha. In rabbinic literature the order of redemption was outlined as follows: (1) the signs of the messiah; (2) the birth pangs of the messiah; (3) the coming of Elijah; (4) the trumpet of the messiah; (5) the ingathering of the exiles; (6) the reception of proselytes; (7) the war with Gog and Magog; (8) the Days of the messiah; (9) the renovation of the world; (10) the Day of Judgment; (11) the resurrection of the dead; (12) the world to come.

On the basis of this eschatological unfolding of history, Jews refuse to accept Jesus as their saviour for several reasons. First, according to Judaism it is obvious that he did not fulfil Jewish messianic expectations. He did not restore the kingdom of David to its former glory; nor did he gather in the dispersed ones of Israel and restore all the laws of the Torah that were in abeyance (such as the sacrificial cult). He did not compel all Israel to walk in the way of the Torah, nor did he rebuild the Temple and usher in a new order in the world and nature. In other words, Jesus did not usher in a cataclysmic change in history. Universal peace, in which there is neither war nor competition, did not come about on earth. Thus for Jews, Jesus did not fulfil the prophetic messianic hope in a redeemer who would bring political and spiritual redemption as well as earthly blessings and moral perfection to the human race.

A second objection to Jesus concerns the Christian claim that he possesses a special relationship with God. In Matthew, for example, we read: "No one knows the Son except the Father, and no one knows the Father except the Son" (Matthew 11:27). In John's Gospel Jesus declares, "I am the way and the truth and the life; no one comes to the Father except through me. If you really know me, you will know my Father as well. From now on, you do know him and have seen him"

(John 14:6–7). Such an idea undermines the Jewish conviction that God is equally near to all.

A third objection to Jesus arises from his attitude to sin and sinners. The traditional task of the prophets was to castigate Israel for rejecting God's law, not to forgive sin. Jesus, however, took upon himself the power to do this. Thus he declared with regard to a paralytic: "Which is easier: to say, 'Your sins are forgiven,' or to say, 'Get up and walk'? But I want you to know that the Son of Man has authority on earth to forgive sins.' So he said to the paralysed man, 'Get up, take your mat and go home'" (Matthew 9:5–6). When Jesus said to a woman of ill repute, "Your sins are forgiven", his companions were shocked. "Who is this, who even forgives sins?" they asked (Luke 7:48–49). It is not surprising that this was their reaction since such a usurpation of God's prerogative was without precedent.

Finally, Jesus' teaching is rejected by Jews because his interpretation of Jewish law is at variance with rabbinic tradition. Though at one point in the Gospels, Jesus declared that no change should be made in the Law (Matthew 5:17), he disregarded a number of important precepts. Several times on the Sabbath, for example, he cured individuals who were not dangerously ill, in violation of the rabbinic precept that the Sabbath law can only be broken for the saving and preserving of life. In a similar vein Jesus rejected the biblical and rabbinic teaching regarding dietary laws: "What goes into someone's mouth does not defile them," he stated, "but what comes out of their mouth, that is what defiles them" (Matthew 15:11). Is it any wonder then that for Jews, Christian claims about Jesus' messiahship are incomprehensible?

3(C) DAWOUD:

Despite the fact that Islam recognizes the virgin birth of 'Isa (Jesus), on balance I think the Muslim view is probably closer to the Jewish opinion than it is to the Christian position, although for different reasons. As I mentioned previously, 'Isa is held in very high regard by Muslims. He is mentioned by name in the Qur'an some twenty-five times, while the Prophet Muhammad is only mentioned by name four times. The word "Masih" is attached to him and is obviously related to the Hebrew word *mashiah* that Dan mentions and has similar meaning. What is completely anathema to Muslims, however, is the suggestion that Jesus is the incarnation of God, or the Son of God. Nowhere in the Qur'an is this suggested. Moreover, the notion that he died on the cross is explicitly repudiated.

The Qur'an goes into some detail with regard to the circumstances of his birth and provides a prologue describing the birth of Maryam (Mary). Maryam was born into the House of Amran (from which *Sura* 3 derives its name). Her mother made a vow before she was born that she would dedicate her child to the service of God and, when a girl was born, sought refuge in God and protection from Satan, for her and her descendants. There is considerable emphasis on Maryam's virtue and the honour accorded to her above all women, although she is not considered holy or to have any intercessory powers. *Sura* 19, named after Maryam, describes the annunciation and birth of 'Isa and the events surrounding this are deemed to be miraculous. Maryam was visited by an angel who informed her that she was to bear a pure son, and when she asked how this was possible when no man had touched her the angel informed her that this was easy for God. She withdrew from her community and was overcome with birth pangs by the trunk of a palm tree. As she cried out wishing that she had died before enduring this, a voice told her that God had put a stream below her feet and that she should shake the tree so that ripe dates would fall. She should eat, drink, and be of quiet mind. On returning to her people she vowed not to speak and when they accused her of immorality she pointed to the infant who spoke and told them:

"Indeed, I am the servant of Allah. He has given me the Scripture and made me a prophet and He has made me blessed wherever I am and has enjoined upon me prayer and zakah as long as I remain alive and [made me] dutiful to my mother, and He has not made me a wretched tyrant, and peace is on me the day I was born and the day I will die and the day I am raised alive." (19:30–33)

'Isa is one of the most important prophets in Islam. Twenty-five prophets are named in the Qur'an, many of them corresponding to or linked to the prophets of the Torah. Five in particular are identified as the most important historical figures: Nuh (Noah), Ibrahim (Abraham) and Musa (Moses), and then 'Isa (Jesus) and Muhammad, for whose lives there is more documentary evidence. Each of them is sent by God as a messenger to remind humanity to worship the One God and to obey His law. For each of the prophets there is a story of triumph in adversity, strength in upholding the faith, and reward for standing up for the right against the wrong. This is the reason why Muslims believe that the Christians must have changed the scriptures and invented the story of the crucifixion because to them it is unthinkable that one of God's prophets should be so humiliated and defeated by human beings. The Qur'an says:

> *And [for] their saying, "Indeed, we have killed the Messiah, 'Isa, the son of Maryam, the messenger of God." And they did not kill him, nor did they crucify him; but [another] was made to resemble him to them. And indeed, those who differ over it are in doubt about it. They have no knowledge of it except the following of assumption. And they did not kill him, for certain. (4:157)*

Some translations say: "… but it was made to seem so to them", and there have always been different opinions as to whether it was made to appear that he was crucified while he was not, or whether another man was substituted for him and made to look like him.

I understand that Christians may think that Muslims have completely missed the point of the whole story.

3(D) GEORGE:

The problems that Dan and Dawoud have identified are first, that Jesus did not bring about any remarkable political or social change, and second, that Christians ascribed divinity to him. Dawoud expresses well the Islamic view of Jesus, and his summary of the virgin birth story is an attractive one. However, he seems uncritically to accept what the Qur'an says. Here we have an important difference between Christian and Muslim scholarship: ever since the European Enlightenment Christian scholars have critically examined the historical issues surrounding the life of Jesus of Nazareth. We cannot accept unquestioningly that he was born of a virgin. As I mentioned previously, such stories surround the birth of many religious leaders, and signal that we look for their meaning rather than their historicity.

Christian scholars have put much effort into the quest for the historical Jesus. This does not mean that we accept that the Gospels were corrupted – a view for which we can find little evidence – but rather that we want to separate out their religious message from their historical value. While no agreed answers have emerged from the debate, it is surely important that the believer – whether Jew, Christian, or Muslim – is able to face critical questions, rather than rely on blind faith.

Dawoud says that he cannot believe in the crucifixion, but the alternative accounts suggested by the Qur'an are both highly improbable. Christians would hardly have invented a story that deprecated their leader if it were not true. I am not at all sure what it would mean for Jesus simply to "appear" to be crucified. How would one organize a mock-up of a crucifixion in the first century?

The idea that someone else took Jesus' place, however, does have a precedent. Some of the ancient Gnostics put forward the notion that when Simon of Cyrene was compelled to carry Jesus' cross (Matthew 27:32), he was mistakenly crucified in place of Jesus. Needless to say, Christians find problems with this account. Not only is it inherently implausible that the Roman soldiers would have made such a gross blunder, with no one pointing out their obvious mistake, but it is not a story that the Christian Gospels could have distorted. It comes from the Second Treatise of the Great Seth, one of the Nag Hammadi documents, and scholars reckon that it is a third-century piece of writing. The Gospels were completed by the end of the first century.

Turning to the question of whether Jesus' death was a humiliation, it is worth noting that Jesus' last recorded words on the cross were "It is finished" – meaning "accomplished" – (John 19:30). So Jesus' early disciples clearly saw things differently from Dan and Dawoud. Let's imagine what might have happened if the story had a "happier" ending, with Jesus accepting the challenge to come down from the cross (Matthew 27:40), overcoming the Roman authorities, restoring the kingdom of David, and ensuring the continued survival of the Jerusalem Temple. How much better would human history have been? A small community would have been left in peace – at least for a while – to practise their own religion with its complex law code and system of animal sacrifices focused on the Temple.

Christians hold that Christ's death was a greater accomplishment than this. Central to the Christian faith is the concept of atonement – God's way of dealing with sin, which is something of far greater significance than dealing with the Romans. Christian theologians have proposed different explanations of how the atonement took place, but what we can say is that the crucifixion demonstrates Jesus' reconciliation of divine justice with divine forgiveness. It underlines the seriousness of sin, yet demonstrates the possibility of acquittal before God. The Gospel writers state that at the crucifixion the Temple veil was torn in two (Mark 15:38): again, this is not necessarily to be taken as a literal happening, as Dawoud appears to take the Qur'an. It is a powerful symbol that the barriers between God and humanity have been broken down, and that a sacrificial system is no longer necessary. As Paul puts it, "Christ, our Passover lamb, has been sacrificed" (1 Corinthians 5:7).

The story that Dan cites – the healing of a paralysed man (Matthew 9:1–8) – makes two points. First, dealing with sin takes precedence over dealing with physical disability, and Jesus claimed authority over sin. Second, showing human compassion took precedence over ritual obligation. True, the man's life was not in danger, but if someone is ill on the Sabbath day, and it is possible to bring about a cure, then why wait an extra twenty-four hours? Can this really be what the Jewish faith wants us to do, and, if so, why?

3(E) DAN:

I want to begin with what George has just said: "Surely it is important that the believer – whether Jew, Christian, or Muslim – is able to face critical questions, rather than rely on blind faith." George is right about this. Yet, to my mind this is what traditional Christians have failed to do. Christian beliefs about Jesus' divinity are not grounded in historical fact – rather they are based on faith. Precisely because I do not share such a spiritual perspective – which calls for a leap of faith (or what George has referred to as "blind faith") – I cannot accept such religious assumptions.

Through the ages Jesus has been understood as the risen Christ who sits at the right hand of the Father. As I noted previously, the doctrine of the Trinity and the incarnation and the understanding of Jesus as the messiah have separated Jews and Christians and have served as stumbling blocks to fruitful interfaith encounter. In a book I wrote some years ago, *The Crucified Jew: Twenty Centuries of Christian Antisemitism*, I highlighted the ways in which such beliefs generated murderous hostility towards the Jewish community. Nonetheless, I believe it is possible for Jews (and Muslims) today to have a more sympathetic approach to the Gospels. What is crucial for positive Jewish–Christian–Muslim dialogue is the emphasis on understanding Jesus as a first-century Palestinian Jew. It is the flesh-and-blood Jesus – the Jesus of history – who is of fundamental importance. The historical context of the Gospels can in this way be reclaimed for Christians, Muslims, and Jews, and Jesus' teaching in the New Testament can be related directly to God's design as recorded in the Hebrew Bible.

From a historical standpoint (which George has stressed is of key importance), the picture of Jesus that emerges from the Gospel narratives is inextricably connected to his Jewish background. His criticism of the religious establishment, like that of the pre-exilic prophets, should not be understood as a rejection of Judaism but as a call to the nation to return to the God of their ancestors. Seen in this manner, Jesus' teaching stands in the tradition of the ethical prophets of ancient Israel. A central theme of prophecy in ancient Israel was the rejection of ritualistic and sacrificial acts devoid of an accompanying quest for righteousness and justice. The prophets were to be the social conscience of the nation. So too did Jesus see himself as the conscience of Israel.

This vision of Jesus as a prophet of Israel calling the people back to the true worship of God should make it possible for the Jew (and presumably for the Muslim as well) to gain a sympathetic insight into Jesus' ministry. His attack on the scribes and Pharisees can be seen, not as a rejection of the Torah, but as a prophetic renunciation of a corrupt religious establishment. Such a conception of Jesus should enable Jews (and Muslims) to set aside previous Christological barriers to interfaith dialogue and concentrate on a shared prophetic heritage. Instead of rejecting Jesus as a blasphemous heretic (as he has been depicted in rabbinic sources), this emphasis on Jesus' prophetic mission can enable both Jews and Muslims to see in Jesus' life a reflection of the prophetic ideals of Israel. In this way the flesh-and-blood Jesus of the New Testament can be understood as Jesus the Jew, who, like the great prophets of ancient Israel, struggled to rescue the nation from its iniquity and draw the people back to the faith of their ancestors. Here then, in the life of Jesus, is a link that can draw our three faiths together in a mutual quest for the elimination of oppression and injustice in the modern world.

3(F) DAWOUD:

George is right to point out that Muslims have been reluctant to engage in critical questioning of Qur'anic accounts and this is no doubt something that we will discuss at greater length when we examine the texts and scriptures of our faiths. While it would be inaccurate to say that there is no critical scholarship of the Qur'an, essentially for Muslims worldwide, the Qur'an is the literal word of God which cannot and should not be challenged. Where the meaning of a verse is unclear, cryptic, ambiguous, or requires further explanation, there is room for exegesis and interpretation, but in the case of a narrative such as the description of the birth of Jesus or a clear statement such as the denial of the crucifixion, Muslims simply cannot do other than to believe it to be the truth. The Qur'an itself answers the question of how Maryam could have given birth to a son while still a virgin, saying that when God wills a thing He only has to say "be" and it is. The debate as to how it was merely made to appear that Jesus was crucified does not suggest any kind of human deception or the staging of the events but rather that God created the illusion that he was crucified. God intervened in this in a manner similar to his intervention in the sacrifice of Isma'il by his father Ibrahim. Having been asked by God to sacrifice his son, with complete submission to God's will, Ibrahim prepared to do so. Only at the last moment did God substitute an animal for Isma'il.

Dan suggests that all three faiths might examine Jesus as a historical figure – as a first-century Palestinian Jew who came to call people to return to the true God – and this is essentially in keeping with Muslim belief, although Muslims believe that like the other prophets he was *muslim* (in the sense of "one who submits to God"). The Qur'an emphasizes the fact that Jesus was one in a line of prophets sent to do just this, and crucially, Jesus predicts the coming of the Prophet Muhammad:

And [mention] when Jesus, the son of Mary, said, "O children of Israel, indeed I am the messenger of Allah to you confirming what came before me of the Torah and bringing good tidings of a messenger to come after me, whose name is Ahmad." But when he came to them with clear evidences, they said, "This is obvious magic." (61:6)

There is little detail of Jesus' life or description of his actions in the Qur'an, but we do find in the description of the annunciation,

And [He will make him] a messenger to the Children of Israel, [who will say], "Indeed I have come to you with a sign from your Lord in that I design for you from clay [that which is] like the form of a bird, then I breathe into it and it becomes a bird by permission of Allah. And I cure the blind and the leper, and I give life to the dead – by permission of Allah. And I inform you of what you eat and what you store in your houses. Indeed in that is a sign for you, if you are believers." (3:49)

Here Jesus' miracles are acknowledged but no detail is offered. This is unusual in comparison with other narratives of the lives of the prophets in the Qur'an, which are often detailed and didactic.

Nevertheless, Jesus is extremely important to Muslims and is revered by some groups particularly in parts of the Middle East. In Syria, for example, the monastery of Sidnaya has been a centre of pilgrimage for Christians and Muslims alike for centuries. Jesus has a particular place in Sufism, the mystical dimension of Islam. In his *The Muslim Jesus*, Tarif Khalidi discusses the body of hagiographic literature that developed over several centuries after the rise of Islam. There are reports of Jesus' life and sayings collected and discussed by Muslim scholars, sometimes referred to as the Muslim gospels, which resemble the *hadith*, the reports of the life of Muhammad.

Khalidi emphasizes that while other prophets in the Qur'an form part of detailed narratives, Jesus is the focus specifically of a theological argument against the Christian claim of his divinity. While there is, no doubt, much in the reverence for Jesus to bring Muslims and Christians together, this is a fundamental stumbling block to agreement.

CHAPTER 4

SACRED TEXTS

All three faiths are "religions of the book". Christianity adds to Jewish scripture, and Muslims claim that the texts of the two older faiths were corrupted in the course of time, and that the true definitive message of Allah was communicated through the revelation to Muhammad. Both Christianity and the liberal branches of Judaism have been influenced by the European Enlightenment, which has encouraged a critical attitude to scholarship, which has been resisted by Orthodox Jews and by Muslims.

4(A) DAN:

For thousands of years Jews have believed that the Torah (Genesis, Exodus, Leviticus, Numbers, and Deuteronomy) was communicated by God to Moses on Mount Sinai. In the twelfth-century Jewish philosopher Moses Maimonides' formulation of the thirteen principles of the Jewish faith, this belief is the eighth tenet:

> The Torah was revealed from Heaven. This implies our belief that the whole of the Torah found in our hands this day is the Torah that was handed down by Moses, and that is all of divine origin. By this I mean that the whole of the Torah came unto him from before God in a manner which is metaphorically called "speaking"; but the real nature of that communication is unknown to everybody except to Moses (peace to him!) to whom it came.
>
> **(Maimonides, *Commentary to the Mishnah*, Sanhedrin, X, I)**

In rabbinic literature a distinction is drawn between the revelation of the Five Books of Moses and the prophetic writings. This is frequently expressed by saying that the Torah was given directly by God, whereas the prophetic books were given by means of prophecy.

These books are: Joshua, Judges, 1 and 2 Samuel, 1 and 2 Kings, Isaiah, Jeremiah Ezekiel, Hosea, Joel, Amos, Obadiah, Jonah, Micah, Nahum, Habakkuk, Zephaniah, Haggai, Zechariah, and Malachi. The remaining books of the Bible (Psalms, Lamentations, The Song of Songs, Proverbs, Job, Ecclesiastes, Ruth, 1 and 2 Chronicles, Esther, Ezra, Nehemiah, and Daniel) were conveyed by means of the Holy Spirit rather than through prophecy. Nonetheless, all these writings constitute the canon of scripture. The Hebrew term referring to the Bible as a whole is "*Tanakh*"; this word is made up of the first three letters of the three divisions of scripture: Torah (Pentateuch); *Neviim* (Prophets); and *Ketuvim* (Writings). This is the "written Torah" (*Torah She-Bi-Katav*).

According to the rabbis, the expositions and elaborations of the written Torah were also revealed by God to Moses. Subsequently they were passed from generation to generation, and through this process additional legislation was incorporated. This process is referred to as the "oral Torah" (*Torah She-Be-Al-Peh*). Thus, traditional Judaism affirms that God's revelation was twofold and binding for all time. This means that all 613 commandments in the Five Books of Moses, and the rabbinical expansion of these laws are obligatory for all Jews; further, the beliefs contained in the Torah are true for all time. Committed to this belief, Jews pray in the synagogue that God will guide them to do His will as recorded in their sacred literature.

In modern times, however, it has become increasingly difficult for most Jews to accept the traditional concept of divine revelation in the light of scholarly investigation of the biblical text. Over the last two centuries, biblical scholars have pointed out that the Five Books of Moses appear to be composed of different sources. Within non-Orthodox circles, it is widely accepted that the Torah is a composite work, consisting of various sources from different periods in the history of ancient Israel. In addition, textual studies of ancient manuscripts highlight the improbability of the traditional view of the Torah. A final aspect of modern studies which bears on the question of Mosaic authorship concerns the influence of the ancient Near East on the Bible: there are strong parallels in the Jewish Bible to laws, stories, and myths found throughout the ancient Near East.

Not surprisingly, traditionalists regard such investigations as irrelevant. Orthodox Judaism today remains committed to the view that the written as well as the oral Torah were imparted to Moses on Mount Sinai: this act of revelation serves as the basis for the entire legal system as well as doctrinal beliefs about God. There is a wide gap between Orthodox and non-Orthodox Jews. Yet, despite such differences of interpretation, non-Orthodox and Orthodox Jews join ranks in continuing to regard the Hebrew Bible as fundamental to the faith. As the liturgy used in all synagogues proclaims: "It is a tree of life to those who hold fast to it."

4(B) GEORGE:

It's interesting that Dan acknowledges the possible composite nature of the Torah. Some years ago I had a conversation with an Orthodox rabbi on the subject, and I asked him whether he thought the last 150 years of Christian scholarship had simply been a waste of time. His answer was, bluntly, "Yes."

Of course, Christians are similarly divided. While many Christians, like me, would share Dan's view about how scripture was compiled, Christian fundamentalism remains strong. The famous evangelist Billy Graham once said that the Bible was a book dictated by God to thirty secretaries. However, many Christians would not accept that the Bible came about through such a mechanical process. They prefer to see it as the work of human hands, written by fallible authors about fallible people. The Bible provides us with a record of God's dealings with His people throughout their history – a record that is not always to their credit, but which illustrates God's patience and forgiveness, and, most importantly, His plan of salvation for the world.

Christians accept all the books of the Bible that Dan itemizes. The Christian Bible arranges them in a slightly different order, but this is not particularly important. However, we don't accept the tradition of the oral Torah, and indeed the majority of Christians probably have not even heard of it. Christians, of course, add their own scriptures: the four Gospels, the Acts of the Apostles, letters by Paul and other early Christian leaders, and the somewhat enigmatic book of Revelation. To these Roman Catholics add the Apocrypha – a further fifteen books written during the inter-testamental period.

The New Testament is usually regarded as more important, since it tells of Christ's ministry, his death and resurrection, and his exalted status as the messiah. While many Christians believe that the Gospels were the record of eyewitnesses, many scholars are not so sure. Mark's – the earliest – was possibly written between 60 and 70 CE , and he may have been informed by Jesus' disciple Peter. Matthew and Luke draw on his account, and John's Gospel is the last, possibly written between 90 and 100 CE. We cannot be certain how much of their narratives can be traced back to Jesus himself, but we are confident that there are no extant earlier traditions that these Gospel writers distorted. The books of the Bible of course were copied many times by scribes. Inevitably, a few mistakes occurred, but scholars have usually been able to decide on the original wording, and discrepancies between ancient manuscripts are fairly unimportant.

One conservative Christian once used the expression "bulldozing the Bible" to describe scholarly attempts to question traditional views on biblical authorship and authenticity. However, Christian scholars do their work not to discredit the Bible, but out of love and fascination for it. They would acknowledge, with more traditional Christians, that the Bible has authority – although they would disagree about precisely what that means. At the very least it means that the Bible contains all the truth that is needed for salvation, and its use in worship – to the virtual exclusion of all other literature – is a testimony to the importance that Christians attach to it.

Something should be said about how we regard the Old Testament. Some Christians, particularly in the Adventist tradition, continue to observe the Jewish dietary laws, the Sabbath, and the major festivals, but they are a minority, and most Christians hold that such requirements have now been superseded. Many of its teachings still stand: the Ten Commandments, of course, being endorsed by Jesus, continue to be regarded as authoritative moral teaching.

Christians hold that the Old Testament in some sense points to Christ, although there are different understandings of this idea. Conservative Christians claim that the ancient prophets were speaking of Jesus, for example when Isaiah tells of the "suffering servant" who was "pierced for our transgressions" (Isaiah 53:5), perceiving in this a foretelling of Jesus' crucifixion. Many scholars question whether the biblical prophets had clairvoyant powers that enabled them to see centuries into the future, preferring to view the ancient sages' expectations of a coming golden age as fulfilled and surpassed by Christ's redeeming work.

One compelling reason for retaining the Old Testament is that the New Testament makes little sense without it. Without the Old Testament, we would be unable to understand Jesus' dialogues with the Pharisees, Paul's discussions about faith replacing the Law, or the "hall of fame" in Hebrews 11, where the anonymous author enumerates the ancient faithful men and women who paved the way for Christ's coming.

Christians view the Bible as the record of God's final revelation, and react unfavourably to attempts to supplement its teachings with further scriptures, such as the Qur'an or The Book of Mormon.

4(C) DAWOUD:

The Qur'an refers numerous times to the "People of the Book", meaning those peoples, Christians and Jews, to whom the message was revealed before the Prophet Muhammad. There are many references in the Qur'an to the scriptures of Judaism and Christianity. The *suhuf* (sometimes translated as scrolls) of Abraham are deemed to be a lost body of revelation of the same monotheistic message of Judaism, Christianity, and Islam; the *torat* of Moses is identified with the Torah; the *zabur* are the psalms of David; and the *injil* is the gospel of Jesus. All of these are mentioned several times as examples of scriptures revealed to these prophets respectively as a reminder of their message. There is a common received belief among Muslims that the earlier scriptures were falsified, or that they became corrupted over time, and this is to a great extent based on the work of the tenth-century scholar

Ibn Hazm who constructed his arguments on analysis of incongruities in the texts and on scrutiny of their transmission. Other scholars, such as Ibn Qutayba and al-Tabari (ninth century CE), however, suggest that there was no corruption of the texts themselves but only errors and distortion in their interpretation. The Qur'an itself says: "Do you covet [the hope, O believers], that they would believe for you while a party of them used to hear the words of Allah and then distort the Torah after they had understood it while they were knowing?" (2:75).

In contrast Muslims believe the Qur'an to be the literal and uncorrupted word of God as revealed to the Prophet Muhammad through Jibril, the Angel Gabriel. Miracles of various kinds are attributed to other prophets, while the Qur'an is the miracle that marks the Prophethood of Muhammad. Much is made of his illiteracy as proof of its divine nature, although at this time very few people could read and write. There was little written literature in Arabic but a substantial corpus of orally transmitted tribal history and poetry.

The revelation of the Qur'an took place over a period of more than twenty years. During the initial period in Mecca the verses were primarily concerned with the call to faith and reward and punishment, including didactic narratives of the prophets and previous generations. Later, during the establishment of the community in Medina, they came to include more detailed prescriptions of rules and principles for the governing of the community, often in answer to situations that arose or questions asked by the community. It was initially memorized and gradually written down piecemeal on whatever materials came to hand, but it was not collated as a manuscript until some time after the death of Muhammad when many of those who had memorized it during his lifetime had died or been killed in battle and it was feared that its arrangement or even parts of the text might be lost.

The Qur'an exists in Arabic and even defines itself as such: "And thus We have revealed to you an Arabic Qur'an" (42:7). This is the only form in which it may be recited or used in prayer. Translations are not recognized as Qur'an but only as a way of understanding its meaning. Early copies of the Qur'an did not have the complex pointing of the script which only appears to have been standardized in the ninth century as Arabic grammar as we know it today was extracted from the Qur'an. It is this that has meant that Arabic in the form in which it was spoken in this part of the Arabian Peninsula in the sixth/seventh centuries is now the written language of the entire Arabic-speaking world and has remained essentially unchanged since the time of the revelation of the Qur'an. The Qur'an is absolutely central to the belief of Muslims and is held in great reverence. It is the ambition of most devout Muslims to memorize the Qur'an, and many people do so, even when they do not understand Arabic.

The complement to the Qur'an which provides guidance to Muslims where more explanation or detail is required is the *Sunna*, the example of the Prophet as described in the *hadith*, the records of his words, deeds, and tacit acceptance. There is a greater range of opinion among Muslim and non-Muslim scholars about its origin and authenticity, although there are canonical collections of *hadith* compiled in the ninth century according to a complex method of scrutiny of their content and chains of transmission which are accepted by the majority of Sunni Muslims.

4(D) DAN:

Paralleling the Muslim view of scripture, traditional Judaism maintains that God has revealed Himself to His chosen people through the revelation of the Torah on Mount Sinai. Nonetheless, throughout history Jews have adopted a relatively tolerant attitude towards other religions. In the biblical period the ancient Israelites were encouraged to view the gods of other peoples as nonentities. Yet foreign peoples were not condemned for their beliefs. Furthermore, it was the conviction of the prophets that in the end of days all nations would recognize that the God of the Israelites is the Lord of the universe. Thus, there was no compulsion to missionize among non-believers. There is hope even for pagan peoples in the unfolding of God's plan of salvation.

In the rabbinic period this tradition of tolerance continued to animate Jewish life. According to the rabbis, all non-Jews who follow the Noahide Laws (the laws that Noah observed) are viewed as acceptable to God. In this context even those who engage in polytheistic practices are admissible as long as the gods they worship are conceived as symbolically pointing to the One God. In the medieval period such writers as Rabbenu Tam applied this rabbinic conception of symbolic intermediacy to Christian believers. In his opinion Christianity is not idolatry, since Christians are monotheists despite their belief in the Trinity. Other writers such as Judah Halevi formulated an even more tolerant form of Jewish inclusivism: for these thinkers Christians as well as Muslims have an important role in God's plan for humanity by spreading the message of monotheism.

Such a positive stance towards other faiths continued into the early modern period due to the impact of the Enlightenment. In the eighteenth century the Jewish philosopher Moses Mendelssohn argued that the Jewish people were the recipients of a divine revelation consisting of ritual and moral law. Nevertheless, Mendelssohn was convinced that God's reality can be discerned through human reason. Thus, all human beings – regardless of their religious persuasion – are capable of discerning God's nature and activity. During this period other thinkers offered a sympathetic appreciation of Christianity and other faiths while at the same time adhering to the belief that Judaism is the superior religion.

Today it is possible to go even further. As I noted previously, within non-Orthodox Jewish circles there has been a widespread acceptance of the findings of biblical scholarship. No longer is the Torah regarded as God's unalterable revelation to the Jewish people: instead the Pentateuch is viewed as a composite work containing the spiritual reflections of Jews through many centuries. In this light, many progressive Jews would regard the world's religions as different human responses to the one divine reality. Such a view of the Divine in relation to the world's faiths can be represented by an image of alternative paths ascending a single mountain. Each route symbolizes a particular religion, with Divine Reality floating like a cloud above the mountaintop. The routes of these faith communities (in our case Christianity, Judaism, and Islam) are all different, yet at various points they intersect: these intersections should be understood as those areas where religious conceptions within the differing traditions complement one another. Thus as pilgrims of different faiths ascend to the summit, they will encounter parallels with their own traditions. But the Divine Reality they all pursue is in the end unattainable by these finite quests.

I wonder what you both will make of this interpretation of religious history. As you can see, such a progressive view of revelation is far removed from the way in which traditional Jews, Christians, and Muslims have regarded their scriptural inheritance. Instead of viewing the Hebrew Bible, the New Testament, and the Qur'an as God's full and final revelation, these sacred texts should be seen as human attempts to make sense of divine reality. Such a shift from the absolutism of the past can free us from the barriers that have separated us, and provide a new basis for fruitful interfaith dialogue and discussion.

4(E) DAWOUD:

As Dan and George have both explained, since the Enlightenment many Jews and Christians have been more open to questioning the origins and meanings of the scriptures, and the Torah and Bible have been subjected to the academic rigour of higher criticism.

The obstacle to this, however, is that Muslims are not open to this kind of criticism of the Qur'an. Instead of encouraging Muslims to look at the Qur'an critically using these methods, however, the conclusions drawn from the analysis of the Jewish and Christian scriptures have simply confirmed Muslims in their belief that these texts were altered or falsified and that the Qur'an alone is infallible and was revealed to rectify the previous scriptures and to bring humanity back to the true message. Muslims are very resistant to anything that calls the Qur'an into question. There are studies by non-Muslim scholars that subject the Qur'an to this kind of historical, literary, and linguistic analysis, notably those by John Wansbrough, Patricia Crone, Michael Cook, and Andrew Rippin. Earlier Western scholars of Islam had generally looked at the Qur'an and *hadith* and early Islamic history through the medium of traditional Islamic scholarship and the classical Islamic histories, but Wansbrough's *Quranic Studies: Sources and Methods of Scriptural Interpretation*, published in 1977, caused uproar by suggesting that Islam evolved from a Judeo-Christian sect and that the Qur'an developed from Jewish and Christian scriptures which became Arabized over time. He suggests that the history of the origins of Islam, as it has come down to us, was put together by later generations with the aim of creating a unique religious identity and asserting its superiority. For Muslims, however, this is completely unacceptable. Anything that challenges the belief in the revelation of the Qur'an and the received view of early Islamic history is heresy. Acceptance of the revelation of the Qur'an is fundamental to the faith. In several verses the divine origin of the Qur'an is asserted within the text itself with emphasis is on its inimitability:

Say, "If mankind and the jinn gathered in order to produce the like of this Qur'an, they could not produce the like of it, even if they were to each other assistants." (17:88)

And if you are in doubt about what We have sent down upon Our Servant [Muhammad], then produce a surah the like thereof and call upon your witnesses other than Allah , if you should be truthful. (2:23)

There are methods of textual analysis within the Islamic sciences, but they all start from the base line of faith and unquestioning acceptance of the revelation. Muslims believe that the Qur'an contains the essential wisdom and practical guidance required for all peoples and for all time and that it is the duty of the Muslim community to seek to understand it and to draw the meanings appropriate to any circumstance. Over centuries, Qur'an scholars and exegetes have produced complex rules and methods for interpreting and understanding the Qur'an. These include detailed linguistic analysis of the text, exploration of the implications of its grammatical intricacies and unique stylistic elements, internal structural and content analysis, historical contextual analysis based on the *hadith* and the *sira* (the biography of the Prophet), and reference to other scriptures. On this basis the whole structure of Islamic doctrine, worship, and law has been constructed, and while there are differences in interpretation between Sunni and Shi'i Islam and between the schools and divisions that each comprises, the Qur'an itself is beyond all question.

Dan presents an intellectual view of the way in which the doctrinal barriers between our faiths might be overcome. I think this perhaps underestimates the profound cultural and emotional attachment of many people of all religions to their founding texts. George has noted the reaction of some evangelical Christians to any challenge to the divine nature of the Gospels and the adherence of Adventists to Old Testament rules. For Muslims absolute belief in the Qur'an underpins their faith and their identity and I suspect the same may be true for many Christians and Jews.

4(F) GEORGE:

Dan and Dawoud have highlighted a number of important and possibly irreconcilable issues. My main disagreements relate to the Muslim view of scripture, but also to the Orthodox Jewish approach, which Dan rejects. I think there are several issues that divide Dan and me from Dawoud. First, Jews and Christians acknowledge that their scriptures are anthologies, rather than a purportedly single-authored work like the Qur'an. Second, we acknowledge human authorship, rejecting the idea of divine dictation, and acknowledging human fallibility in its composition. Consequently, we believe that our scriptures should be subjected to critical scholarship, like any other sacred or secular text, with no special pleading that they bear divine authority. This contrasts with the Islamic view that, because the Qur'an is sacred, any attempt to look for multiple sources, discrepancies, or stages of compilation is irreverent, and seeks to undermine its authority.

If there were evidence, Christian scholars would consider seriously the idea that there were primordial gospels that became distorted at an early stage of Christian history – but there is no such evidence. We acknowledge that Gospel writers borrowed from each other, and drew on oral tradition – but there has been no discovery of a primordial gospel that predates the biblical ones, let alone one with a radically different message. The only ground for such belief can be the authority of the Qur'an itself. Here we have an impasse between Western and Islamic scholarship: Western scholars, influenced by the European Enlightenment, favour a historical–critical approach to the sacred texts, and hence it is understandable that they should wish to analyse the Qur'an in a similar way. Muhammad lived in the sixth and seventh centuries in Mecca in the middle of a trade route, so might he not have heard ideas from Jews, Christians, Zoroastrians, and followers of local religions? The idea is unacceptable to Muslims because they want to give special status to their scripture and exempt it from this kind of critical questioning.

It is true that there are discrepancies in the Christian Bible, but these are not particularly worrying, and generally concern points of detail rather than disagreements about the fundamental Christian message. One example is Jesus' triumphal entry into Jerusalem. According to Mark, Luke, and John, he rides into the city on a single donkey (Mark 11:7; Luke 19:35; John 12:14). By contrast, Matthew tells us that two animals were involved (Matthew 21:7). Matthew here is probably trying to portray Jesus as fulfilling Jewish prophecy, and tailors his account to suit his purpose, since Zechariah mentions both a donkey and "a colt, the foal of a donkey"(Zechariah 9:9). Mark, Luke, and John opt for plausible description, while Matthew endeavours to portray Jesus as the messianic king foretold by the prophets.

Some Christian scholars have distinguished between *kerygma* (the church's essential proclamation) and "myth" – the incidental details surrounding the message, which may or may not be historically true. Some incidents may have been created by the early church to deal with issues that arose in the Christian community, while other pieces of narrative may go back to Jesus. Scholars continue to argue about which stories and sayings are authentic, but the Christian message does not stand or fall on their answers. The key message is that God sent His son into the world to redeem it from sin, and that he rose again to offer new life to those who believe in him.

Dan's suggestion that our three faiths are the routes to the same reality is interesting. A few fundamentalists have denied that Muslims share the same God as Jews and Christians, and say that Allah is therefore a false god. This is absurd, since Jews, Christians, and Muslims all acknowledge God's dealings with the same patriarchs and prophets, and share many important claims about God, with each faith offering a path to gain access to Him. The idea of a progressive view of revelation has its problems, however. Christians would certainly not see the truth as progressing from Judaism, through Christianity, and on to Islam. Christians have always been open to new ways of understanding its theology and scriptures, and have used many intellectual ideas from the ages in which they have lived. However, scripture implies finality. The canon of scripture is closed, and Christians typically dissociate themselves from groups that have new scriptures, whether it be The Book of Mormon, the Urantia Book, or the Qur'an. Christian history has had its problems with those who have claimed new revelations, whether it is a prophecy, a vision, or some other kind of spiritual experience. John urges his readers not to believe every new revelation, but to "test the spirits to see whether they are from God, because many false prophets have gone out into the world" (1 John 4:1).

PART II

RELIGIOUS PRACTICE

CHAPTER 5

INITIATION

How does one gain entry into the faith? Jews and Muslims favour circumcision, which Christians reject as belonging to the "old covenant", and often regard it as inflicting unnecessary suffering on an infant. For Christians the means of entry to the faith is baptism, which involves a public confession of one's faith, either by the candidate or by his or her parents.

5(A) DAN:

The first thing to remember, as we have seen, about the Jewish faith is that Jewish identity is traditionally based on maternal descent. A person is Jewish if his or her mother is Jewish, and Jewish descent is passed through the maternal line. This has been the practice through the centuries. Therefore an individual is viewed as Jewish regardless of belief or practice. This means that in the modern world, there are many Jews who see themselves as Jewish (and are perceived as such by the Jewish community) despite having no formal identification with the faith or observing any Jewish laws or ceremonies. In recent years, however, the Reform movement (followed by other branches of non-Orthodox Judaism) has redefined the criteria of Jewish identity. According to these movements, a person is Jewish if either parent is Jewish as long as he or she observes Jewish timely acts.

Of course, conversion to Judaism is accepted as well. In ancient times conversion was practised to assimilate conquered people as well as those who came to live within the Israelite community. Later the

Talmud laid down a complex procedure. The key requirement is a willingness to become part of the Jewish community and observe the Law. Traditionally both male and female candidates are obliged to be immersed in a *mikvah* (ritual bath) as part of the process, and men are to be circumcised. Orthodox Judaism specifies that there should be no coercion involved; further, the desire to marry someone Jewish is regarded as an unsuitable motive. Non-Orthodox movements have developed variations of this rabbinic procedure, in some cases dispensing with attendance at a *mikvah* and circumcision. Frequently conversion takes place for the purpose of marriage.

The most important Jewish initiation procedure for boys is circumcision (although I should note that unlike baptism within the Christian community, a person is Jewish regardless of whether he undergoes this ceremony). According to Jewish law, all male children are to be circumcised in accordance with God's decree, and as a sign of the covenant between God and Abraham's offspring. As Genesis 17:9–11 relates:

> *God said to Abraham... "This is my covenant with you and your descendants after you, the covenant you are to keep: every male among you shall be circumcised. You are to undergo circumcision, and it will be the sign of the covenant between me and you."*

Jewish ritual circumcision involves the removal of the entire foreskin. It is to be performed on the eighth day after the birth of the child by a person who is properly qualified. Traditionally it is to be performed in the presence of a quorum of ten adult Jewish men (*minyan*). Within the Jewish community this ceremony has retained its original religious significance. Yet it is striking (and perhaps surprising) that circumcision has remained a universal practice among even the most secular Jews. It is rare for Jews to question this practice on health or moral grounds. Instead, nearly all Jews regard circumcision as a form of Jewish identification and insist on the retention of this ancient custom.

For Jewish girls, there is no parallel ceremony. Instead a naming ceremony takes place in the synagogue. Baby boys are named at the circumcision; Jewish girls are named in the synagogue on the first time the Torah is read after their birth. The Hebrew form of the individual's name consists of that person's name followed by "*ben*" (son) or "*bat*" (daughter) of the father. This form is used in all Hebrew documents as well as for the call to the reading of the Torah. In modern times it is still the practice to give a child a Jewish name in addition to a secular one. At the age of thirteen a boy attains the age of Jewish adulthood: from this point he is accounted as part of a *minyan* (the quorum for prayer). This is the stage at which a *bar mitzvah* ("son of the commandment") takes place. The essentials of the *bar mitzvah* involve reading from the Torah and the prophetic books of the Bible in a religious service. Unlike *bar mitzvah* there is no legal requirement for a girl to take part in a religious ceremony to mark her religious majority (at the age of twelve). Nonetheless, a ceremonial equivalent of *bar mitzvah* (*bat mitzvah*) has been designed for girls. It should be noted, however, that these religious initiation ceremonies do not make a person Jewish – rather a person is Jewish either because of descent or conversion.

5(B) GEORGE:

In its early days Christianity was a form of Judaism, and the earliest Christians would of course have been circumcised as Jews. There was early controversy about whether converts to the Christian faith should be required to become Jews first by undergoing circumcision, but Peter, Paul, and Barnabas persuaded the more conservative Jewish followers, and thus enabled Christianity to emerge as an independent faith, without circumcision being a requirement (Acts 15:1–11). I'm pleased about that – it would be a great disincentive for me to have to undergo circumcision if I ever wanted to become a Jew or a Muslim! Circumcision may originally have been justified on the grounds of health, but I am not convinced that this is true in the twenty-first century. (Christians certainly disapprove of female circumcision, and it would be interesting to hear Dawoud comment on this.)

Instead, one enters the Christian faith through baptism – a rite that Jesus himself underwent when he was immersed in the River Jordan by John the Baptist. From what we gather, John promoted a reform movement in which Jews were asked to reaffirm their commitment by immersion in water, to signify purification. Using water for Jewish recommitment may be associated with the use of *mikvah* for Gentile converts to Judaism, to which Dan refers, but we cannot be sure. Whatever the nature of John's movement, Christians have followed Jesus' own example, and his final commission to his disciples included the instruction that they should baptize (Matthew 28:19). In many Roman Catholic and Anglican churches, the baptismal font is found at the entrance, to indicate that, just as the font is at the entrance of the church building, baptism is one's point of entrance to the wider church.

Since the earliest converts to Christianity were adults, baptism was administered to those who were old enough to understand the commitment they were making. The Baptist churches, together with Adventists and Pentecostals, believe that baptism should only be administered to those who are old enough to understand, and that it should be done in the same way as Jesus' – by immersion. Other Christians take a different view, holding that children are also part of the church, and that their inclusion should be marked by baptism. Their parents take vows on their behalf, undertaking to bring them up in the faith and to provide them with spiritual nourishment. In the Roman Catholic tradition and among Protestants (with the exceptions mentioned above) infant baptism is normally administered not by immersion, but by the sprinkling or pouring of water over the baby (the latter is known as "affusion"). When the children are old enough to understand the faith and make a commitment, they can "confirm" their baptism in a further ceremony, in which they take vows for themselves, and become entitled to participate in Holy Communion (also known as the Eucharist or the Mass, according to one's tradition). Eastern Orthodoxy has a different set of conventions: the baby is baptized by immersion, and is immediately eligible to receive the sacramental bread and wine.

Baptism is one of the church's sacraments – special rites in which the visible elements of the ceremony symbolize an underlying hidden reality. In baptism, the water symbolizes the washing away of sin. This does not mean that the candidate is automatically and instantly freed from sin, but rather that the sacrament points to the salvation that Christ offers. The traditions that believe in immersion typically see the act of going down into the water and being brought back up as paralleling Christ's dying and rising again – a comparison made by Paul (Colossians 2:12).

A person is baptized into the church as a whole, not into a congregation or denomination. This is important, because one's Christian life transcends denominational barriers. Someone who had been baptized, say, in the United Reformed Church would not have to undergo re-baptism if he or she decided to become an Anglican or a Roman Catholic. Some Christians have sometimes felt that, because their baptism was carried out at an early stage in life that they do not remember, they ought to undergo a further adult baptism. Many Christians disapprove of this practice, since baptism is traditionally a once-and-for-all event, and undergoing a new baptism is tantamount to saying that one's previous life as a Christian did not count for anything.

Religions have always provided the opportunity for marking important life-cycle events, such as birth, marriage, coming of age, admission to the religious community, admission to holy orders, and finally death. Depending on one's tradition baptism can mark either birth or coming of age, but either way it signifies the entry into the Christian community, and symbolizes the cleansing from sin that is offered by Christ and his church.

5(C) DAWOUD:

There is no ceremony or rite required for entry into Islam. There is nothing resembling baptism either for those born into the faith or for those who embrace it. A child of Muslim parents is automatically considered to be a Muslim and should be raised as such and the same applies to a child of a Muslim father and non-Muslim (Christian or Jewish) mother. As Muslim women are not permitted to marry non-Muslim men and cannot legally do so in any Muslim country, the reverse situation should not occur. If such a marriage occurs under a civil jurisdiction in a non-Muslim country, this marriage will not be recognized by the Muslim community or by the law in any Muslim country. The main reason for the prohibition of marriage to a non-Muslim man is that a Muslim woman might be drawn away from her faith and because it is assumed that the father will have greater influence over the children and that they would not be brought up as Muslims.

It is common for the call to prayer to be recited by the father into the right ear of a baby at birth, but this does not affect whether or not the child is considered to be a Muslim. There are also a variety of naming ceremonies, but these are cultural practices and not Islamic requirements. One that is common in some countries and said to be based on the practice of the Prophet is the *Aqiqa*, which is normally held on the seventh day following the child's birth. The child's head may be shaved or a lock of hair cut. The hair is weighed and its weight in silver given in charity. A sheep or goat may be slaughtered for a baby girl or two for a boy and the meat distributed among the family and to the poor. Although this may still take place within the community in many countries, in urban settings and particularly in Western countries it is possible to pay for this sacrifice through Internet-based charities which arrange the slaughter and for the meat to be distributed in poor Muslim countries.

Circumcision is not mentioned in the Qur'an but only in the *hadith*. Most Muslim boys are circumcised although there is no specific age at which this must happen. Again this tends to vary according to local custom, and in urban communities it commonly takes place in hospitals. Female circumcision is a cultural practice in some countries; it predates Islam and is certainly not a requirement. Many argue against it on the basis that according to Islamic law a woman is entitled to sexual gratification in marriage and that anything that prevents this must be forbidden. There are, however, some *hadith* that permit it, although these are not among those considered most authoritative according to classical *hadith* scholarship.

There are no rites of passage resembling *bar* or *bat mitzvah*, confirmation or first Holy Communion. Muslim children are gradually introduced to the practices of Islam as they become old enough to be involved and to understand.

Islam is a proselytizing religion that welcomes new converts and encourages Muslims to call others to faith. There is a current trend to refer to converts from Christianity and Judaism as "reverts", as they are considered to have rediscovered the original and true faith.

All that is really required for a person to become and to be deemed a Muslim is that he or she make the profession of faith: "I testify that there is no god but God and I testify that Muhammad is the Prophet of God." Once a person has made this profession, his or her Islam may not be challenged. This is the first pillar of faith and he or she is then expected to adhere to the other four: *salat* or prayer; fasting during Ramadan; paying *zakat* or alms tax, and performing the *hajj* or pilgrimage at least once in a lifetime if he or she is able to. Although it is not essential, new Muslims will often adopt a Muslim name that they use instead of or alongside their original name, or sometimes just a forename that they use with their own surname. It is usual for them to select a name that has some religious or historical significance, and in some cases the Arabic equivalent of their original name, such as Yusuf for Joseph, Dawoud for David, or Maryam for Mary. There is no definitive ruling with regard to circumcision for male converts and this is a matter of personal choice.

5(D) DAN:

We have discussed the various initiation rites of our three faiths, and it is clear that there are some crucial differences. As I explained, Jewish identification is based on descent: traditionally this has been understood as maternal descent, but in modern times paternal descent has been accepted as well. Conversion too is another route to Jewishness, yet the various movements have specified different procedures. Today the vast majority of members of the Jewish community are of either maternal or paternal descent, but the number of converts has increased considerably from previous centuries. Hence, Jews define themselves largely in ethnic terms. Belief and practice are of secondary significance as far as Jewish identity is concerned, although the various Jewish religious denominations stress their significance. Like Judaism, Muslim identity (as Dawoud explained) is inherited, although conversion is of key importance. Non-Muslims are welcomed into the fold, and today there are millions of converts to Islam. As Dawoud has made clear, in these cases religious belief is a key factor. For Christians, belief in Jesus is critical, and it makes little sense to identify oneself as a Christian without accepting the central tenets of the faith. Although baptism of infants is a widespread practice, Christianity is a religion where belief and practice play a fundamental role.

What happens if a Jew, Christian, or Muslim wishes to separate from the religious family into which he or she is born? In the case of Christianity, the answer is clear: individuals are free to either accept the religious teachings of their faith or not. It is a personal choice of conscience. There may be disappointment if a person ceases to be a Christian, particularly from family members or members of the community, but it is ultimately a matter of conscience. The same is not true in the case of Judaism (and I assume in Islam). According to Orthodoxy, a person who is born a Jew remains a Jew, even when that individual converts to another religion. According to *halakah* (Jewish law), it is technically impossible for a person born to a Jewish mother or converted to Judaism through the traditional procedure to change his or her status. Even when a Jew undergoes the process of admission to another faith and formally renounces the Jewish religion, that person remains a Jew, even though he or she is deemed a sinner. In the view of the medieval scholar Nahmanides, this attitude is based on the fact that the covenant between God and Israel was made "not only with you who are standing here with us today in the presence of the Lord our God but also with those who are not here today" (Deuteronomy 29:14–15).

For an individual who is born a Jew, Jewish identity is thus not a matter of choice: that person remains a Jew regardless of his religious beliefs. However, if a person embraces another faith, he or she is treated differently from other Jews. Technically such individuals are known as *mummer* (from the Hebrew root meaning "to change"), or *mushumad* (from the Hebrew root meaning "to persecute or force abandonment of faith"), or *apikoros* (heretic), or *poshe'a Yisrael* (rebellious Jew). Some authorities insist that if a person eventually reverts to Judaism, that individual must confess his or her sins before a rabbinic court and declare that he or she will keep Jewish law. What this means in effect is that once a Jew, always a Jew. Within the progressive branches of Judaism, however, there is a degree of flexibility about the status of an individual who has abandoned Judaism or converted to another faith. In general, if such a person ceases to identify as a Jew or to adopt another religion, it is accepted that he or she has voluntarily left the community. And if they wish to return, no expression of remorse is regarded as necessary.

Islam is obviously very different and far less tolerant. Even though the Qur'an states that there should be no compulsion in religion (2:256), it is clear that those who reject the faith are in serious jeopardy:

How shall Allah guide those who reject faith after they accepted it and bore witness that the Apostle was true and that clear signs had come unto? Allah is not the God of unjust people. The reward of such people is the curse of Allah, the angels and all humanity is upon them. They shall remain under it forever; neither will their punishment be lightened nor will they be given respite. But for those who mend their ways, then Allah is forgiving, Merciful. (3:86–91)

As a liberal Jew, I find such a stance disturbing, particularly when individuals are persecuted or even killed. Perhaps Dawoud can enlighten us.

5(E) GEORGE:

This discussion, which began with issues about entry into one's faith, has now moved on to questions about exit. I'd like to remark on both.

First, I shall comment on the practice of circumcision. Although I can appreciate that religions want to maintain their traditions, circumcision seems a cruel – not to say barbaric – practice in this day and age. Its biblical origin relates to God's covenant with Abraham (Genesis 17:10). A covenant is invariably accompanied by a physical sign, and in this case God's reminder of His promise to Abraham is the mark on one's body, which one bears for the rest of one's life.

However, Jewish scriptures also make reference to a "new covenant", which is "a law in their minds and... on their hearts" (Jeremiah 31:33). Its recipient has so fully appropriated God's law that there is no need of outward symbols, such as circumcision or tablets of stone, like Moses is said to have brought down from Mount Sinai. Saint Paul wrote about the "circumcision of the heart" (Romans 2:29), arguing that the Jewish law is impossible to keep to the letter, and hence external observance is now superseded by the grace that Jesus Christ offers. The true Jew, he claims, "is one inwardly" (Romans 2:29). For the Christian, it is one's heart that is important, not keeping meticulous rules or undergoing outmoded rituals. As for a tangible guarantee of the covenant, this is Jesus himself: his death on the cross is a symbol of the divine grace that this covenant mediates, made physical in the bread and wine of the Eucharist, which symbolizes his body and blood which was offered on the cross. Circumcision is therefore an obsolete practice for Christians, who would only undergo it as a clinical procedure, if there were a compelling medical reason. It has no longer any ritual justification.

Turning now to the question of disengagement from one's faith – Christianity and Islam have traditionally been proselytizing religions. Dan points out that by contrast Judaism accepts, but does not actively seek, converts. For all three religions, however, it is understandably a matter of regret when someone decides to abandon his or her faith. What, then, should we do when this occurs? Although the rest of one's community might deeply regret someone's decision to abandon the Christian faith, such a decision cannot be prevented. What happens to a lapsed Christian is in God's hands. One's baptism is something that is lifelong: one cannot be "de-baptized", and a lapsed member returning to the church would not have to undergo baptism to be readmitted.

It is therefore a matter of regret, to put it mildly, that Islam should show such hostility to those who decide to embrace some other faith. In many Muslim countries the penalties for apostasy are severe. In Saudi Arabia and Afghanistan, the punishment is death, and I understand that most Muslim scholars hold the view that this is the appropriate penalty under *Shari'a* law. In other countries one can be imprisoned and fined for abandoning Islam, and in countries such as Egypt and

Malaysia there are legal impediments to changing one's faith and seeking appropriate recognition. As for those who have espoused the Bahá'í faith, Muslim persecution has been relentless. They have been subjected to arrests, imprisonment, torture, execution, confiscation and destruction of property, including sacred shrines. They have been denied employment, access to education, and other civil rights and benefits. This has not merely occurred in Iran, but in various Islamic countries, and their persecution has repeatedly been condemned by the United Nations, Amnesty International, the European Union, and numerous national governments.

Article 18 of the Universal Declaration of Human Rights states:

Everyone has the right to freedom of thought, conscience and religion; this right includes freedom to change his [*sic*] religion or belief, and freedom, either alone or in community with others and in public or private, to manifest his religion or belief in teaching, practice, worship and observance.

So I have to echo Dan's concerns. The Qur'an states, "Make war on [unbelievers] until idolatry is no more and Allah's religion reigns supreme" (8:39). Does Dawoud agree with the Qur'an here, or with the UN Declaration? Can Muslims truly justify these penalties? Since Islam teaches that Allah is the ultimate controller of all affairs on earth, should one not leave unbelievers and apostates in His hands, letting the Islamic faith speak for itself, resorting merely to invitation and non-violent persuasion? Can one have true and sincere acceptance of religion if one embraces it simply out of fear or compulsion?

5(F) DAWOUD:

I understand George's point about circumcision, but I think that the custom of circumcision of boys is so deeply entrenched in the culture in Muslim countries that there is little likelihood of change. A boy or man who is not circumcised may feel somehow deficient or excluded from his community and may then suffer emotionally and spiritually due to this. Male circumcision has been practised in many cultures historically, and although it is forbidden by Catholicism it has appeared as a trend at various times in Western countries. It was common in England in the late nineteenth and early twentieth centuries and it remains a common practice in the United States. The usual term for circumcision in Arabic is *tahara*, meaning "purification". Most Muslims believe it to be *Sunna* or recommended practice based on the *hadith* of the Prophet Muhammad and going back to the Prophet Ibrahim. It is argued that it promotes hygiene and cleanliness and makes it easier for a person to achieve the level of cleanliness by ablution required for the performance of the *salat*, the regular prayers.

Male circumcision may be argued to have some medical benefit in terms of hygiene and protection from infection, but the same cannot be said for female circumcision or female genital mutilation in any of its forms which can never be anything other than harmful. Although it is mostly practised by Muslims in a few but by no means all Muslim countries, it is also practised by some Christian communities including Egyptian Copts (although not universally) and by Ethiopian Jews. There are many Islamic scholars who consider it to be prohibited but who recognize that references to it occur in the *hadith*. These argue that it should be prohibited on the same legal basis as the prohibition of slavery. The argument goes that it was a practice which existed at the time of the Prophet which was not immediately forbidden but which with the progress of society is totally unacceptable in the modern world.

Both Dan and George have questioned the consequences for a person who leaves the faith. Naturally I would not condone any form of violence in this case. It is true that many jurists have upheld the view that the penalty for apostasy should be the death penalty, or imprisonment until the person repents and returns to Islam, but there are those who point out that the Qur'an states quite clearly that there is to be no compulsion to faith:

There shall be no compulsion in [acceptance of] the religion... (2:256)

And had your Lord willed, those on Earth would have believed – all of them entirely. Then, [O Muhammad], would you compel the people in order that they become believers? (10:99)

Not upon the Messenger is [responsibility] except [for] notification.
(5:99)

Conversion from Islam is relatively uncommon among Muslims because faith, identity, and community are so intertwined, and renunciation of Islam can lead to estrangement from family and friends. In Egypt, for example, where there is no legislation prohibiting conversion, in cases where it does occur people may face harsh treatment by their families and immediate communities. There have been a number of reported cases where converts to Christianity have faced ill treatment by the police, lawyers, and their own families and may be detained indefinitely or confined to psychiatric facilities. While conversion as such is not strictly illegal in some Muslim countries, proselytizing to Muslims by members of other faiths is prohibited in most.

Who except God can know what is in a person's heart, however? A person may perform every religious duty as part of membership of a community but have no genuine belief in their heart. What a person actually believes cannot be enforced upon them. All that can be enforced is compliance with the physical practices of the religion, which is meaningless without belief. If a person explicitly rejects the faith or behaves in a manner that is interpreted as such, including adopting another faith, punishment will serve no purpose. While a person is alive there is always the hope that they will be guided to return to the faith.

CHAPTER 6

WORSHIP

Christians attach great importance to the Eucharist, regarding it as a sacrament. Dan thinks it's cannibalistic. Why do Christians consume Christ's body and blood, and what is the point of this rite? Why can't Jews, Muslims, and Christians pray in the same way? Is it possible for them to pray together?

6(A) DAN:

For the Jewish people, prayer has served as the vehicle by which they have expressed their joys, sorrows, and hopes; through the centuries, it has played a major role in the religious life of the Jewish nation. Jews have constantly turned to God for assistance. In the Bible the patriarchs (Abraham, Isaac, and Jacob), Moses, and the prophets addressed God through personal prayer. In addition, Jews turned to God through communal worship. In ancient times Jewish communal worship centred on the Temple in Jerusalem. Twice daily – in the morning and afternoon – the priests offered prescribed sacrifices while the Levites chanted psalms. On Sabbaths and festivals additional services were added to this daily ritual.

With the destruction of the Second Temple in 70 CE, sacrificial offerings were replaced by the prayer service in the synagogue, referred to by the rabbis as "*avodah she-be-lev*" (service of the heart). To enhance uniformity, they introduced fixed periods for daily prayer which corresponded with the times sacrifices had been offered in the Temple: the morning prayer (*shaharit*) and afternoon prayer (*minhah*) correspond with the daily and afternoon sacrifice; evening prayer (*maariv*) corresponds with the nightly burning of fats and limbs. By the completion of the Talmud in the sixth century, the essential features of the synagogue service were established, but it was only in the eighth century that the first prayer book was composed by Rav Amram, Gaon of the Academy of Sura in Babylonia.

In the order of the service, the first central feature is the *Shema* prayer, which begins with the phrase "*Shema Yisrael*" (Hear O Israel). This verse teaches the unity of God, and the paragraph emphasizes the duty to love God, meditate on His commandments, and impress them on children. The second major feature of the synagogue service is the *Shemoneh Eshreh* (eighteen benedictions). From earliest times the Torah (Pentateuch) has been read in public gatherings; later regular readings of the Torah on Sabbaths and festivals were instituted. The Torah itself is divided into fifty-four sections – each section is subdivided into portions. Before the reading of the Torah in the synagogue, the Ark is opened. After the reading of the Torah, a section of the prophetic books (*Haftarah*) is recited. Another feature of the traditional synagogue service is the *Kaddish* prayer. Written in Aramaic, it takes several forms in the prayer book and expresses the hope for universal peace under the kingdom of God. Since the thirteenth century the three daily services have concluded with the recitation of the *Alenu* prayer, which proclaims God as king over humankind.

The central liturgy of the synagogue for weekdays, Sabbaths, and holy days remained essentially the same until the Enlightenment. At this time reformers in Central Europe altered the worship service and introduced new prayers into the liturgy in conformity with current cultural and spiritual developments. Influenced by Protestant Christianity, these innovators decreed that the service should be shortened and conducted in the vernacular as well as in Hebrew. In addition they introduced Western melodies to the accompaniment of a choir and organ and replaced the chanting of the Torah with the reading of the Torah portion. Prayers viewed as anachronistic were eliminated, and those of a nationalistic nature were changed so that they were more universalistic in scope. In recent times all groups across the religious spectrum have introduced new liturgies (such as those that commemorate Holocaust Remembrance Day, Israel Independence Day, and Jerusalem Reunification Day). Among non-Orthodox denominations there is a growing emphasis on more egalitarian liturgies with gender-free language and an increasing democratic sense of responsibility. For example, inclusive pronouns such as "we" are used to emphasize that both men and women are included in religious services. Thus prayer and worship continue to be of vital importance to the Jewish people, yet there have occurred a variety of alterations to its nature within all branches of the Jewish faith.

Given this background, it is natural for Jews to respect liturgical practices of both Christianity and Islam. Yet there are certain rites which they find difficult to understand. The Eucharist service, for example, with its references to eating the body and blood of Christ, appears somewhat cannibalistic. Despite the Jewish background to this observance based on Jesus' words to his disciples as recorded in the New Testament, it appears strange and primitive. Perhaps George can enlighten us.

6(B) DAWOUD:

I do not think that Muslims perceive the ritual of Holy Communion in the terms that Dan describes but as we discussed earlier they do object to what appears to them to be a form of worship of a being other than God.

In Islam worship centres around what are known as the Five Pillars, which are the religious duties of all Muslims. The first requirement before any other is the profession of faith whereby a person testifies that there is no god but God and that Muhammad is the Prophet (or Messenger) of God. Although a person only needs to say this once in a lifetime, it is commonly repeated and constitutes part of the *adhan*, or call to prayer, made by the *mu'adhdhin* (often rendered as "muezzin" in English).

Prayer is the second pillar, and for practising Muslims it forms part of the structure of their daily activity. The Qur'an does not specify the number of daily prayers or their times; this is derived from the *hadith* and is based on the practice of the Prophet. Muslims are required to perform the ritual prayers five times a day: at dawn, noon, mid-afternoon, sunset, and nightfall. They may pray anywhere as long as it is clean – at the mosque, at home, or in the workplace. In many cultures women only pray at home but where they do pray at a mosque they will either do so in a separate section or behind the men in order not to distract the men from their prayer. Where family members pray together at home, the women will pray behind the men. The prayer consists of repetitions of the *rak'a*, which is a sequence of movements comprising standing, bowing, prostration, and kneeling, accompanied by formal wording and recitation of passages of the Qur'an. The number of *rak'at* is different for different times of day. Where people pray in a group, one person acts as *imam*, or prayer leader, and stands in front of the group or congregation, facing the same way, that is, with his back to the others. The group will then follow his lead, or her lead if it is a group of women and children. Muslims pray in the direction of Mecca and mosques always have a *mihrab* or prayer niche indicating the direction of prayer. Special compasses exist to help Muslims away from home to find the direction of prayer. Today there are smartphone "apps" to help with this and to indicate the prayer times. In Muslim countries, the call to prayer is broadcast at each of the formal prayer times from the *ma'dhana* (usually inaccurately translated in English as "minaret", which is an Anglicization of *manara* or beacon).

Prayer is obligatory and those who do not pray are considered by most schools of law to be sinners, although the Hanbali school goes further and considers them to be unbelievers. Pregnant, lactating, or menstruating women are not required to pray and the same goes for people who are seriously ill or travelling. Before prayer a person must be clean. They must perform *wudu*, or ritual ablution, which requires washing, in a specified order, the hands, mouth, nasal passages, head, and feet. A person cannot pray after using the toilet or having sexual intercourse without bathing and if they do so their prayer is void.

The most important prayer of the week is the noon prayer on Friday and Muslims, or at least Muslim men, should try to pray in congregation at a mosque. There are two names for a mosque: *masjid* literally means place of prostration and may refer to any mosque regardless of size. *Jami'*, or place of gathering, usually refers to a larger congregational mosque. The Friday prayer is accompanied by a sermon on a meaningful topic.

During Ramadan, after the breaking of the fast at sunset, many people perform *tarawih* or supererogatory prayers which consist of numbers of extra *rak'at* until late into the night.

Ritual prayer is intended to bring a person into direct contact with God at regular intervals during the day, and in this way they should keep God in their hearts and minds in their daily activity. It does not involve personal prayer or supplication, *du'a*, which is distinct from ritual prayer and entirely an individual matter.

The other pillars of faith which are an essential part of worship for Muslims are *siyam*, or fasting from dawn until sunset during the month of Ramadan, *zakat* (sometimes referred to as "alms tax"), or the giving in charity of one-fortieth (2.5 per cent) of one's wealth, and *hajj*, the performance of the ritual pilgrimage to Mecca which a Muslim is expected to do at least once in a lifetime, if his or her health allows and if he or she has sufficient financial resources.

6(C) GEORGE:

Dan and Dawoud both provide insightful accounts of worship in their respective traditions. It is particularly interesting that Dawoud itemizes the physical gestures involved in prayer. Christians are divided on the question of how much physical activity should go into worship, and how much should come from the heart. Roman Catholics and Orthodox Christians emphasize the former, while Protestants tend to dislike elaborate ritual, and many of them favour extempore prayer rather than prayers composed by others over the centuries. Christian public worship also normally includes reading from scripture, and – at major services – a sermon and hymns.

All traditions, however, believe in the importance of a relationship with God, which is expressed in prayer and worship, and encourage private as well as public devotion. Private devotion enables Christians to express their feelings in their own words. Dawoud's tradition seems to have a highly prescribed way of praying, and I would be interested to know what place he finds for believers expressing their personal feelings and concerns to God in their own words.

Dan mentions the Eucharist (also known as Holy Communion, or the Mass in Roman Catholicism), which is the church's principal sacrament. The different Christian traditions have different views on the sacraments. In the Protestant tradition, in which I was brought up, it is held that the sacraments are rites that Christ himself instituted, and that they are signs of the benefits of Jesus' new covenant (*Shorter Catechism*, A.92). The notion of "sign" is important: spiritual truths can be difficult to grasp, and hence the sacraments present something that can be experienced by several senses – sight, sound, touch, and taste.

The Bible recounts that, on the last night of Jesus' life, he had a meal with his disciples – it may have been a Passover meal, but the Gospel accounts are unclear – in which he took bread and wine, and offered them to his disciples, instructing them to continue celebrating this rite. The idea of eating flesh and drinking blood of course would be offensive to Jews, since the Torah teaches that the blood is the life, and is not to be consumed (Genesis 9:4). By celebrating the sacrament, therefore, Christians were dissociating themselves from the Jewish community.

However, the sacrament also has a positive role: because the church is often described as "the body of Christ", the sacrament demonstrates the Christian's mystical participation with Christ and with each other. Saint Paul points out that the Eucharistic bread is "participation in the body of Christ", adding, "Because there is one loaf, we, who are many, are one body, for we all share the one loaf" (1 Corinthians 10:16–17). What we eat goes to make up our body, and hence, if we partake – symbolically – of Christ's body, it becomes part of us, and we all share in this "one body".

The traditional Roman Catholic view is that the bread and wine of the Eucharist are miraculously transubstantiated, but of course this does not imply that they turn into real physical flesh and blood. The Mass is not a horror movie, and if this really happened I doubt many Christians would be willing to take part! Today, many Roman Catholics would acknowledge that the traditional understanding of the Mass draws on Aristotle's metaphysical system, appropriated by the church through scholars such as Saint Thomas Aquinas (1225–74), which many believe is no longer acceptable in the twenty-first century.

The Eucharist has a further significance. In Luke's account of the Last Supper, he links the meal with a future occasion, in which Jesus will share this meal in the coming kingdom of God. Jesus takes the cup and says, "I will not drink again of the fruit of the vine until the kingdom of God comes" (Luke 22:18). Jesus often compares the coming kingdom to a feast, to which all are invited. We have not yet reached this kingdom, but in the sacrament of the Eucharist, it is as if a small part of that celestial banquet reaches down to Christ's community of followers who are still on earth awaiting the celebration of this new kingdom. The fact that the Eucharist is not a full meal as we would normally recognize one is an indication that it is a symbol of something much more that is yet to come.

Some people outside the church find it strange that people should come to church to eat a small piece of wafer and have a sip of wine. Clearly they have not yet grasped the sacrament's full meaning. But it is certainly not a meeting of cannibals, and any visiting cannibal would be seriously disappointed!

6(D) DAN:

We have outlined the myriad rites and practices in our respective faiths, and it is clear that worship in its many forms plays a fundamental role in our three faiths. There is overlap, as well as important differences. Throughout our discussion, we have often focused on the ways in which Jews, Christians, and Muslims disagree, and we will continue to do this in the rest of the book. But I think that we all concur that in our monotheistic traditions, worship is of critical importance in the life of believers. At times such prayer is private and the relationship with God is intimate; at other times communal worship serves to unite the community.

Given the centrality of worship in our traditions, it seems to me that there is the possibility today for Jews, Christians, and Muslims to engage in interfaith worship, and that such activity can bind us together rather than create barriers to dialogue and encounter. In this regard, a distinction should be made between three different types of interfaith worship:

1. Services of a particular religious community in which members are invited as guests. On such occasions, it is usual to ask a representative of the visiting faith community to recite a suitable prayer or preach a sermon but the liturgy remains the same.

2. Interfaith gatherings of a serial nature. At such meetings representatives of each religion offer prayers or readings on a common theme. Those present constitute an audience listening to a liturgical anthology in which the distinctiveness of each religion is acknowledged, but everyone is free to participate as well.

3. Interfaith gatherings with a shared order of service. In such situations all present are participants, and there is an overarching theme.

These various kinds of services possess their own particular characteristics. In the first type, where adherents of one faith invite others to attend, they are not seeking to make converts – rather there is a conscious recognition of the integrity of other faith traditions. In the second type of worship service, in which there is a serial reading by representatives of other religions, participants actively join in the liturgy from other traditions when appropriate. Such serial services are based on mutual respect and allow each community an equal part in worship. In the third form of worship, participants pray with members of other faiths. In services of this type the distinctiveness of each religion is acknowledged – there is no attempt to replace the implicit assumption that in worship the followers of the monotheistic faith traditions stand before God.

These three modes of interfaith worship are designed to bind Jews, Christians, and Muslims together on a practical level. No longer should members of our faiths stand aloof from one another. Instead, there is a conscious recognition that each faith is an authentic path to God. Interfaith worship as I have described it should pave the way to a sympathetic appreciation of the riches of other religions.

So far we have frequently stressed the differences between us, and we will continue to do so as our dialogue continues. As far as theology is concerned, there are major areas of disagreement. Similarly, when we explore ethics and lifestyle as well as societal issues, we will inevitably discover serious points of disagreement. Yet, in the sphere of worship we can find common ground where our differences can be set aside as we stand together – brothers and sisters – in prayer and meditation before the One God, transcendent and imminent, the Lord of all.

6(E) DAWOUD:

I appreciate Dan's ideas regarding interfaith worship but I think they are a little idealistic. I suspect that this would appeal to a self-selecting congregation of well-meaning people predisposed to this kind of religious meeting of minds, and only in a multi-faith society such as British society. However I am afraid that this would not reach the majority. If you will pardon the pun, I think he is preaching to the converted. Nevertheless, I think he makes a very good point, in line with George's question, about the importance of both personal and ritual worship. The ritual prayer for Muslims, far from being simply a sequence of physical movements, should allow a person to empty their mind of everything in their daily lives and focus entirely on God, and in theory carry this inner tranquillity with them through the rest of their day. As Dan says, where people pray together it helps to unite the community. There is also private supplicatory prayer in Islam by which people seek forgiveness or pray for something specific. The Qur'an says: "And your Lord says, 'Call upon Me; I will respond to you.'" (40:60). Some people use books of prayer, including prayers believed to have been used by the Prophet or well-known prayers by scholars of later periods.

Reading or reciting the Qur'an is a form of worship and many people do this on a regular basis as part of the practice of their faith. It is not simply a book of guidance but has a spiritual value beyond the words on the page. To read the Qur'an, a person should be clean and many perform ablution as they would for prayer. This is not only out of respect for the Qur'an but also a form of mental preparation for reading. Some people read or recite it systematically as it has divisions marked to enable people to divide it over the thirty nights of a month or seven larger sections to read over the course of a week. Sometimes they may seek guidance from specific passages, or they may open the Qur'an at random, having offered a supplication for guidance on something that is troubling them. The words of the Qur'an and the lyrical nature of its recitation combined have the power to move people deeply, and it is not uncommon to see people weeping as they listen to recitation of the Qur'an.

I have not yet mentioned Sufism, the mystical form of Islam. This takes many forms, but Sufi worship is aimed at purifying the heart and bringing the individual into the divine presence through forms of individual or group worship which include *dhikr* – the repetition of the name of God – songs or chants such as the Indian *qawwal*, and sometimes forms of dance or whirling that are said to take those participating to a higher level of consciousness of the Divine. There is a corpus of Sufi mystical poetry such as that of Al-Rumi that aims to capture the ecstasy of the union with the Divine. Sufism is complex and diverse and too large a topic to discuss in detail here, but Sufi worship has been important throughout the history of Islam and remains so in the present.

The *hajj* or pilgrimage is an important form of worship and all Muslims hope to perform this at least once during their lives. During the *hajj*, pilgrims enter into a state of ritual purity or *Ihram*. Women are to maintain their modest dress but men must wear only two unhemmed white sheets and sandals. During the *hajj* they may not shave, cut their hair or nails, argue or use offensive language, or have sexual relations. They perform a number of rites that reflect episodes in the life of the Prophet and narratives from the Qur'an.

The pilgrimage brings people from all over the world together in a shared experience of worship. Many Muslims describe the *hajj* as an overwhelming and life-changing experience that brings them closer to God and makes them think about their lives, their deeds, and the hereafter.

6(F) GEORGE:

We agreed that in our discussion we would be frank and highlight points of disagreement between our three faiths. But there are times too when it is appropriate to acknowledge common ground for possibilities for conciliation. Interfaith worship affords one such opportunity, and the threefold distinction that Dan mentions was endorsed by the British Council of Churches (now Churches Together in Britain and Ireland) in its 1983 booklet, *Can We Pray Together?: Guidelines on Worship in a Multi-Faith Society*. It seems reasonable that those who acknowledge the same God as Father should be able to address Him and listen to Him together.

There are occasions where common worship seems appropriate. Different faiths may have worked together on a common project – for example in a school, hospital, or locality. They may wish to express common concerns, such as care for the environment or the elimination of prejudice. Where there have been disturbing news items, such as terrorist attacks, multi-faith devotion not only shares common concerns, but is a firm indicator that we share a common aversion to hatred and violence.

It is only fair to say that there are Christians who have reservations about interfaith worship. I have to agree with Dawoud that only a small proportion of Christians take part in interfaith activity, and we need to encourage greater involvement. However, many Christian evangelicals adopt an exclusivist standpoint, and are opposed to all interfaith activity, fearing that another faith's contribution would tarnish true devotion to God. There are those who stereotype other faiths: one evangelical Christian organization ends its discussion of interfaith worship with the comment, "Allah says: 'Die for me.' Jesus says: 'I died for you.'" We need to break through this naïve confrontational stereotyping. This same organization argues that interfaith worship is not possible because Christians and Muslims worship different gods. This claim is also strange: Christians believe that there is only one God, so how can there be different ones? Admittedly, the three of us claim different things about the One God and worship, but we belong to the Abrahamic tradition, acknowledging God's dealings with Abraham, Moses, and the ancient Hebrew prophets.

Avoiding offence in interfaith worship, however, can cause each of us to strip away what is truly important to our faith, in the interests of world ecumenism. One solution is to devise new pieces of ritual that are not tied to any specific faith. One such example involves placing a bowl of water on a table, and inviting participants from each faith to place a pebble in it, possibly symbolizing that each faith has something to contribute towards an understanding of God. However, care is needed to avoid creating a bland anaemic event, which a friend of mine once described as "decaffeinated religion".

Different participants in interfaith events have different views on what inspires them and what does not, and I would not want to be prescriptive about the ingredients of interfaith worship. What is important is that everyone should feel comfortable, while affirming and respecting the various traditions. This is where Dan's second model has an advantage: each participant can bring something from his or her own faith, without having to find a lowest common denominator. I certainly have no objections to hearing things with which I do not personally agree, and it is often salutary to discover aspects of another tradition which are thoroughly resonant with my own.

Supporters of interfaith worship often mention the importance of using silence in such events. We do not need to talk incessantly to God all the time, and I think all our faiths would acknowledge that there is an important role for spiritual practice that does not rely on words. This observation fits in well with Dawoud's mention of Sufi mysticism. Christians too have a role for contemplation, and like Muslims, they often make pilgrimages, and – in some traditions – have dancing. Spoken and written ideas tend to divide, but when elements of worship transcend words, they can serve to unite us.

Obviously, careful thought needs to be given to the rationale for interfaith worship. Whether religions that do not pray to a creator God (for example Buddhists or Jains) can take part comfortably along with Jews and Muslims is a question that needs to be resolved. They do not share the same God, and hence we need to consider what is happening when they take part in rites and ceremonies with other faiths. I would not wish to exclude them, but we cannot overlook the need to develop a theological understanding of what is taking place.

CHAPTER 7

HOLY DAYS

Why do we celebrate different festivals from each other, and observe different days of the week as our special day? What is the role of fasting? Although some Christians may make minor sacrifices during Lent, the observation of Ramadan might seem to make life needlessly miserable.

7(A) DAN:

As you know, the Sabbath, which celebrates God's creation and rest on the seventh day, takes place every week, and is the most important holy day for Jews. You may be familiar with other Jewish festivals such as Passover, *Purim*, and *Hanukkah*. These are holy days too. But I want to focus on the High Holy Day Festivals that begin the Jewish spiritual year: *Rosh HaShanah* (New Year) and *Yom Kippur* (The Day of Atonement). *Rosh HaShanah* is celebrated for two days in the autumn (either in September or October depending on the Jewish calendar). It marks the start of the Ten Days of Penitence which end on the Day of Atonement. In the Bible the festival is described as the Day of Solemn Rest, a day of memorial to be proclaimed with the blast of a ram's horn (*shofar*). The Mishnah (the first code of rabbinic law) teaches that all human beings pass before God on the New Year – consequently, self-examination is an essential element of the day. It is said that every individual stands before the throne of God and is subject to judgment. A very small proportion are judged to be fully righteous, and another tiny group is rejected as irredeemably wicked. The vast majority, however, are the middling sort. They have the Ten Days of Penitence to repent of their folly and evil ways because final judgment is not sealed until the Day of Atonement. For ten days their fate hangs in the balance and, in view of the seriousness of the situation, these ten days are also known as the Days of Awe.

Like the New Year, the Day of Atonement (*Yom Kippur*) is prescribed in scripture. According to the book of Numbers: "On the tenth day of this seventh month hold a sacred assembly. You must deny yourselves and do no work. Present as an aroma pleasing to the Lord a burnt offering…" (29:7–8). This was the practice in ancient times when Jews worshipped and sacrificed in the Temple in Jerusalem. *Yom Kippur* is a solemn day of self-denial, and five services take place in the synagogue. Every male over the age of thirteen and every female over twelve, unless there is a medical reason against it, is obliged to fast from sunset until nightfall the next day. The usual laws of fasting apply, and the rabbis taught that through this affliction atonement could be made for sins against God. Transgressions against others, however, can only receive pardon if forgiveness has been sought from the person injured. Therefore, just before the Day of Atonement, it is usual for people to seek reconciliation with anyone whom they might have offended. During the course of the day itself, five services take place, all with their characteristic liturgies.

Yom Kippur highlights a central principle of Judaism: Jews can be forgiven for their misdeeds as long as they are truly repentant, resolve not to sin in the future, and seek God's mercy. Yet, as I noted, forgiveness for transgressions against others is conditional. It is imperative that the sinner asks the person who has been injured for forgiveness and makes restitution if at all possible. Here, I believe, there may be a crucial difference between Judaism and Christianity. In the Jewish faith, sins can be forgiven only if the sinner truly seeks God's pardon and resolves not to transgress again. But it is essential that the sinner must also seek reconciliation with the person who has been harmed. Forgiveness is not automatic. This is a crucial distinction and is critical in understanding Jewish attitudes towards contemporary issues such as the Middle East conflict. The Jewish community, for example, does not automatically forgive the Palestinians for their role in the bloody history of Israel/Palestine. On the contrary, they blame them (and the Arab nations) for their unwillingness to accept the legitimacy of the State of Israel. Without an expression of remorse for their determination to drive the Jewish nation into the sea and an attempt to make some form of restitution, peaceful reconciliation is impossible.

7(B) GEORGE:

The topic of festivals and holy days might seem relatively uncontentious. It might seem as if we ought simply to say that we celebrate different festivals, and go our own ways. However, Dan raises a number of points that merit further discussion.

The Jewish festivals are based on a calendar whose year begins on the purported date of creation, and which uses the traditional Hebrew months and year numbers. Christians, however, regard Christ's coming as even more significant than the world's creation, and its impact is underscored by the fact that the entire world uses a calendar based on Jesus' birth. But Christians also have a liturgical calendar, punctuating the year with their distinctive festivals. It begins with Advent – the four-week period leading up to Christmas – and continues in uneven sections: Epiphany, Lent, Easter, and finally the longer Pentecost/Trinity season.

Most Christians hold that the Jewish festival calendar, prescribed by the Jewish law, has been superseded with the coming of Christ. A few Christians – particularly Seventh-day Adventists – continue to celebrate the Sabbath from Friday evening through to Saturday as their holy day, and also celebrate the Passover. However, the vast majority of Christians replaced the Jewish Sabbath with Sunday – the first day of the week – it being the day associated with Christ's resurrection. The New Testament records that Christians met on the first day of the week to "break bread" (that is, celebrate what is now the Eucharist) (Acts 20:7), and the early Christians were instructed to set aside money for the church's work on that day (1 Corinthians 16:2).

Religious festivals – in any tradition – serve a number of functions. As well as punctuating each year with landmarks, they make us aware of the major events of our faith. Most obviously, in the Christian tradition, these are Christmas, Easter, and Pentecost. The date 25 December is the conventional date assigned to Jesus' birth, although it is unlikely that this was his real birthday. Because the Orthodox use the Julian rather than the Gregorian calendar for liturgical purposes, they celebrate Christmas on 6 January, and they have a slightly different way of calculating Easter, so that it is usually (although not always) a week apart from the date of Western churches. Pentecost celebrates the coming of the Holy Spirit upon the early disciples (Acts 2:1–13), the event that is generally regarded as the birth of the church. In addition, Orthodox Christians, Roman Catholics, and Anglicans celebrate dates assigned to saints and to the Virgin Mary, although Protestants are not keen on this practice.

Not all events in the church calendar are causes for celebration. In the Orthodox tradition, the entire liturgical year consists of an alternation between eight feasting and fasting periods. Dan is right to say that Christians can choose how – or indeed whether – they want to fast during Lent. Many Christians decide to use Lent as a weight-watching period, often giving up fattening items such as chocolate or alcohol, but, apart from this practical function, fasting serves to demonstrate that we are able to control our bodies, rather than that they control us.

Festivals have a further function. They enable believers to place themselves within their tradition's story, by symbolically re-enacting some of its features. For example, on Palm Sunday – the day of Jesus' triumphal entry into Jerusalem (Mark 11:1–11) – Christians often take part in a "Procession of Palms", when the congregation processes around the church grounds waving palm branches. Some congregations go so far as to acquire a real donkey (the animal Jesus rode) for this event. To outsiders this may sound silly, but it is a way in which Christians can identify with Jesus' early supporters who welcomed Jesus to the holy city, and demonstrate this in a physical way. Fasting during Lent, likewise, is a means of identifying oneself with Jesus who fasted in the desert, tempted by Satan (Matthew 4:1–11).

It is interesting that Dan mentions repentance, forgiveness, and reconciliation. They are not typically associated with major festivals, although Ash Wednesday is particularly associated with penitence.

Nonetheless they are extremely important to Christians: repentance and forgiveness are frequently mentioned in the New Testament, and are frequently mentioned in sermons. I remember one occasion in my childhood, when my mother came back from a Friday evening service. She told us that the minister had urged the congregation that, before coming to Holy Communion that Sunday, they should make peace with anyone with whom they had quarrelled. My mother took the message to heart, and promptly wrote a letter to an aunt with whom the family had a long-standing quarrel. This led to a reconciliation, and my brother and I acquired a new aunt whom we had not previously met!

7(C) DAWOUD:

In Islam, as in Judaism and Christianity, the major festivals mark important and formative events in the history of the early Muslim community, and as George has described, they involve people in this community experience in forms of ritual re-enactment of important and symbolic events.

The Islamic calendar is dated from the year of the *Hijra*, or emigration, in 622 CE, when the first Muslims fled from Mecca to Medina to escape persecution. This was enacted retrospectively in 638 CE by the Caliph Umar when dates became necessary for administrative purposes. The Islamic calendar is a lunar calendar which in most Islamic countries is based on sighting of the crescent moon according to specific rules (unlike other lunar calendars based on astronomical calculations). This means that it has 354 or 355 days and does not correspond with the Gregorian calendar, or the seasons, so the feasts and other notable dates fall ten to twelve days earlier each year as measured by the international calendar, moving round the year over a period of approximately thirty-three years.

Muslims keep Friday, *Yawm al-Jum'a* (day of gathering) as the day of obligatory congregational prayer. There is no clear evidence for the choice of Friday and it may simply have been established to distinguish it from Sabbaths of the other religions. In Islam there is no belief in it being the day of rest following the labours of creation and therefore no prohibition on working. It is, however, normally the day of the week on which offices and banks and many other businesses close in most Muslim countries.

There are two major feasts in the Islamic calendar and these are celebrated universally. *Eid ul-Fitr*, the feast of the breaking of the fast, takes place at the end of Ramadan, which itself is a hugely important part of the Islamic calendar. Ramadan begins with the sighting of the new moon and for a month Muslims are required to abstain from all food, drink, smoking, and sexual intercourse from first light until sunset. Obviously, the further one moves away from the equator, the greater the difference in the length of the fast depending on what time of year the month falls. The sick, people who are travelling, and pregnant, lactating or menstruating women are exempt. Young children are not required to fast, but by eight or nine they may begin gradually to become involved by fasting for part of the day. By the time they reach their early teens, many will fast the whole day like their parents. The feast begins at sunset on the last day of Ramadan as determined again by the sighting of the crescent moon, and the next morning, *Eid* prayers are held in the early morning, after which families and communities gather for a celebration meal. New clothes are worn and gifts are given, particularly to children. Money or food is given to the poor and needy as *Zakat ul-Fitr*, with particular emphasis on enabling the poor to celebrate the feast along with the rest of the community.

Eid ul-Adha, the feast of the sacrifice, takes place at the end of the *hajj*, the annual pilgrimage. It marks Ibrahim's willingness to obey God by sacrificing his son Isma'il, for whom God, having tested Ibrahim, substituted an animal at the last minute. Notably, contrary to Jewish belief, Muslims hold that it was Isma'il and not Ishaq whom Ibrahim was to sacrifice. All who are able should sacrifice an animal according to their means. Depending on where they live, they may carry this out themselves or have it done on their behalf. Normally a proportion of the meat is distributed to the poor. Pilgrims on the *hajj* previously performed or supervised the slaughter themselves and the scale of this in the conditions in Mecca meant that vast amounts of meat were left to rot in the desert. Then, in the mid-1980s, the Saudi government established a voucher scheme so that meat slaughtered on behalf of pilgrims in abattoirs could be distributed to poor Muslim countries.

Many Muslim communities celebrate *al-Mawlid al-Nabawi*, the birth of the Prophet, although Wahabis and Deobandis consider it heresy. This is a joyful festival where homes and businesses are lit up with coloured lights and sweet stalls appear outside regular shops. People tell stories of the life of the Prophet and in some countries there are parades and national celebrations.

These are some of the main festivals of the Sunni calendar and I have not yet touched upon those of the Shi'a. As I have mentioned, while Sunni and Shi'i Islam have much in common there are also important differences, some of which are marked in the holy days of the Shi'a.

As for Dan's points regarding forgiveness as part of the process of atonement, I think this may have to wait until we discuss the issues of the Middle East.

7(D) DAN:

Dawoud mentioned that the Muslim calendar is lunar – this is so in Judaism as well. So far I have focused on *Rosh HaShanah*, which celebrates the New Year, and *Yom Kippur* (the Day of Atonement) that takes place ten days later. In addition there are three pilgrim festivals that commemorate historic events in the life of the Jewish nation. The first is Passover (*Pesach*), which takes place for eight days and commemorates the exodus from Egypt. The festival begins with the Seder meal when the narrative of the exodus is recited, and during the eight days of Passover only unleavened bread (*matzoh*) is eaten. This symbolizes the unleavened bread the ancient Israelites took with them as they fled from the Egyptians. The second pilgrim festival – *Shavout* (weeks) – is celebrated for two days. Symbolically it commemorates the culmination of the process of emancipation which began with the exodus at Passover. It is concluded with the proclamation of the Law on Mount Sinai. The word "*Shavuot*" means weeks – seven weeks are counted from the bringing of the *omer* (wheat offering) on the second day of Passover. The liturgical readings for the festival include the Ten Commandments. The third pilgrim festival is *Sukkot* (booths), which commemorates God's protection of the Israelites during their sojourn in the desert. During this festival it is customary to build a booth with a roof covered with branches of trees or plants. During the seven days of the festival Jews are commanded to eat meals inside the *sukkah*.

In the Jewish calendar there are a number of festivals of joy:

- **Hanukkah:** This festival (meaning "dedication") is celebrated for eight days and it commemorates the victory of the Maccabees over the Seleucids in the second century BCE. The central observance of this festival is the kindling of the festive lamp on each of the eight nights.

- **Purim:** This festival of joy commemorates the deliverance of Persian Jewry from the plans of Haman, the chief minister of King Ahasuerus. In the evening and morning of Purim the Esther scroll is chanted to a traditional melody. In most congregations Purim resembles a carnival – children frequently attend the reading from the scroll in fancy dress, and whenever Haman's name is mentioned, worshippers stamp their feet and whirl noisemakers.

- **Rosh Hodesh:** This festival occurs with the new moon each month. Since the Jewish calendar is lunar, each month lasts a little more than twenty-nine days. Special services take place on this day.

- **The New Year for Trees (*Tu Bi-Shevat*)**: It is customary to eat special fruits during this festival. In Israel trees are planted as part of the celebration.

- **Fifteenth of Av:** In ancient times bachelors selected their wives from unmarried maidens. In modern times this festival is marked only by a ban on eulogies or fasting.

- **Israel Independence Day:** This is Israel's national day, which commemorates the proclamation of its independence in May, 1948. The Chief Rabbinate of Israel declared it a religious holiday and established a special order of service. It is celebrated by Jews around the world.

The Jewish calendar also includes fast days in addition to *Yom Kippur*. Pre-eminent among these fast days is the Ninth of Av (*Tisha B'Av*), the day when Nebuchadnezzar destroyed the Temple in 586 BCE. Other fast days include the Seventh of Tammuz, which commemorates the breaching of the walls of Jerusalem during the First Temple period and in Second Temple times by the Romans. The Tenth of Tevet is a fast commemorating the commencement of the siege of Jerusalem by Nebuchadnezzar. The Fast of Gedaliah commemorates the fate of Gedaliah, the governor of Judah, who was assassinated on this day. The Jewish calendar also includes a number of other fasts decreed by the rabbis. There are also private fasts such as the fast for brides and grooms on their wedding day.

In addition to the Sabbath, there are a number of special Sabbaths which take place throughout the year such as the Sabbath of Blessing, the Sabbath of the New Moon, the Sabbath of Return, the Sabbath of Genesis, the Sabbath of *Hanukkah*, the Sabbath of Song, the Sabbath of the Shekel Tax, the Sabbath of the Red Heifer, the Great Sabbath, the Sabbath of Prophecy, and the Sabbath of Comfort.

These various festivals are fundamentally different from holy days in the Christian and Islamic traditions. There is a central feature I should mention which is characteristic of a number of these days of commemoration. Passover and *Purim* in particular celebrate the victory of the Jewish people over their enemies. These holidays stress that we Jews have been persecuted through the centuries – from ancient times to the present. Yet, the constant theme is that with God's help, we can triumph over adversity and continue to endure.

7(E) GEORGE:

Dawoud and Dan have each given interesting and informative accounts of their respective festivals. I have already outlined the Christian ones, so I would like to take the discussion a stage further, and ask to what extent it is possible for us to share our various celebrations. When I have spoken to Muslim students at university, some of them tell me that at Christmas they also exchange presents, and sometimes hang up stockings and put up Christmas trees. One of the local *imams* used to send me a Christmas card annually, and I suppose all this makes sense since Jesus is acknowledged within Islam as one of the important prophets.

I only wish my Jewish friends were more generous in acknowledging the birth of Jesus. I know that they cannot accept his messianic or divine status, but he was a Jewish rabbi whose unsurpassable teachings were rabbinic expositions of the Torah. I usually have to find a *Hanukkah* card for Jewish friends, instead of a Christmas one – in fact, I have been told that the celebration of *Hanukkah* acquired recent popularity, since Jewish children felt they were missing out on Christmas celebrations! (The two festivals almost coincide in our calendars.)

I am not sure, however, that I would wish to join with Muslims in celebrating *Eid-ul-Adha*. Sacrificing animals seems to me unnecessary and cruel. If they are used for food, then there is some justification, but the idea of animals rotting away because worshippers felt an obligation to engage in ritual slaughter seems quite appalling to me. In my previous section, I mentioned the role of festivals as re-enacting events in our faiths, but surely there are some stories relating to our past that are not appropriate to recreate symbolically centuries later. Christians made a point of distancing themselves from the Jewish sacrificial system, and of course the Jews themselves ceased such practices after the destruction of the Jerusalem Temple in 70 CE. I know many of them dislike intensely the idea that is championed by a small minority of Jews, that there should be a Third Temple in Jerusalem, with the restoration of the sacrificial system.

One event in which we can all participate, however, is International Holocaust Remembrance Day, which is marked in many countries of the world on 27 January each year. Although we designed this book to highlight points of disagreement between Jews, Christians, and Muslims, there are some matters on which there has to be consensus. One such matter is Adolf Hitler's attempt to exterminate Jews in Nazi Germany. One can only express the utmost horror at the pseudo-scientific attempts to show that Jews were subhuman, the subsequent persecution, and their removal to extermination camps.

The Christian church has sometimes been criticized for its failure to act against Hitler. Certainly Pope Pius XII did not publicly speak out against the Nazi regime, and this is not to his credit. The Vatican has subsequently expressed remorse about this; although, during the war years, the Pope did speak against the persecution of Jews and encouraged the church to offer refuge to them. A number of Protestant clergy, most notably the Lutheran pastor Dietrich Bonhoeffer, were courageous enough to speak out against Nazism, and Bonhoeffer was prepared to suffer the penalty of being imprisoned and subsequently hanged in a Nazi concentration camp.

Although Holocaust Day is a sombre event, it is a powerful reminder of events that should never be forgotten, and of the power of religious believers to do both good and harm. It is certainly an event that all faiths can share in, and it was a privilege for me to be asked to speak at such a gathering in Wolverhampton some years ago.

I should like to add a couple of caveats about Holocaust remembrance, however. Dan has made the point that Jews have been victims throughout the centuries. While this is undoubtedly true, I think this can disguise the fact that some Jews can also adopt a very different role, particularly in the context of the Palestinians in the West Bank. This raises issues about persecution, forgiveness, and reconciliation, as Dawoud acknowledges, and this is something to which we shall return. I think too that, while there continues to exist a great deal of prejudice against Jews, it is important to avoid the opposite extreme in which, by typecasting Jews as victims, any criticism of Jews – and particularly Israelis – becomes construed as anti-Semitism.

I wonder if we would agree that while all our three faiths teach love, peace, harmony, and forgiveness, we have all at various times been persecutors, as well as victims who have suffered persecution for our faith?

7(F) DAWOUD:

I think George makes an interesting point about joining in with each other's festivals. It reminded me that when Dan and I worked together at the University of Wales Lampeter we would often exchange Christmas cards. It is not unusual for those living as minority cultures within a larger community to join in naturally with the feasts and festivals of the majority and to want to wish their neighbours well. Muslims in the West, as well as those of other religions, can hardly avoid the celebrations of Christmas and many have no problem in joining in with the general season of festivity. Muslims who do so, however, despite their reverence for the Prophet 'Isa (Jesus), do not do so as a celebration of the birth of Jesus but rather in the way of being part of a national culture. Some Muslims deliberately refuse to recognize or celebrate Christian or other religious festivals, believing that this would be a kind of heresy. Many hold the celebration of birthdays in general to be un-Islamic, and so find the celebration of the birth of Jesus particularly inappropriate. Some will ask that their children be excluded from worship and from Christmas or Easter activities at school. Those who are secure in their faith, however, should not feel threatened or undermined by acknowledging the beliefs and culture of others and for this reason many Muslims embrace the Christmas season and take the opportunity to spend time with their family and friends and exchange gifts.

It is not always easy for Muslims to celebrate their holy days in non-Muslim countries. In many cities with large Muslim populations it is possible for them to feel part of something bigger, particularly where there are communities with a relatively homogenous culture. In other places they may come together to share the parts of the feasts that are common to all Muslims; however, the real soul of any feast comes from family and culture, so Muslims from different countries may have no more in common with each other than Christians from different European and New World countries, each having their traditional foods and social customs.

The same applies to non-Muslims in Muslim countries. During Ramadan, for example, one can hardly fail to be aware of the daily cycle of fasting and breaking the fast and the night-time activity and entertainment. Many non-Muslims will find it inappropriate to be seen eating, drinking, or smoking in public during the day, merely out of politeness and consideration for those who are fasting. The feasts are part of national culture in the same way as Christmas in Western countries, and in most Muslim countries, it is perfectly possible for non-Muslims to enjoy the atmosphere of celebration.

Perhaps I gave the wrong impression regarding the sacrifice of animals for *Eid ul-Adha*. It does not take place on an altar or in a specific ritual place but simply by the normal method of slaughter (which I am aware is a topic for debate in itself), and it is extremely important that the meat should be used as food and in particular given to the needy. It was for this reason that the voucher scheme was introduced in Mecca to avoid the waste where it had not previously been logistically possible to deal with the amount of meat produced.

I do agree with George that all of us can, and should, mark International Holocaust Remembrance Day. It is essential for our common survival that we recognize each other's humanity and each other's suffering. In the incomparable scale of the calculated atrocities of the Holocaust and in other genocides and attempts at ethnic cleansing that have taken place around the world in the years since that time, we have seen that it is all too easy for ordinary people to lose sight of the humanity of their neighbours. When we begin to see people of faiths, races, or nationalities different from our own as "the other", and fail to understand their suffering and feel their pain in the same way as we feel for "our own", then we are not far away from the Holocaust. As George points out, Jews, Christians, and Muslims have been both victim and oppressor. It is particularly important in our current times that we remain vigilant against this.

CHAPTER 8

EVANGELISM

Christians and Muslims traditionally have been committed to spreading their faith. Jews have been less inclined to proselytize, although they have regarded themselves as God's chosen people. Has the interfaith movement changed things in this regard? What do we see as the strengths and limitations of interfaith activity?

8(A) GEORGE:

Jesus' last recorded words to his disciples were, "Go and make disciples of all nations, baptising them in the name of the Father and of the Son and of the Holy Spirit" (Matthew 28:19). This saying is known as the "Great Commission", and Christian missionaries have seen themselves as obeying Christ's commandment. The fact that the West was more advanced in medicine, education, technology, and military power than the countries it colonized helped to fuel the assumption that Christians also had a superior spiritual message.

There are many Christians who still believe that they have this role, and that the church's task is to bring the whole world into the Christian fold. Others are not so sure, and several factors have called for a reappraisal of Christian mission. Many of us are uncomfortable with the stark division of eternal destinies – heaven and hell – about which the church has traditionally taught. Could a loving God really consign most of the human race to eternal torment that serves no obvious purpose? Would it be fair to condemn billions of people who, through no fault of their own, never heard the gospel message?

Traditionally the church has taught the doctrine of *nulla ecclesiam salus est* (no salvation outside the church), but during the twentieth century, a number of theologians came to re-evaluate this position. The missionary J. N. Farquhar wrote a book entitled *The Crown of Hinduism*. The book was influenced by evolutionary theory, and claimed that other religions of the world – particularly Hinduism – were ultimately leading up to and pointing to Christ. Although this view might seem somewhat disparaging of Hinduism, it nonetheless acknowledged that other faiths are not in total darkness, as some missionaries in previous years had suggested.

Some Christian theologians have also assigned positions to other faiths that suggest that they can have important insights into spiritual truth. The Roman Catholic theologian Karl Rahner proposed the idea of "anonymous Christianity": if Jesus Christ is a universal presence, then he must also somehow be present in other faiths, even if he is not explicitly acknowledged. In the same tradition, Hans Küng distinguished between "ordinary" and "extraordinary" ways of salvation. By this he meant that there is a possibility of salvation outside the church, but the Christian faith provides a special – and best – path. Although these attempts at inclusiveness are well intentioned, they still relegate other faiths to a lower division.

The Protestant philosopher of religion, John Hick, suggested a somewhat different idea. We are saved, he contended, not by any religion, but by God Himself. He described this as a "Copernican revolution" in theology: instead of seeing Christianity as the centre, around which other faiths revolve, we should regard God as the centre of all faiths, bringing them all to salvation or liberation. This may seem more magnanimous, although it does have problems in accommodating Buddhism, in which a creator God is of little interest, and it also raises the question of whether any faith at all leads to salvation – the Ku Klux Klan, Satanism, the Church of the Flying Spaghetti Monster?

In Britain, the substantial immigration that took place from the early 1960s marked a shift in attitudes towards other faiths. These faiths were no longer to be found in remote countries, but were now on our very doorstep. While missionaries such as the early nineteenth-century Reginald Heber had written words like "The heathen in his blindness / Bows down to wood and stone", such stereotypes became much less plausible when Christians came to know members of other faiths personally. Some of them – particularly Hindus and Sikhs – needed premises in which to worship, and approached Christian congregations to seek the use of church halls. The major denominations in Britain expanded the remit of their central committees assigned to mission, and widened them to include relationships with other faiths. The main concern became interfaith dialogue, rather than conversion.

The interfaith movement undoubtedly has its value, although, as Dawoud pointed out earlier (6E), only a small handful of members of each faith are involved. It has undoubtedly served a purpose in creating friendships and dispelling misconceptions. However, I think that there is a danger that it reduces all faiths to a common denominator, or blurs differences between them. The nineteenth-century Presbyterian poet George Matheson wrote words that are often used at interfaith gatherings. (The "seven" to whom he refers below were Buddhists, Christians, Hindus, Jews, Muslims, Sikhs, and Parsees.)

Each sees one color of Thy rainbow light,
Each looks upon one tint and calls it heaven;
Thou art the fullness of our partial sight;
We are not perfect till we find the seven.

It's a nice idea but, while I have gained much from relationships with people of other faiths, I don't think I can accept that my own faith is incomplete without them.

8(B) DAWOUD:

And let there be [arising] from you a nation inviting to [all that is] good, enjoining what is right and forbidding what is wrong, and those will be the successful. (Qur'an 3:104)

Islam is an unashamedly proselytizing religion. The concept of the revelation is fundamental to Muslims as it marks the watershed between the *Jahiliyya*, the time of ignorance, and the era of Islam. For Muslims, Islam was revealed for all humankind and all peoples are to be invited to Islam. The *shahada* or profession of faith says, "I witness that there is no God but God and I witness that Muhammad is the Messenger (*Rasul*) of God." Although it is sometimes translated as "prophet" (and a word meaning prophet is often used to refer to Muhammad), the word *rasul* in the second part of the *shahada* means "messenger", the one chosen to bring *ar-Risala*, "the Message", to the world.

Da'wa (literally "call" or "invitation") or mission in Islam is of two kinds. One is aimed at inviting non-Muslims to Islam, with the ultimate aim of bringing all humankind to the faith. The other is aimed at encouraging Muslims to be more devout and knowledgeable about their faith. Da'wa is something that can be undertaken by any individual and is considered highly meritorious, but there are also many da'wa organizations that encourage and support Islamic mission. Some of these are on a small or local scale, but there are several significant large international organizations such as the Tablighi Jamaat, originally formed in India, which organizes large-scale missionary work worldwide and encourages members to participate in regular missionary activity on a weekly, monthly, and an annual basis. In the UK there is a sizeable and highly active da'wa movement concentrated in higher education institutions that aims both to invite non-Muslims to Islam and to strengthen the faith of Muslims and encourage them in participation in the Muslim community. It is important, however, to distinguish here between valid religious education and the more alarming phenomenon of radicalization.

Muslim doctrine is much more absolute and has far fewer qualms about the "division of eternal destinies" that George refers to or about relegating other faiths to a lower division. Muslims are much less reticent in claiming the monopoly on truth. As discussed previously, they believe that Islam is the one true faith; however, while Judaism and Christianity are considered its inferior predecessors, they are nonetheless given the status of religions "of the book" and recognized as sharing the central belief in one God. Conversion from these to Islam is welcomed, but the reverse is deemed to be apostasy. Other religions such as Hinduism and Sikhism, or the native religions of other countries, are not recognized as valid religions, however, and their practitioners are considered to be *mushrikin* or idolators who will not be saved unless they are brought to Islam. In 2006 an Egyptian legal ruling went as far as to declare that Islam, Christianity, and Judaism were the only legitimate religions, thereby depriving Egyptians of other faiths, or no faith, an aspect of their civil status (as there is no option for a person to identify themselves otherwise in their civil identity documentation, thus forcing them either to falsify their religious affiliation or suffer the penalties of having no national identity card).

Attitudes to religious practice and proselytizing by other religions vary in different Muslim countries, but in many of them proselytizing to Muslims by other faiths is illegal. In Malaysia in 2006 the Education Ministry ordered the closure of a tuition centre following allegations that it was trying to convert Muslim children to Christianity, and in February 2013 a number of foreign nationals including Egyptian Copts were arrested in Libya on charges of proselytization of Muslims, a crime that could lead to the death sentence as it involves encouraging a Muslim to commit apostasy.

The Qur'an contains a great deal of rhetorical material concerned with calling people to Islam and away from idolatry. This is particularly true of many of the sections revealed during the first years of Islam in Mecca, where the emphasis was on monotheism and acceptance of the message itself. As we have already mentioned, the Qur'an makes it clear that there is no compulsion in religion (2:256).

8(C) DAN:

Through the centuries both Christianity and Islam have been missionary religions. On the whole this has not been the case with Judaism. With the exception of the Hellenistic period, Jews have not been anxious to bring Gentiles into the fold. Conversion has always been an option, but since the rise of Christianity, Jewry has been content to coexist with other religious traditions. This is due to the generally tolerant attitude towards other religions. In biblical times the ancient Israelites were encouraged to view the gods of other peoples as nonentities. In this respect ancient Israelite faith was exclusivist in orientation. Yet, foreign peoples were not condemned for their pagan practices. Although the religion of the Jewish people was perceived as the one true faith, there was no harsh condemnation of idolatry. Furthermore, it was the conviction of the prophets that in the end of days all nations would recognize that the God of the Israelites was the Lord of the universe; thus, there was no compulsion to missionize among non-believers. There was hope even for pagan peoples in the unfolding of God's plan of salvation.

In the rabbinic period this tradition of tolerance continued to animate Jewish life. According to the rabbis, all non-Jews who follow the Noahide Laws (the laws kept by Noah in the Bible) are viewed as acceptable to God and can enter into the world to come. Hence salvation exists for those outside the Jewish fold. In this context even those who engage in polytheistic practices are admissible as long as the gods they worship are conceived as symbolically pointing to the One God. In the medieval period such writers as Rabbenu Tam applied this rabbinic conception of symbolic intermediacy to Christian believers. In his opinion Christianity is not idolatry since Christians are monotheists despite their belief in the Trinity.

Such a positive stance towards other faiths continued into the early modern period due to the impact of the Enlightenment. In the eighteenth century the Jewish philosopher Moses Mendelssohn argued that the Jewish people were the recipients of a divine revelation consisting of ritual and moral law. Nevertheless, Mendelssohn was convinced that God's reality can be discerned through human reason. Thus all human beings – regardless of their religious persuasion – are capable of discerning God's nature and activity. During this period other thinkers offered a sympathetic appreciation of Christianity, while at the same time adhering to the belief that Judaism is the superior religion.

For nearly four millennia Judaism has in various ways espoused a generally indulgent attitude towards other religions. Unlike Islam and Christianity, which have had a long tradition of exclusivism, Jews have been encouraged to grant other religions a role in the unfolding of God's purposes. Such Jewish inclusivism presupposes the superiority of the Jewish tradition; however, it recognizes that God's purposes have been served by other nations and that He has had an authentic encounter with other peoples. Such ideas have been largely confined to a consideration of Christianity and in some cases Islam. Yet, there is no denying the inclusivist thrust of centuries of Jewish teaching. Religious tolerance has been the hallmark of Judaism through the ages.

In the post-Holocaust world, Jews have been uncomfortable with the kind of missionizing that George and Dawoud described. Given the threat posed by the Nazis to Jewish existence, Jewry is determined to survive. Hence, evangelism is regarded with deep concern. It is the fervent wish of Jews worldwide that we be allowed to continue to practise our faith in the way we choose without outside interference. Although we can understand the religious motives that animate Christian and Islamic evangelism, we would prefer that our Christian and Muslim brothers and sisters adopt the kind of religious tolerance that we Jews have exhibited through the centuries.

8(D) GEORGE:

There is a joke about a native in a remote village who asks a Christian missionary, "Is it true that we won't go to hell if we haven't heard about Jesus?" "Yes, that is true," the missionary replies. "Then why did you tell us about him, then?" the native asks.

This dialogue illustrates some of the problems of Christian mission. If we thought that anyone who had not accepted Jesus Christ was doomed to spending eternity in hell, then missionizing would make sense. However, as I mentioned earlier, many Christians now feel that the idea of eternal punishment goes against the notion of a loving God. So I would like to challenge Dawoud on the idea that God will eternally punish not merely the wicked, but also those who cannot accept the Islamic faith. Surely the ninety-nine names of Allah include the Beneficent, the Merciful, and the Forgiving. He is described as the Reckoner and the Avenger, but are these really commendable attributes of a deity, and are they compatible with mercy and forgiveness?

I am rather puzzled by Dawoud's notions of "valid religions" and "legitimate religions". He seems to imply that Judaism and Christianity are somehow superior to Hinduism and Sikhism, but I'm not clear on what grounds. If his claim is that the non-Abrahamic religions use "idols" or images in worship, this is not true of Sikhism, where the sole focus of worship is the holy book the Guru Granth Sahib. Conversely, some Christians make use of images, although they do not directly address worship to them. And when Dawoud implies that Hinduism and Sikhism are not "legitimate religions" in Egypt, does this mean that they can be subjected to discrimination or even persecution? Dan offers a different slant on mission. As he points out, the Jews have regarded themselves as having an important role in the salvation of the world. It's a nice idea that a relatively small religious community should take upon itself the burden of bringing about salvation for the entire world by their own obedience to God's law. However, it is difficult to see how obedience to a large number of very detailed rules achieves this purpose. I was once at an interfaith gathering, where one of the rabbis had gone so far as to bring his own crockery – presumably because of his understanding of Jewish food laws. I find it really hard to see how this can have any role in bringing about the world's salvation! I know that, as a Reform Jew, Dan takes a more relaxed view of interpreting the Torah, but it would be interesting to know how he thinks that Jewish legal observance can secure salvation.

Dan's mention of the Noahide Covenant is interesting. Probably few Christians know about this, although they realize that God made a covenant with Noah, with corresponding obligations to be fulfilled (Genesis 9:1–17). For the benefit of readers who are unfamiliar with the idea, this covenant was made before Israel became a nation – it is at a later stage that God gives Jacob the name of "Israel" (Genesis 35:10) – and hence it is traditional Jewish teaching that God gave seven commandments to Noah that are binding on all people, and not just Jews. These are: to refrain from idolatry, murder, theft, adultery, blasphemy, and eating of live animals, plus the more positive obligation to adopt a system of just laws. There is certainly nothing here with which Christians could disagree.

However, the Christian faith holds that, although the Noahide Covenant offers simpler and clearer sets of obligations than the complexities of Jewish law, the religious life entails more than observing detailed rules. Christ's death on the cross is described as God's final sacrifice because it brought the Jewish system of rules and regulations to an end. Forgiveness of sin and reconciliation with God become paramount, and these are not brought about by deeds, but can be accepted as an act of faith. This should be good news, and it is understandable that Christians should want to share it with others.

Christian mission has changed over the centuries, however. Many Christians have come to recognize that it is unnecessary to go abroad to find "heathen" who are in need of the gospel. In a society that is beset with materialism, consumerism, violence, prejudice, sexual misconduct, breakdown of family life, and declining interest in religion, there is a need to look beyond human solutions. This, I believe, is a mission for all the people of faith, and not just Christians. However much we may part company on other matters, perhaps this is something on which all three of us might agree.

8(E) DAWOUD:

Of course I agree with both Dan and George that interfaith dialogue is important, and, as reasonable people, there is probably little in practical everyday terms that the three of us would disagree on. As George points out, there is nothing to disagree with in the Noahide commandments, which represent key principles on which a civilized society can be based. We can hold our own beliefs in our hearts and communicate with our God in the way that is comfortable and familiar to us, that is imprinted in our ways of thinking and our sense of self, and that patterns our lives in ways of which we are not always aware. The three of us are happy to try to explain our faiths to each other and none of us feels the need to convince the others of our belief or our way of worship. We simply want to understand, explore our common ground, and establish the boundaries of where we will simply have to agree to differ – without condemning the others for what they believe or considering their faith or form of worship less valid or less acceptable to God. While we may be representative of those of our social and professional circles, however, many of our co-religionists – and I refer in the main where evangelism is concerned to Christians and Muslims – do not feel the same, so I understand Dan's concerns that Jews, and all other peoples for that matter, should be allowed to practise their faiths freely, in peace and without interference. In our comfortable world, in a society that has worked for generations to eliminate discrimination in public life, we are able to discuss things as we are doing now, but much of the rest of the world is not so "politically correct".

In some parts of the world, Muslims, Christians, and Jews have lived together for hundreds of years in different states of peaceful and less than peaceful coexistence, and what stands out is that for the most part they have maintained their distinct religious and cultural identities, some going back many centuries, with only relatively marginal movement between the faiths. Religion binds these communities together internally and provides a focus of identity, being inseparable from culture and community, so where this is undermined the whole community is threatened.

Many Muslims are active in interfaith movements and dialogue and are involved in important work in promoting understanding and friendly relationships between communities, but others (as is no doubt the case with members of other religions) seek to isolate themselves from the influences of other faiths, as if religion were contagious.

This is perhaps something of an overreaction to the following verse:

And it has already come down to you in the Book that when you hear the verses of Allah [recited], they are denied [by them] and ridiculed; so do not sit with them until they enter into another conversation. Indeed, you would then be like them. Indeed Allah will gather the hypocrites and disbelievers in Hell all together. (Qur'an 4:140)

They may withdraw their children from school assemblies involving other religions or philosophies, or classes that they believe may undermine the beliefs of their children such as lessons about sex education or evolution. They may discourage or prevent their children from socializing with children of other backgrounds, or the structures of their own communities may simply make it almost impossible for children to meet and socialize with children of other faiths. This is to do our next generations an enormous disservice. It should be our duty to lighten their load, not to pass on to them a historical burden.

If we are secure in our own faiths, then why should we feel threatened by the beliefs of others? What has to be most important then is not that we try to convince or convert each other, but that we try to understand and accept each other. It is only knowledge and understanding that will enable us to live together.

> *O mankind, indeed We have created you from male and female and made you peoples and tribes that you may know one another. Indeed, the most noble of you in the sight of Allah is the most righteous of you. Indeed, Allah is Knowing and Acquainted. (Qur'an 49:13)*

8(F) DAN:

In this book we have attempted to explore the various points of contention that separate Jews, Christians, and Muslims. Arguably it is in the area of evangelism that disagreement is most acute. As I noted, we Jews do not believe that salvation is only for the Jewish people. George asked why Jews believe that they are a light to the nations. The standard answer is that God revealed the moral law to the ancient Israelites, and that the Hebrew Bible is a beacon to all peoples. As far as our three faiths are concerned, the Five Books of Moses, the Prophetic Books, and the other books of scripture serve as the foundation and anchor of our faiths. Traditionally the Jewish people contend they have offered to the world ethical teachings by which every individual can live. It is not ritual law (which is binding only on Jews) that is crucial, but the moral commandments which provide a basis for civilized living. The Noahide Laws offer Gentiles a path of righteous living and a means of entry into the world to come.

Jewish tolerance of the possibility that non-Jews might enter into eternal life is, however, at odds with traditional Christian teaching.

Matthew 28:19 states: "Go and make disciples of all nations." Christianity has always been a missionary faith. In this it is unlike Judaism from which it sprang. Christians are committed to sharing the good news of God's saving love revealed in Jesus. From the beginning of their history, Christians have believed that they possess ultimate truth about God's providential action – to share this good news can bring hope, confidence, and courage to all humanity. In the 1980s church leaders began to consider appropriate ways of marking the new millennium. Pope John Paul II suggested the 1990s should be a Decade of Evangelization, and the 1988 Lambeth Conference of Anglican Bishops worldwide declared a "Decade of Evangelism". Most mainstream churches supported these initiatives, with their vision of a renewed and unified effort to make Christ known to the peoples of the world.

You must remember that for twenty centuries Jews have suffered at the hands of Christians who used every means possible including torture and murder to convert them. Today we live in the shadow of the Holocaust, and these kinds of initiatives to convert us are perceived by many Jews as a silent form of Holocaust – a further Christian attempt to wipe out Judaism and the Jewish people from history. It is inevitable that such a form of evangelism with its triumphant proclamation of Jesus' transformation of history is regarded with suspicion and fear. The rise of militant Islam with its endorsement of *Shari'a* law and its sense of mission is also regarded with anxiety. Coupled with the growth of Jew-hatred within the Arab world, this form of Islam has caused widespread distress among Jews worldwide. Today there are, of course, some Messianic Jews who believe that Jesus (or Yeshua, as they call him) is the long-awaited messiah. This movement has been widely rejected as a valid interpretation of Judaism by all the major Jewish movements, and they are a small minority.

I appreciate that neither of you seeks to compel Jews to convert. What Dawoud has described in his last exchange – an endorsement of interfaith activity – is to be welcomed and acknowledged. Similarly George's outreach to all faith communities embraces the same spirit of ecumenism. But what both of you must see is that such a view is unrepresentative of the attitudes of millions of Christians and

Muslims. We Jews are outnumbered. We regard ourselves as a minority faith, beleaguered and bloodied over centuries by Christians and Muslims who seek to wipe us off the religious map. Is it not surprising that we live in fear for our future?

PART III

ETHICS AND LIFESTYLE

CHAPTER 9

DECLARING IDENTITIES

Religious believers often want to indicate their identity. Increasingly in the West, Muslim women have taken to wearing the veil. Some Jewish men reveal their faith by not cutting their beards and by acquiring locks on their hair. Christians sometimes identify themselves by wearing crosses as jewellery, or by displaying WWJD ("What would Jesus do?") or fish symbols either on their person or on possessions. This has sometimes given rise to controversy, as in the case of the flight attendant who took her case to the European Court of Human Rights in 2012. To what extent is it "politically correct" to minimize one's religious identity? Is it unduly confrontational to reveal one's religious identity, or is it a fundamental human right to be able to do so?

9(A) DAWOUD:

Why do some people of religion feel the need to dress in certain ways or to display certain religious symbols? Do they do so because of faith itself, or as a statement and marker of community identity, or perhaps a combination of both?

For Muslims the most visible aspect of this is the *hijab*, the head veil worn by women, or its more extreme forms the *niqab* or the *burqa*. There are differences of opinion among Muslims as to whether or not the veil is required. It is not prescribed, as such, in the Qur'an but there are some general requirements:

And tell the believing women to reduce [some] of their vision and guard their private parts and not expose their adornment except that which [necessarily] appears thereof and to wrap [a portion of] their headcovers over their chests and not expose their adornment except to their husbands, their fathers, their husbands' fathers, their sons, their husbands' sons, their brothers, their brothers' sons, their sisters' sons, their women that their right hands possess, or those male attendants having no physical desire, or children who are not yet aware of the private aspects of women. And let them not stamp their feet to make known what they conceal of their adornment. (24:31)

The main dress requirement for women, and for men, is modesty. Outside the home, women should dress so as not to attract male attention and this in general terms means avoiding wearing close-fitting or revealing clothes and jewellery, make-up, and perfume.

The Arabic word *hijab* may mean a cover, curtain, or screen, while the related word *muhajjaba* ("veiled" – in the feminine form) implies not just a physical covering, but a way of life in which interaction with men outside a woman's immediate family is strictly regulated.

For Muslim women in many parts of the world, dress is purely a matter of culture and is not an issue. In many Muslim countries, however, the *hijab* had seen a steep decline particularly among the urban middle classes during the middle years of the twentieth century. Since the 1970s, however, there has been a gradual return to the *hijab*, even among women whose grandmothers discarded it, both in Muslim countries and in the West.

This has accompanied an Islamic resurgence, and the rise of political Islam. For many, adopting and wearing the veil signifies a desire to put Islam at the centre of their lives in personal terms, and to become part of something larger. For women who convert to Islam it is a part of the rites of passage. It is both a personal undertaking and a statement that signifies the assuming of a whole new way of life, and many say they feel it enables them to live and work without being defined by their physical attractiveness. Naturally, however, it defines the terms in which both other Muslims and non-Muslims interact with them to a very great extent.

There has also been a change in which many Muslim men choose to define their identity. Many follow what they believe to be the *Sunna*, or custom of the Prophet, which involves wearing a beard. There are certain groups of Salafis who cultivate a particular style of beard without a moustache. They may also adopt the wearing of the *jilbab* or *galabiyya* – a long-sleeved robe, many choosing to wear it in a form which reaches mid-calf length rather than floor length in emulation of the Prophet who is said to have worn this length to avoid becoming too comfortable. Whereas the parents and grandparents of many of the men and women who choose to dress in this way rejected traditional dress several generations ago, this appears to be a choice to become part of a larger movement. In the West, however, many Muslims feel that they are prejudged by their choice of dress and face discrimination.

9(B) DAN:

One of the most distinctive signs of masculine Orthodox Jewish dress is the skull-cap (*yarmulke* in Yiddish; *kippah* in Hebrew). In fact the practice of wearing a skull-cap only goes back to about the twelfth century CE, and may have been introduced to distinguish Jewish from Christian prayer. Christian men traditionally pray with their heads uncovered. Jews, on the other hand, came to wear a head covering as a matter of custom. Today all strictly Orthodox men keep their heads covered at all times. Members of Conservative and Reform congregations generally wear a head covering in the synagogue, but go about bare-headed on secular occasions. Similarly Jewish men who do not affiliate with any religious movement have abandoned this practice.

According to the book of Leviticus, it is forbidden to cut the corners of the beard (19:27). Throughout the Middle Ages, it was the custom of Jewish men to wear beards, and the Talmud describes the beard as an "ornament of the face". Later the biblical verse was interpreted to mean that Jews should not shave, but it was permissible to cut facial hair. Today many Jewish men are clean-shaven; they dispose of their beards either by clipping with an electric razor or with a chemical depilatory. Among the Hasidim and the strictly Orthodox, this passage from Leviticus is also understood to mean that men should allow their side-locks to grow. These are known as *peot*, and are frequently seen on young boys. Adult men tend to curl the locks round and tuck them behind their ears so that they are almost invisible. Male members of non-Orthodox movements as well as secular Jewish men, however, have abandoned these practices.

Another element of Orthodox Jewish appearance is fringes (*tzitzit*). According to the book of Numbers, God told the Israelites "to make tassels on the corners of your garments... so you will remember all the commands of the Lord" (15:37–39). Orthodox men wear an undergarment with fringes on the four corners; these are tied in a particular way to symbolize the numerical value of the name of God. Known as the *tallit katan*, the garment is largely hidden, although the fringes are brought out above the trouser waistband and are discreetly tucked into a pocket. Again, non-Orthodox and secular Jewish men do not follow these practices.

Orthodox Jewish women's dress is characterized by modesty. Married women traditionally cover their heads and the Orthodox continue this practice either by wearing a wig or by swathing the head in a large scarf. Skirts cover the knee and sleeves the elbow. The non-Orthodox ignore these customs and, particularly in Israel, it is not unknown for the strictly Orthodox to vent their disapproval on young women whom they perceive to be improperly dressed.

A final law concerning clothing is that of *shaatnes*, or forbidden cloth. The Law states: "Do not wear clothes of wool and linen woven together" (Deuteronomy 22:11). This regulation is one of several laws against mixing. Vineyards should not be sown with two different types of seed, and an ox and a donkey should not be yoked together at the plough. Today modern technology can be employed to determine the precise composition of fabrics, and there are several "*shaatnes* laboratories" which can carry out tests and certify the legality of a particular material. In any event the commandment is only understood to forbid the mingling of linen and wool. Any other combination, such as wool and acrylic or cotton and silk, is permissible. Again, this law is ignored by the non-Orthodox.

In the past Jews were all too often compelled by secular governments to wear distinctive emblems. From the seventh century CE,

Muslim rulers insisted that Jews wear special clothing and the same provision was made by the Christian church in the thirteenth century. The practice was revived by Hitler's Nazis in the Holocaust period, when all Jews were compelled to wear yellow Stars of David. Today, however, the vast majority of Jews are indistinguishable from the general population. Those who wear distinctive dress, such as the skull-cap, do so only as an expression of their own personal religious convictions.

9(C) GEORGE:

An anonymous second-century author wrote a letter to someone by the name of Diognetus, in which he says the following about the early Christians: "They live in both Greek and foreign cities, wherever chance has put them. They follow local customs in clothing, food, and the other aspects of life."

Christians are under no obligation to wear any special dress or identification, and prefer to blend into the societies in which they live. One or two communities wear distinctive clothing, for example the Amish, and members of the clergy and religious orders like monks and nuns are often readily identifiable. These special forms of dress indicate a separation from the world, whereas most Christians recognize that they are part of it.

Less ostentatious forms of religious identification have gained popularity in recent times, such as the fish symbol, frequently seen as a lapel badge or car bumper sticker. (This fish is an ancient Christian symbol, the Greek word *ICHTHUS*, meaning "fish", being an acronym for "Jesus Christ, Son of God, Saviour" in Greek.) Another popular piece of Christian paraphernalia comes from the WWJD movement. The letters stand for "What Would Jesus Do?" and can be found on wristbands, necklaces, ties, and other articles of clothing. The idea is to remind the wearer to reflect on how Jesus might have behaved, when they are faced with moral decisions.

Some Christians use tattoos to express their religious identity, and a quick Internet search of "Christian tattoos" reveals an amazing assortment: Christian symbols, biblical texts, pictures of Jesus, and scenes from the Gospels. One man even sports a tattoo of the Last Supper across his back! Not all Christians approve, however: some cite the book of Leviticus, which states: "Do not cut your bodies for the dead or put tattoo marks on yourselves" (19:28). Others argue that this command belongs to the old covenant, and is no longer valid for Christians.

The most traditional mark of identity is of course the cross or crucifix. The 2006 incident involving the British Airways flight attendant who was asked to cover up a necklace displaying a Christian cross – a case that went as far as the European Court of Human Rights – was more of a human rights issue, however, than an issue about freedom to practise her religion, since Christians can practice their faith fully, without displaying such symbols.

Visible religious symbols enable others to correlate believers' behaviour with their faith. If a car cuts in on me when I am driving, and I see a fish symbol on its tailgate, this tells me that at least one Christian is a discourteous driver! Saint Paul wrote about being Christ's ambassadors (2 Corinthians 5:20) and wearing a Christian symbol enables others to judge whether we are good ones or bad.

Regarding Jewish and Muslim dress, I have no problems about religious or ethnic minorities dressing differently, but one's dress sends out signals. Dan mentions the Hasidim. I have never quite understood why they dress in a costume that originated in nineteenth-century Poland, and I always think they look somewhat unapproachable. That's a subjective judgment, I know, and they certainly have the right to dress as they do.

The wearing of the *burqa* is more controversial, however. Dawoud indicates that it is not a requirement of Islam, and I must confess that I have a number of problems with the practice. Given the prejudice against Islam that exists in certain Western circles, I would have thought that Muslim women would integrate better into Western society if they did not cover themselves up totally. As Dawoud points out, the wearing of the *burqa* stems from a society in which women have limited contact with men outside the family. However, women who wear the veil and simultaneously pursue a career seem to place themselves in a paradoxical position: they don't want to stay in the home as housewives, yet they adopt dress customs appropriate to a traditional unliberated role.

There are practical problems too. If they are in careers in which they interact with people, facial expressions and eye contact are very important – especially if they are working with children, who may find a fully veiled woman intimidating. In my own profession, there are problems of possible impersonation in exams, where staff cannot identify a student's face, and one Western convert to Islam refused to have an ID photograph taken. If one reason for veiling is that women should not look sexually provocative, then perhaps part of the problem lies with men (Muslim and non-Muslim), some of whom may need to change their behaviour. Public sexual harassment of women in Islamic countries such as Egypt is widespread, and causes many Western women to be unable to work there.

9(D) DAWOUD:

I think George makes some valid points regarding some of the forms of dress worn by Orthodox Jews and by Muslims who adhere to an Islamic dress code, as well as perhaps some of the more distinctive although rarer forms of dress adopted by Christian groups such as the Amish. Controlling what people wear allows a degree of social control, and schools, armies, and other organizations have always used this as a way of creating a corporate identity, loyalty, and pride. Forms of dress that are specific to certain religions may be looked at as a kind of uniform which signifies belonging to something bigger and more important than the individual. Many would say that, like the standardized dress of communist China, religious costume indicates the suppression of individuality and the importance of conformity for the greater good of the group. For many people, the notion of an Islamic society requires people to conform to a set of rules that puts individual gratification second to the interests of the community, promising thereby a more profound contentment in living in a stable and ordered world based on a solid family life and clear boundaries. I imagine that this is very similar in the Jewish Orthodox and other religious communities. For Muslims in non-Muslim countries, the adoption of the *hijab* or the growing of a beard and the wearing of one of the many cultural forms of dress for Muslim men marks a person as being of that group and therefore separated in some respects from the outside community. It establishes a boundary which may not easily be crossed in either direction and indeed, as George points out, it can make people appear unapproachable. For some communities this is the external expression of their desire to live separately and to minimize their interaction with other communities.

I agree with George that people should be free to wear whatever form of dress they choose, but I also agree that sometimes there appear to be logical contradictions in this. The *burqa* or *niqab*, for example, is representative of a segregated society in which women's interaction with the wider community is strictly limited. The culture that expects a woman to dress in this manner is a culture that also expects her to accept a specific role in society as wife and mother and does not permit her to work outside the home or even to speak to men to whom she is not related. Logic would suggest that a woman who chooses to adopt this form of dress should also accept all that goes with it, including these restrictions on her activity. I am not referring here to women who are born into societies where these customs apply and who still have a very long way to go even to be able to discuss such matters.

George also makes a very good point that dress in itself cannot protect women from the unwanted attention of men. Sexual harassment of women in Muslim countries is not restricted to Western women or to unveiled Muslim women, but is also experienced by veiled Muslim women and women of all ages. Here the problem lies entirely with the men and boys responsible, and with the society that allows and encourages such attitudes towards women.

I think that the UK has on the whole a model approach to allowing people to dress as they believe their religion requires them to and avoiding the imposition of restrictions on dress other than those justified by objective operational or safety reasons. I would like to hope that this tolerant society will resist pressure to impose restrictions on dress in the manner of the French law on the wearing of religious symbols in schools and colleges and the ban on the wearing of the *niqab* in public places. Inevitably, such laws have the opposite of the desired effect. As the issue becomes politicized, many people feel obliged to take sides. Even people who would not previously have had a strong opinion on religious dress may feel that their religion and culture are under attack and this may lead to more entrenched attitudes. The result of the French law has been that more women have adopted the *hijab* or *niqab* in solidarity with their sisters. To take liberties with Voltaire, he might have argued: "I disagree with what you wear but I will defend to the death your right to wear it."

9(E) DAN:

I think we all agree that religious laws and customs regarding dress pose serious issues in modern society. In many cases they reflect unliberated attitudes towards women, and reinforce isolation between members of different faiths. In the case of Judaism, this has been deliberate. And it is not simply in the area of dress that Jews are obliged to remain aloof from non-Jews: laws of *kashrut*, for example, make it impossible for strictly Orthodox Jews to eat with Gentiles unless kosher food is served. The aim of such legislation is to ensure that the Jewish community continues and survives. Jews are to marry within the fold, and contact between Jews and the outside world is viewed as dangerous and a threat to survival.

You must remember that we Jews are an ancient religion. There are relatively not many of us – perhaps about 15 million worldwide – yet we have endured for over 3,000 years. The Assyrians and Sumerians have disappeared from history; the Egyptian religion has vanished, as have the Greek and Roman faiths. But we – the descendants of Abraham, Isaac, Jacob, Moses, and the prophets – continue to worship in synagogues as did our ancestors. Despite thousands of years of Jew-hatred, the Jewish people and the Jewish faith continue. It is amazing, don't you think? Hitler tried to annihilate us, but Nazism is no more. We are now faced with the threat of annihilation from Arab nations who detest Israel and seek its destruction. In a post-Holocaust world, we remain determined to triumph over our enemies as we have always done.

It is understandable then why traditionalists are anxious to continue the practices of the past. Assimilation is perceived as a menace and dire threat. Personally, however, I do not accept such arguments even though I understand the reasoning of the critics of modernity. In my view, it is far healthier for Jews to integrate into the societies in which they live. As you may know, this has been the ideology of Reform Judaism from its inception in the nineteenth century.

The Reform movement arose early in nineteenth-century Germany. Having had the benefit of Western secular education and mixing freely with Gentiles, these German Jews were embarrassed by traditional Jewish practices, including distinctive Jewish dress and food laws. They created a liturgy that was more dignified and more in keeping with Western ideas. They called their places of worship temples rather than synagogues, and discarded those practices and beliefs that they viewed as antiquated and irrelevant. Their aim was to integrate into the society in which they lived. This ideology quickly spread to other countries throughout the Jewish world.

Today the Reform movement is the largest Jewish denomination in the world, and other non-Orthodox movements have been created which similarly espouse the integration of Jewry into the mainstream community. Hence, it is only among the strictly Orthodox (referred to as the Haredim) that you will find the kind of isolating features of Judaism that we have been discussing. These Orthodox Jews (including the Hasidim) are adamant that the traditional lifestyle of the Eastern European ghetto and the *shtetl* (Jewish village) continue into the modern world to protect Jews from the corrupting features of contemporary society.

In Israel there are hundreds of thousands of Haredim who are determined to keep Orthodoxy alive. Yet, the vast majority of Israelis – despite their determination to preserve the Jewish identity of the State – have largely discarded the customs of the past. Like their Jewish counterparts in the diaspora, they have embraced modernity and seek to live as modern men and women. I believe they are right. The liberation of Judaism from the fetters of the past is a liberation long overdue.

9(F) GEORGE:

The discussion of dress and identity has highlighted several reasons for publicly observable expressions of one's faith. It may be a requirement of one's religion: Dan quotes the Torah, and Dawoud the Qur'an as the basis for their faiths' respective practices. Signs of identity may also have the function of separating the believer from the rest of the world, avoiding undue assimilation by visibly expressing one's solidarity or "corporate identity". One may be keeping up a tradition, not wanting one's faith or even its symbols to die out. It may serve as a reminder of our faith, causing us to watch our behaviour, if we can be readily identified as Jews, Muslims, or certain types of Christian.

I think we are agreed on the right to express our faith in the way we dress, and on the need to respect each other's traditions by observing appropriate dress codes on each other's premises. The use of religious jewellery, lapel badges, car bumper stickers, and tattoos indicates one special feature of the Christian faith. Christianity is firmly "incarnational" – that is to say, it holds that God entered the world in human flesh, becoming involved in human life and earthly affairs. Christians have therefore recognized that aspects of the physical world can be legitimate – indeed important – ways of expressing the Divine. According to Saint John, Jesus teaches his disciples that, although they are in the world, they "do not belong to the world", but that he has chosen them out of the world, and that this may make them unpopular in it (John 15:19).

Living in the world entails that we are encouraged to draw on what is potentially good in it in order to express our faith – whether that is art, music, drama, or aspects of popular culture such as car bumper stickers and tattoos, if Christians find these meaningful ways of expressing their faith. However, because the world is "fallen" and sinful, it presents temptations which the Christian must avoid: we should "participate in the divine nature, having escaped the corruption in the world caused by evil desires" (2 Peter 1:4).

The Bible portrays Christians as belonging to two different worlds, or countries – a physical one and a spiritual one. The book of Hebrews describes the ancient Hebrew patriarchs as being on a journey towards a promised land, but the author adds, "God had planned something better for us" (11:40), and the book of Revelation speaks of a New Jerusalem, the heavenly city, which those who overcome the world will inherit (21:7).

Saint Augustine (354–430) later made use of the imagery of the two cities in his monumental work *City of God*. He was writing at a time when there was much dispute about who were true believers, and who were heretics. Could the true Christian be identified by visible signs, such as having been baptized, affirming the creeds, receiving the Eucharist, or standing firm in the face of persecution? Augustine's answer was that visible criteria did not conclusively determine who the true Christians were. Christians live within earthly political systems, but they are also – invisibly – members of God's kingdom, the "heavenly city". Their real identity is known only to God, who will reveal it at the end of time, when we reach the final goal.

So one's identity as a Christian cannot be determined by what we wear, what we eat, or what customs we observe, and the Christian has no special obligations or prohibitions that should not be expected of people of other faiths, or no faith. Ideally, Christians should be honest in their dealings, do a fair day's work, be truthful, trustworthy, and charitable – but these characteristics also define the good Jew and Muslim.

If Christianity does not dictate an observably different lifestyle, and if its followers are indistinguishable from others, and known only to God, then could it be that upright Jews and Muslims might also be included in God's kingdom?

Orthodox and Catholic Christians hold that their identity lies in belonging to the church, outside which there is no salvation, whereas evangelical Protestants emphasize a personal conversion experience as the hallmark of the true Christian. Recently, a number of more radical modern theologians who have addressed interfaith issues (such as Karl Rahner, Raimon Panikkar, and John Hick) have been more inclusive, suggesting that it is God who saves and recognizes the identity of His followers, rather than any one specific religious identity. No doubt we shall find out at the end of time.

CHAPTER 10

DIET

Traditional Jewish dietary laws include the avoidance of pork and shellfish, and devout Muslims are committed to the avoidance of alcohol. For both these religions, animals must be slaughtered in the prescribed manner. To the Christian the perceived necessity to stick to kosher or *halal* foods seems unduly inconvenient, and prohibitions on mixing meat and milk seem to be unnecessary. The practice of strict Orthodox Jews in refusing to use the same plates as Gentiles seems to pose needless barriers to commensality and friendship. Does not Peter's vision in Acts 2 suggest a much more open attitude to table fellowship between Jews and Gentiles, and a breaking down of dietary barriers between faiths?

10(A) DAWOUD:

Food is an important part of most cultures and the sharing of food brings people together as families and communities, whether it is in the routine of daily life or to mark important events.

Dietary regulations are important to Muslims, but although there are a number of similarities, they are relatively straightforward compared with those of Judaism. They are based primarily on a single verse from *Surat al-Baqara*:

He has only forbidden to you carrion, blood, the flesh of swine, and that which has been dedicated to other than Allah. But whoever is forced [by

*necessity], neither desiring nor transgressing, there is no sin upon him.
Indeed, Allah is Forgiving and Merciful. (2:173)*

The verse is simple and clear. The prohibition of pork is common to Islam and Judaism. Muslims consider pigs to be unclean and the aversion to pork is deeply culturally entrenched.

The Arabic word "*al-mayita*", translated here as carrion, means any creature found dead or that dies of natural causes or by accident. It also refers to meat that has not been slaughtered in the correct manner. Correct slaughter – *dabiha* – requires the animal to be killed by a single cut to the throat and all blood to be drained from the carcass. For this reason animals such as cows and sheep that have been stunned prior to slaughter (such as by captive bolt) are considered *mayita* because they are effectively dead prior to having their throat cut, as are smaller creatures such as birds killed by having their necks broken.

The process of *dabiha* required for Islamic slaughter, similar to that required by Judaism as Dan will no doubt tell us, is controversial in many non-Muslim countries as many people consider it unnecessarily cruel to cut the throat of an animal and allow it to bleed to death. Many Muslims will claim, however, that performed correctly it is not cruel, as the cutting should be done cleanly and quickly with a very sharp blade.

In the process of slaughtering an animal the butcher should pronounce the formula "*Bismillah'ir-rahman ir-rahim*", in the name of God the Compassionate, the Merciful. Where this is not done, or if the name of any other deity is invoked in the process, the meat is considered prohibited.

There are no restrictions on the consumption of fish and seafood, and fish are not subject to the rules required for slaughter of mammals. Foods that are permissible for Muslims to eat are referred to as *halal* – which simply means "permitted".

Islam prohibits the consumption of alcohol. The Qur'an refers to this in several places. This prohibition was introduced in stages, the first being concerned with the proper approach to prayer: "O you who have believed, do not approach prayer while you are intoxicated until you know what you are saying" (4:43). The second reference to alcohol to be revealed states: "They ask you about wine and gambling. Say, 'In them is great sin and [yet, some] benefit for people. But their sin is greater than their benefit'" (2:219). Later again we find a clear and definitive prohibition which is accepted as an absolute by the majority of Muslims: "O you who have believed, indeed, intoxicants, gambling, [sacrificing on] stone alters [to other than Allah], and divining arrows are but defilement from the work of Satan, so avoid it that you may be successful" (5:90).

Naturally in Muslim countries it is not difficult to adhere to dietary rules and it does not require a great deal of thought as these are the norms. It is a little more difficult for Muslims in the West, but while *halal* meat used to be found only in Muslim butchers' shops, it has become increasingly common to see foods labelled "halal" in major European supermarkets, restaurants, and fast-food outlets. Some supermarkets even have dedicated *halal* butchery counters.

While sourcing *halal* meat is relatively easy, observant Muslims do have to be careful if they want to avoid consuming non-*halal* substances accidentally. Animal products may be found in all kinds of processed foods, food supplements, and medications. Gelatine, which may be from pork or non-*halal* beef, is commonly found in sweets, sometimes in puddings and certain brands of yoghurt, and in the gel casings of capsules such as cod-liver oil.

10(B) DAN:

If there is a single factor that has kept the Jewish people separate from other peoples, it is the food laws. Because certain foods are forbidden, because even permitted animals must be slaughtered in a particular way, and because there can be no mixing of certain categories of food, observant Jews cannot eat in secular restaurants nor in the houses of Gentiles. As the Jew Shylock puts it in Shakespeare's *Merchant of Venice*: "I will buy with you, sell with you, talk with you, walk with you... but I will not eat with you, drink with you nor pray with you" (Act I, Scene 3).

According to the creation account in Genesis, the earliest human beings were vegetarians: "Then God said, 'I give you every seed-bearing plant on the face of the whole earth and every tree that has fruit with seed in it. They will be yours for food'" (1:29). Only after the great flood did God allow Noah and his family to eat meat. Nonetheless, the eating of meat is hedged about with many restrictions, and several authorities teach that in the days of the messiah, both human beings and animals will return to vegetarianism.

In the first place, not all animals or birds may be eaten. The book of Deuteronomy specifies that for an animal to be permitted as food, it must have a cloven hoof and chew the cud (14:6). Pigs are forbidden because they do not chew the cud; rabbits fail on both criteria, and a camel may not be consumed because the camel has a pad for a foot. Therefore the only animals commonly eaten are oxen, sheep, goats, and deer. No rules are offered for birds, but the biblical list of forbidden species consists largely of birds of prey.

The creature must be slaughtered in a prescribed manner. Because of the prohibition against eating blood, the ritual involves getting rid of as much blood as possible from the carcass. A Jewish ritual slaughterer has to undergo considerable training. The knife must be perfectly smooth and razor-sharp. The creature is killed by a quick downward slicing of the throat. Then the body is suspended to drain off its blood. After slaughter is completed, the carcass is inspected and if there is any evidence of internal injury or disease, then it is pronounced forbidden. It is frequently argued that the Jewish method of slaughter is the most painless one possible. This was certainly the case in the past, but today some authorities on animal welfare argue that the modern practice of pre-stunning is more humane. Unfortunately, due to Jewish law, it is not possible to stun the animal or bird before slaughter since this would constitute a blemish and would render the carcass forbidden.

There are no rules for the slaughter of fish, but not all sea creatures may be eaten. According to the book of Deuteronomy: "Of all the creatures living in the water, you may eat any that has fins and scales. But anything that does not have fins and scales you may not eat; for you it is unclean" (14:9–10). This means that all shellfish (oysters, lobsters, mussels, shrimps) are forbidden, as are eels and turtles. The roe of forbidden fish, like the eggs of forbidden birds, is also not permitted.

It is also not permitted to eat both meat foods and dairy products at the same meal. This prohibition grows out of the rabbinical interpretation of the verse, "Do not boil a kid in its mother's milk", which appears no fewer than three times in the Bible (Exodus 23:19;

34:26 and Deuteronomy 14:21). This may have originally been designed to counter the pagan practice of seething a new-born creature in the milk of its own mother. However, it has been understood to mean that neither meat nor poultry may be mixed with milk or with anything made from milk. Again, this ruling does not apply to fish. It should be noted, however, that in the modern world, there is considerable variation about the observance of these laws. Strictly Orthodox Jews are insistent that these biblical and rabbinic commandments are followed. Among non-Orthodox Jews, however, the majority of these regulations have been abandoned although it is not uncommon for even the most secular Jews to refrain from eating pork.

10(C) GEORGE:

The Gospel of Mark records that on one occasion Jesus' disciples violated the Jewish food laws. Jesus defended them, saying, "Nothing outside a person can defile them by going into them. Rather, it is what comes out of a person that defiles them" (7:15). Jesus meant that our external behaviour was more important than the compliance with rules and regulations about food, and Mark adds: "In saying this, Jesus declared all foods clean" (7:19).

In the early years of Christianity it was unclear whether the Christian faith was simply a form of Judaism, whose followers accepted the Jewish law but acknowledged Jesus as a rabbi and as the messiah. It was therefore understandable that some of the early leaders, like Peter, took a conservative view regarding the Torah, and advocated acceptance of its food laws, among other things.

The book of Acts recounts an incident in which Peter had a vision of a net descending from heaven, containing a large assortment of animals, reptiles, and birds. A voice instructed him to "Kill and eat" (10:13). When the Council of Jerusalem met to resolve disputes between Peter and the more liberal innovator Paul, they decided that Jewish and non-Jewish Christians alike should "abstain from food polluted by idols, from sexual immorality, from the meat of strangled animals and from blood" (Acts 15:20) – a set of rules bearing similarities to the Noahide Covenant, which Dan mentions earlier (8c).

Apart from Seventh-day Adventists (see 4B), the majority of Christians see themselves as free from the constraints of the Jewish law, and allow themselves to eat and drink like everyone else. It is hard to see the need, in this day and age, for rules prohibiting pork and shellfish. In the ancient Middle East eating such foods may have incurred the risk of disease, but in the twenty-first-century West it is relatively safe to do so.

Dan mentions vegetarianism as the original diet prescribed for God's people, and as the possible ideal in God's coming kingdom. Some Christians, including me, are vegetarian, but they are vegetarian through choice, and not through any obligation that the Christian faith imposes. I think there can be little doubt that Jesus ate meat. Some of his disciples were fishermen, and he saw no problem about eating some of their catch (John 21:1–14).

Dawoud mentions alcohol. Again, there can be little doubt that Jesus drank alcohol. According to John, his first miracle was to turn six large stone jars of water into around 150 gallons of wine at a wedding at Cana in Galilee. It must have been some party! Teetotallers have sometimes suggested that the wine Jesus drank was unfermented, but this is highly unlikely, given the hot climate, in which fermentation of grapes is inevitable. Paul (or another author using his name) instructs Timothy, "Stop drinking only water, and use a little wine because of your stomach and your frequent illnesses" (1 Timothy 5:23).

Some Christians, it must be said, are firmly opposed to alcohol, and Christians were largely at the forefront of the temperance movement of the eighteenth and nineteenth centuries, and in much of the US Bible Belt it is virtually impossible to buy alcohol. Other Christians, however, see little harm in drinking socially, or using alcohol to liven up a party. Most would agree that they should drink responsibly, however, avoiding drink-driving, and recognizing the dangers of alcohol dependence.

In matters of food and drink, Christians rely on a number of biblical principles. The first of these is conscience. Paul states that the Gentiles have a "law... written on their hearts, their consciences also bearing witness" (Romans 2:15). By this he means that Gentiles are not exempt from moral requirements, but can act morally without necessarily being subject to all the rules and regulations of the Torah. So much of Christian behaviour is determined by what one's conscience will allow. Second, in matters of diet, one's health is important. Paul writes, "Do you not know that your bodies are temples of the Holy Spirit?" (1 Corinthians 6:19). We should treat our bodies with respect, just as we would treat a sacred building, avoiding gluttony and greed – two of the seven "deadly sins". Third, Paul says that one should not "put any stumbling-block or obstacle in the way of a brother or sister" (Romans 14:13). In other words, if I have a friend who is an alcoholic, I can help her by avoiding alcohol in her company. Perhaps too, if I know a friend is on a weight-watcher's diet, I should avoid putting temptation in his way, or even encourage him by making the same choice from a restaurant menu. It would probably do me good too!

10(D) DAN:

Many years ago when I was living in Canterbury I taught an adult education class, with the Dean of the Cathedral, about worship. On one occasion we took our group to a convent for a day of silence. In the afternoon, the Lady Superior wanted to see me in her study. Over a cup of tea she said, "You know, our Lord was the first Reform rabbi." I had never thought about this before, but in a sense she was right. Jesus' view about the dietary laws which George mentioned is similar to the position of Reform Judaism.

From its earliest origins in the nineteenth century, the Reform movement discarded the laws of *kashrut*, believing, as Jesus said, that what comes out of one's mouth is much more important than what goes in. Throughout its history, Reform Judaism has maintained that biblical and rabbinic laws that are irrelevant and anachronistic in the modern age should be set aside. As early as 1888, Reform Judaism adopted the Pittsburgh Platform in which is contained the following declaration:

We hold that all such Mosaic and rabbinic laws as regulate diet, priestly purity, and dress originated in ages and under the influence of ideas entirely foreign to our present mental and spiritual state. They fail to impress the modern Jew with the

140

spirit of priestly holiness; their observance in our days is apt to obstruct than to further modern spiritual elevation.
(Jacobs 1999: 127–128)

Far more important than such ritual is the moral law. Hence, I share George's reservations about the various dietary commandments that I described. Like most Reform Jews (and for that matter most Jews today), I do not find the myriad laws of *kashrut* spiritually meaningful. Of much greater significance are the moral commandments contained in the Hebrew Bible and the rabbinic tradition.

Let me turn to the issue of vegetarianism to which George has referred. From earliest times Judaism has held vegetarianism to be the ideal God-given diet for human beings. Isaiah 11, for example, hopes for a messianic age in which the "wolf will live with the lamb", and humans "will not harm nor destroy on all my holy mountain" (11:6, 9). Although vegetarianism has never been the ethical norm within the tradition, it has invariably been accepted as the better ethical option, one that more clearly approximates to the original will of the Creator. Indeed, some Jewish scholars have suggested that ethical vegetarianism lies at the heart of the Torah. One highly respected Talmudic scholar, Abraham Isaac Kook (former Chief Rabbi of Israel) maintained that the biblical constraints concerning killing are themselves preparation for a state of higher ethical awareness. He wrote:

The free movement of the moral impulse to establish justice for animals generally and their claim for rights for mankind are hidden in the natural psychic sensibility in the deeper layers of the Torah.
(Clark 1993:59)

Such a view is of profound importance in shaping our relationship with the animal world. If animals are spiritual beings – in the sense of being creatures with their own relationship to the creator – then it follows that in our encounter with them we apprehend to some degree the workings of the creator. In God's providential ordering of the world, we can see in other creatures something of the creator's own self-power and grace. Such a rich relationship cannot be expressed in terms of utility and subordination. Rather it provides a basis for formulating moral limits in relation to our treatment of animals. This means in practice that we should avoid wanton acts of cruelty: this idea is expressed in the rabbinic concept of *tasaar baalei hayyim* (not acting cruelly to animals). Further, such an understanding of animals challenges a wide range of contemporary practices that make animals suffer in farming, in laboratories, and in abattoirs.

10(E) GEORGE:

I very much welcome Dan's description of Jesus as the first Reform rabbi. If only all Jews were as generous! Jesus certainly did not like nitpicking rules, although possibly the Pharisees became stereotyped by the Christians.

As Dan says, vegetarianism may have been the original ideal for humanity, with meat eating being a concession to human fallen nature. It is worth noting, though, that Noah was not commanded to eat meat – only permitted to do so. Jesus expressed no problems about the fattened calf being killed for the Prodigal Son, and it is highly unlikely that when he celebrated the Passover he and the disciples would use some meat substitute! Even Saint Francis, who is renowned for his love of animals, was not a vegetarian. However, just as Jesus did not slavishly follow the rules of the Torah, Christians do not have to follow unquestioningly his first-century Palestinian lifestyle, but must use their reason and conscience for gaining new insights into ethical issues.

There can be a variety of reasons for Christians adopting vegetarianism. Some view it as an animal rights issue: animals have a right to life and enjoyment of it, just as humans do. Some argue that "dominion" over creation entails not permission to do what one likes with animals, but rather responsibility for them. Other issues relate to health: arguably, vegetarians are less prone to heart disease, cancer, and obesity, and – as I mentioned earlier – keeping oneself healthy is a Christian obligation.

There is also the issue of stewardship of the earth's resources. The Christian Vegetarian Association points out that 37 per cent of the world's grain is not eaten directly by humans, but feeds animals for slaughter. The figure is 66 per cent in the US. This, arguably, is a waste of protein, particularly when two-thirds of the world's population is undernourished. On matters of diet, Christians ought to be concerned – as indeed many are – about world hunger, and our Christian obligation to improve the lot of those who are without adequate food (Luke 16:19–31). Again, this is a matter of stewardship: we should not just use the planet's resources for our own selfish benefit.

I have to admit, though, that I think some vegetarians can be unduly fussy, as when they meticulously examine food packaging to ensure that there is not any trace of renin or gelatine, for example. On this point I have to take issue with Dawoud: if we try substantially to fulfil our religious obligations, is that not enough? Does it really matter if we eat the odd bit of food that is technically against our principles? I must confess that there are situations where I support the meat industry. For example, if I invite someone out to a restaurant, I don't veto their choice of food, even if I'm paying the bill. If they choose a meat dish, that is a matter for their conscience rather than mine.

There is also the question of accepting hospitality – another virtue that is important to the Christian. My wife and I were once visiting our aged aunt, who was well into her nineties at the time. Unexpectedly she had prepared lunch for us, but had forgotten that we are vegetarian. There was nothing to be achieved by refusing to eat the chicken. We would only have hurt her feelings, and we would certainly not have revived the chicken! The Bible records that, when Jesus sent out seventy-two disciples, his instructions for accepting hospitality included "eating and drinking whatever [your hosts] give you" (Luke 10:7). I don't think our dietary practices should involve observing over-fussy sets of rules.

Dan mentions the humane treatment of animals, and this is a matter for meat-eaters and vegetarians alike. Many Christians too are concerned with kindness to animals and are becoming aware of some of the issues regarding how food is brought to our tables. We ought to be concerned about factory farming, battery hens, dehorning and debeaking, and painful castration of animals in the meat and poultry industry. There is still a long way to go, however, in persuading the meat industry to treat animals better.

Interestingly, Dan quotes Isaiah on the role of animals in the coming kingdom. Isaiah also writes about the lion lying down with the lamb, the cow and bear living together in harmony, and the little child leading them (11:6–9). Do animals have souls that survive death? I don't know, but they certainly have feelings, and that is a reason for treating them humanely.

10(F) DAWOUD:

There is a perception that Islamic culture is predominantly meat-eating, and to some extent this is true. In many Muslim cultures, particularly in Arab culture, hospitality and celebrations are based on the offering of meat dishes. A family may slaughter (or have slaughtered – or buy from their butcher) a sheep or goat, or several, a cow or even a camel depending on their financial circumstances and scale of the celebration, whether it be a wedding, the birth of a child, a new house or some other good fortune for which thanks are to be given and a portion of this should be given to the poor. As we have discussed elsewhere, in the major festival in the Islamic calendar – *Eid ul-Adha*, the Feast of the Sacrifice, Ibrahim's willingness to sacrifice his son Isma'il is remembered in the slaughter of animals for meat and its distribution between the family and people in need.

There are some who believe that it is actually un-Islamic not to eat meat and often quote the verse: "O you who have believed, do not prohibit the good things which Allah has made lawful to you and do not transgress…" (Qur'an 5:87). While the eating of meat is permitted, however, there is nothing that says it is obligatory. The verse only says that no rule may be enacted against what is lawful, which means that meat-eating may not be prohibited or prevented. The insistence by some religious scholars and communities that vegetarianism is forbidden contains, in some cases, an element of drawing a distinction between Islam and Hinduism and Buddhism, in which vegetarianism can be part of the religion.

What all of this tends to ignore, however, is that for many people in the world including many Muslim communities, meat is a luxury that they cannot afford. Many people do not eat meat or only eat it in small quantities not by choice but by necessity. The national and ethnic cuisines of many Muslim countries and communities have a vast array of delicious and nutritious vegetarian dishes that are not ethically or "politically" vegetarian, but are simply dishes without meat based on the vegetable production of their regions of origin.

There are Sufi orders that practise vegetarianism, notably in South Asia, and there are a growing number of vegetarians and vegetarian associations in many parts of the Muslim world and in Muslim communities in non-Muslim countries. Islam forbids cruelty towards animals and there are numerous *hadith* that demonstrate the Prophet's compassion for animals. Increasingly there are Muslims who are becoming more aware of the ethical questions, and the health and environmental issues involved in meat-eating and the production of meat.

The fast during the month of Ramadan should make people feel, even if only temporarily and in the mildest degree, the hunger and thirst suffered by the poor. It should make them give thanks for what they have and be more willing to share with others. At the time of the breaking of the fast at the end of the day, people should not eat voraciously, but break their fast with a little milk and a few dates in the tradition of the Prophet before praying and then eating together with family and community. There is particular emphasis on providing food for the poor at the time of the major feasts, but this is, in fact, a duty at all times for those who are able. As important as food is the obligation to give water and there are many *hadith* that indicate that it is a sin to withhold water if one has any to spare, either for the relief of immediate thirst or for agriculture or pasturage.

In Islam, human beings are seen as stewards of the earth entrusted with its protection and the fair distribution of its bounty.

And He it is who causes gardens to grow, trellised and untrellised, and palm trees and crops of different [kinds of] food and olives and pomegranates, similar and dissimilar. Eat of [each of] its fruit when it yields and give its due [zakat] on the day of its harvest. And be not excessive. Indeed, He does not like those who commit excess. (Qur'an 6:141)

CHAPTER 11

SEX

This section draws on themes we have explored in our previous book, *Love, Sex and Marriage* (2013). In Western society where attitudes to sex are liberal, do all three religions need to move with the times – or is it important to stick to traditional values? In the light of the feminist movement, and increasing concern to make women more equal with men, do our religions continue to discriminate against women? Islam often attracts the reputation for being particularly reluctant to give women equal rights. To what extent can it defend itself against such criticism?

11(A) GEORGE:

The traditional conservative Christian view about sex and marriage is that sex should be confined to marital relationships, that a Christian should have one marital partner only, and that divorce is only permissible if one's spouse has been unfaithful. This contrasts with the Western societal norm, in which sexual freedom is encouraged, and which perceives positive advantages in sexual experimentation. Sex before marriage can test sexual compatibility with one's partner, and, provided that due precautions are taken, it need not lead to unwanted pregnancy. Some 42 per cent of marriages in Britain and 50 per cent in the United States end in divorce, which has become more socially acceptable. Most people see little point in prolonging an unhappy marriage, when "sequential monogamy" is possible.

While many Christians may believe that the Christian life offers a contrast to modern-day society, this is far from the case. Statistical evidence has shown that the majority of Christians – especially evangelical Protestants – have had sex with their partners before marriage (perhaps as many as 80 per cent), and in 2009 the Church of England bowed to the inevitable and offered a "two-in one ceremony" combining marriage and the baptism of their children. Although the Roman Catholic Church continues to forbid "unnatural" forms of contraception, the majority of Roman Catholics ignore the prohibition.

Christians are also struggling with the issue of homosexuality. While many conservative Christians continue to disapprove of homosexual relationships, more liberal Christians recognize that sexuality is an orientation and that one can enter into a same-sex relationship that is as loving and caring as a heterosexual partnership. In 2012 British law was changed to enable churches to conduct ceremonies of same-sex couples, which could be legally recognized as civil partnerships, if they wish to do so. Some Christians see this as a victory for the lesbian and gay community, although it is unlikely that every Christian congregation will offer this facility to same-sex couples. The Roman Catholic Church and the Church of England are still prevented by canon law from offering such services, and the Orthodox churches still firmly disapprove of practising homosexuals.

The situation regarding monogamy is not clear-cut either. Although many Christians are critical of Islam for permitting a husband to have up to four wives, Christianity has spread to countries where some converts are already polygamously married. This raises the question of whether a polygamous husband should remain in a relationship that the church believes falls short of its ideal, or whether the husband should be asked to send away his "surplus" wives. Within the Church of England debate continues on this issue, with no easy solution.

Apart from recognizing that adulterous relationships are unacceptable, it would probably be no exaggeration to say that Christianity is in a state of turmoil regarding sexual matters. For individual Christians, how they behave in terms of relationships with the opposite sex is a matter of conscience. The key principles are love and responsibility. Christians – and indeed everyone – should certainly avoid entering into relationships which would cause needless suffering to a partner. All pregnancies should result in children that are wanted and able to be cared for. Family bonds are important, and divorce is certainly not something that should be entered into lightly – although it certainly does not carry the stigma that it did half a century ago. Times have changed, and single-parent families are much more common than they once were.

As with sex and marriage, Christians are divided on the subject of sexual equality. The Bible says, "A woman should learn in quietness and full submission" (1 Timothy 2:11), and some have taken this to mean that the man should be in charge of the household, and that women should not have an active role in public worship. Even as I write, there is strong debate in the Church of England as to whether women should become bishops, and in the Roman Catholic and Orthodox traditions the idea of their becoming priests is out of the question. More liberally minded Christians believe that a household should be run democratically, with each partner having an equal say, and that one's gender should be no bar from holding any office in the church or in the workplace. The Bible also teaches, "There is neither Jew nor Gentile, neither slave nor free, nor is there male and female, for you are all one in Christ Jesus" (Galatians 3:28).

The more liberal Christians fear that we might be stuck with a slavish adherence to the Bible – or rather, those parts of it that support the conservative position – while the conservatives feel that the liberals are abandoning the Bible and being led by secular rather than Christian standards. At least there is scope for healthy debate. It would be interesting to know what debates are taking place within the Jewish and Muslim faiths.

11(B) DAN:

George pointed out that traditional Christian attitudes to sex conflict with Western social and cultural norms in which sexual freedom and experimentation are accepted. Traditional Judaism is equally critical. The Hebrew Bible has a positive attitude to sex within marriage, but sex outside marriage is strongly condemned and scripture warns against various forms of sexual perversion. The rabbis declare that it is a religious obligation for men to marry, and that a husband has a duty to satisfy his wife sexually. Yet, rabbinic sources stress that the sex drive must be severely controlled, and there is a tendency in rabbinic thought to curtail too much sexual indulgence, even in the marital bed. Thus the rabbis warn: "There is a small organ in a man's body which when hungry is sated but when sated is hungry." Another rabbinic saying has it that on judgment day a man will be reminded of the frivolous conversations he has had with his wife. Generally speaking the sages welcome the sex drive as a divine gift while acknowledging that, of all human instincts, sex is the most likely to lead people astray.

As a consequence of this perception of the dangers of sexual lust, social intercourse with women was usually taboo: women were perceived by rabbinic scholars as the source of moral danger. The evil impulse – *yetzer ha-ra* – was regarded primarily as the impulse that leads to sexual impurity. In rabbinic sources there are numerous references to proper behaviour during sexual intercourse. While there was an acknowledgment of sexual pleasure, the primary aim of intercourse is reproduction. In this context, both biblical and rabbinic Judaism sternly disapprove of extramarital sex. Indeed, the Talmud states that it is forbidden for a husband to have another woman in mind during intercourse. Adultery is among the most serious of sins, forbidden by the seventh commandment. There is strong disapproval of male homosexuality, although there is hardly any condemnation for lesbianism.

Strictly Orthodox Judaism therefore has an elevated view of sexual relations between a husband and wife. Sexual behaviour is to take place according to highly regulated rules, and its main goal is reproduction. Unlike Christianity, where celibacy is regarded – at least by Paul in his letters – as the ideal state, Jews view the sex act as divinely ordained and holy. Sex outside marriage is strictly condemned, and sexual activity prior to marriage is forbidden. Even today in Orthodox communities it is common for marriage to take place at an early age, and for husbands and wives to produce as many children as possible. While contraception is permitted in certain circumstances, the emphasis is on conceiving children who will remain loyal to the Jewish heritage.

In non-Orthodox circles, however, the restrictive attitudes of the past have been largely set aside. While marriage continues to be extolled as the ideal, most Jews adopt a lenient view about rabbinic legislation regarding pre-marital sex, and generally ignore rabbinic prescriptions regulating sexual activity within marriage. Nonetheless, extra-marital activity is frowned upon. Homosexuality and lesbianism, on the other hand, are widely accepted within the Jewish community, and various non-Orthodox movements such as Reform Judaism have welcomed homosexuals and lesbians into the fold. Today there are practising homosexual and lesbian rabbis who officiate in gay congregations; these rabbis and others are active advocates of legalizing gay marriages in the United States and elsewhere. Yet, despite such fundamental changes in attitude, both religious and secular Jews continue to regard marriage as fundamental to Jewish life and a source of stability within the community.

11(C) DAWOUD:

Both Dan and George have highlighted the differences between traditional attitudes to sex and marriage in Judaism and Christianity and in the communities that still adhere to these values, and the reality of life in Western societies where the majority of men and women have relationships and cohabit before marriage or may not even feel the need to marry. Attitudes among the majority of Muslims remain much more conservative, however, and Islamic communities do not accept cohabitation of men and women without valid marriage. The *Shari'a* is a complete body of law and a way of life and there is no option to select parts of it and reject others.

Rules regarding sex and marriage are enshrined in Islamic law and in this there is little scope for change or negotiation. Although there is considerable diversity today in the environments and ways in which Muslims live, there are certain fundamentals that are untouchable; this is one of the few areas in which the Qur'an goes into some detail. There is no disapproval of sex itself in Islam or of sexual desire or the enjoyment of sex. With regard to sex, Islam is only really concerned that sexual gratification should take place in a lawful context, which means valid marriage. Of course, this does not mean that extra-marital sex does not exist among Muslims, but only that it can never be considered acceptable, and not even liberal Muslims will attempt to claim that it is a valid alternative to lawful marriage.

Within the context of marriage both husband and wife should enjoy a healthy sexual relationship and while procreation is important, there is no notion of shame in the enjoyment of the physical relationship between husband and wife.

There is an absolute prohibition of sexual relationships outside marriage, and adultery and fornication are not merely sins but crimes that entail prescribed punishments:

The [unmarried] woman or [unmarried] man found guilty of sexual intercourse – lash each one of them with a hundred lashes, and do not be taken by pity for them in the religion of Allah, if you should believe in Allah and the Last Day. And let a group of the believers witness their punishment. (24:2)

The threshold of proof of adultery or fornication is high, however, requiring the eyewitness testimony of four men or three men and two women. Hearsay and circumstantial evidence are not acceptable. The false accusation of virtuous women is also a crime and punishable by eighty lashes.

Traditional Islamic culture disapproves of the mixing of the sexes outside the immediate family. While today men and women work and study together, socialization between the sexes, particularly on a one-to-one basis, is unacceptable and relatively uncommon. It is not acceptable for a man and woman who are not married or within the degree of relationship that precludes marriage to be alone in each other's company.

There are also explicit injunctions against homosexual activity and, as is the case with extra-marital sex, this is a crime as well as a sin. While there are some support and campaigning groups for homosexual Muslims, these are small and marginal and have very little influence on mainstream Muslim attitudes.

Islam permits polygyny, and a man may be married to up to four women at once. A husband is required, however, to treat his wives with complete equality in terms of material support and the time that he spends with each. If he is unable to do so, he should limit himself to one, and for the majority of Muslims a monogamous partnership is the norm.

Marriage and the family are at the heart of Islam and the notion that anyone should be single or celibate by choice is completely alien to Islamic culture. There is no virtue in deliberate abstinence from legitimate sexual relations in Islam and no tradition of celibacy or monasticism. According to a tradition of the Prophet, "if a Muslim marries then he has completed half of his religion and that piety makes up the other half".

Marriage should be entered into with the intention of it being a lifelong bond and the founding of a family, but Islam recognizes that this is not always possible and where a marriage is unsustainable divorce is permitted. The *Shari'a* gives the husband a unilateral right of divorce; however, this is not to be used arbitrarily, and a *hadith* of the Prophet states, "Of all things permitted, divorce is the most reprehensible." Access to divorce for women is more difficult, but during recent decades there have been attempts to establish more equitable systems, within the provisions of the *Shari'a*.

11(D) GEORGE:

The sociologist Max Weber said that sexual love was "the greatest irrational force of life" (Gerth and Mills: 343). This did not mean that he thought sex was bad: on the contrary, it contrasted with the "banality of everyday routine". A celibate life in a monastery could well be a bit dull! When Saint Augustine wrote that in the resurrection men and women would retain gendered bodies, but no longer have sexual lusts (*City of God*: 20:17), one cannot help thinking that this would be a serious deficiency!

The problem we are faced with during our earthly existence is reconciling our animal desires with our reasoning faculties. I have to take issue therefore with Dan when he suggests that sex is for procreation. In ancient times it might have made sense to expand one's family and have lots of male warriors to ensure the security of one's tribe, and maybe to guarantee that there were sons and daughters to look after them in old age. Those days have long gone, however, and we are faced with life on an overcrowded planet with dwindling resources. It therefore seems irresponsible when religions teach that we should continue to add to the world's population without proper restraint. This can only result in unwanted children, undue consumption of the planet's resources, and increased poverty.

In saying this, I am conscious that the Christian faith has been as guilty as any other, and I believe some sectors continue to propagate irresponsible attitudes to procreation. Yet, even in the Roman Catholic Church, which still officially forbids "unnatural" forms of contraception, the majority of its Western followers recognize that it is no longer realistic to engage in sexual relationships without controlling the potential consequences.

I think Dawoud could have presented Islam in a slightly more favourable light if he had mentioned that it does not forbid contraception. His comments seem to suggest that one cannot be alone in the company of the opposite sex without the risk of some kind of sexual encounter. Particularly in the twenty-first-century West, where people pursue professional occupations, such prohibitions seem particularly unrealistic. I would be unable to offer help to many of my students if I insisted that the women were chaperoned every time they wanted to discuss their work. In a profession in which women make their contributions as much as men, my work would be greatly impoverished if I could not have one-to-one discussions with colleagues, who frequently include women. And why can't friendship extend to members of the opposite sex as well as one's own? I think we would cut off many fruitful relationships if we adopt such a strait-laced attitude to the opposite sex.

I fully recognize that those who live in the Middle East believe that the West flaunts sex. It pervades our advertising industry, and is prevalent in the media more widely. We certainly do not dress as modestly as those in many other cultures. However, I don't think the remedy is the opposite extreme, and I find the increasingly prevalent practice of Muslim women wearing the veil somewhat problematic. As I understand it, it is not a requirement laid down in the Qur'an (see

9A) and, although people have a right to dress as they see fit, I don't think it is conducive to social integration. Facial expressions are an important part of body language, and particularly in professions where interpersonal relationships are important – such as schoolteaching – such dress does not seem to me appropriate. If Muslim men believe that women might be sexually harassed if they do not cover themselves completely, then perhaps men should change the way they think of women, and come to regard them as potential friends and colleagues, rather than causes of sexual arousal.

It would be wrong to suggest that my own faith treated women equally to men. I wish it did. However, when writing about divorce, both Dan and Dawoud suggest that their faiths make it significantly more difficult for a woman to divorce her husband than vice versa. Although Christianity has never been keen on divorce, at least partners in failing marriages should be in an equal position to remedy the situation.

Dawoud mentions that there might be scope for change in the situation of women seeking divorce, and he also notes that there are campaigning groups of gay and lesbian Muslims. Does this mean that there is scope for change within Islam after all, I wonder, and that the traditional teachings of the Muslim faith are not set in stone for all time?

11(E) DAN:

It is clear from our discussion that there are serious differences between us in this area. Traditionally Judaism, Christianity, and Islam shared many similar attitudes towards sex. Marriage between a husband and wife was viewed as holy and sanctified. Extra-marital affairs of any kind were condemned. The three Abrahamic faiths stood shoulder to shoulder in upholding marriage as a sacred and essential element in society. However, in a post-Enlightenment age, this is no longer the case. Today within both Judaism and Christianity there has been a revolution in attitudes about human sexuality. In this respect, what both George and I have described represents a fundamental difference between modern Judaism and Christianity and contemporary Islam.

Dawoud stresses that there are certain fundamentals in Islam which are untouchable. This is certainly so with regard to the importance of marriage in Jewish life: across the religious spectrum (from strict Orthodoxy to liberal Humanistic Judaism), there is a universal acceptance of the significance of marriage and child rearing. Yet, unlike Islam, progressive Judaism in its various forms does not regard the Torah as immutable. Rather, the Five Books of Moses are viewed as composite works written at different times in the history of ancient Israel. Its laws are therefore not binding on future generations. Over a hundred years ago the Reform movement enshrined this principle in the Pittsburgh Platform, a formulation of the key principles of the movement:

> We recognise in the Mosaic legislation a system of training
> the Jewish people for its mission during its national life in
> Palestine, and today we accept as binding only the moral laws
> and maintain only such ceremonies as elevate and sanctify our
> lives, but reject all such as are not adapted to the views and
> habits of modern civilisation.

Regarding the belief that rabbinic law is similarly binding on Jews in every generation, the movement categorically rejected those practices which are no longer religiously significant:

> We hold that all such Mosaic and rabbinic laws as regulate
> diet, priestly purity and dress originated in ages and under the
> influence of ideas altogether foreign to our present mental
> and spiritual state. They fail to impress the modern Jew with
> a spirit of priestly holiness: their observance in our days
> is apt rather to obstruct than to further modern spiritual
> development.

As we have seen, the Pittsburgh Platform refers specifically to ritual law, but the same applies to commandments regarding sex and marriage. The spirit of this sentiment has pervaded all the branches of modern non-Orthodox Judaism as well as secular Jewish life in

Israel and the diaspora. In modern times, most Jews do not feel bound by the constraints of biblical and rabbinic law. It is in this light that the changes that have taken place in contemporary society can be understood.

As I have mentioned, most Jewish young men and women generally feel no moral constraints about sexual activity before marriage. Many couples live together before being engaged. Homosexuality and lesbianism are widely accepted. The use of sex manuals (and sex toys) is viewed as acceptable. Intermarriage between Jews and non-Jews is frequent, and a significant number of non-Orthodox rabbis are willing to perform intermarriages (although in many cases with a serious commitment to raise offspring as Jews). All this is far removed from the way of life of the past. In the ghettos and *shtetls* (Jewish villages) of Eastern Europe in previous centuries, Jewish life was highly regulated and under the control of rabbinic leadership. In such a setting Jewish law was universally observed and sexual standards maintained. The modern age has changed all this: today each Jew is free to choose his or her pathway through the tradition.

This is clearly not the case with regard to Islam. As Dawoud has explained, Islamic law based on the Qur'an and the *hadith* is rigidly applied throughout the Islamic world. In some countries there is a quest to regulate all aspects of life under *Shari'a* law. How are we to view this state of affairs? In a recent book, *Good and Bad Religion*, the philosopher of religion Peter Vardy outlined a series of criteria for differentiating between good and bad religion. They include the following:

1. Religious imperatives that are not subject to rational scrutiny and interpretation are features of bad religion. Claiming something is the supposed command of God without any rational basis for determining whether such commands do stem from God can no longer be acceptable. Textual fundamentalism needs to be resisted – it leads too easily to closed-mindedness and denies any independent standard for evaluation of good and bad religion. A refusal to acknowledge the discipline of hermeneutics or the influence of the cultural context of any text opens the door to

any group appealing to the supposed will of God, as it interprets its own text free from any rational justification. Religious imperatives can then be imposed, which lead to authority being abused and certainty claimed where none is available.

2. Any good religion must aim to foster human flourishing, to help human beings to develop their full potential, however this may be defined. Any religion that cannot show itself as fostering the fulfilment of potential of all human beings needs to be resisted. This means affirming that human beings must be genuinely free to make choices without being wholly determined – or at least that they have the capacity to come to this degree of freedom.

3. Good religion respects human freedom. It does not seek to coerce people, is willing to educate young people into alternative perspectives other than its own, while being confident in its own position. Good religion rejects indoctrination and is not frightened by alternative possibilities. It respects autonomy and is willing to both accept the possibility of its own error and also confidently affirm its understanding of truth and the relevance of its beliefs and practices to the modern world. Any religion, therefore, that refuses to allow members to listen to alternatives or to understand alternative religious perspectives needs to be resisted. (Vardy 2010: 171–73)

On the basis of these criteria, it is clear that contemporary Islam fails to meet the test. Is it any surprise that in our world Jews, Christians, and Muslims find it difficult to get along?

11(F) DAWOUD:

I understand the points that both Dan and George make with regard to the relationships between men and women, but there are religious and cultural elements within Islam which come together to resist the kind of changes that they describe. The essential homogeneity of Islamic social and sexual mores throughout the Muslim world and among Muslim communities in non-Muslim countries is largely due to the fact that the law regarding marriage, divorce, and sexual propriety is the most clearly defined and universally agreed upon area of Islamic law. Islam is more than just a corpus of beliefs and rules for ritual worship. It is a complete way of life incorporating all aspects of personal and public life and there is no option for individuals to choose the parts that they like and dismiss those that do not suit them, and for the vast majority there is no desire to do so. For the greater part, the law regarding the relationship between the sexes is based on the Qur'an, which, for the majority of Muslims, is the literal and infallible word of God as revealed to the Prophet Muhammad. To challenge those parts of Islamic law that are derived from the Qur'an would be tantamount to apostasy. The Qur'an is at the centre of the faith and not open to selective application. In this, the Islamic view of marriage and sexuality probably has more in common with strict Orthodox Jewish teaching than with contemporary Christianity and Judaism. There is nothing comparable to the Pittsburgh Platform that Dan mentions whereby certain parts might be considered as no longer binding in the modern world.

In addition to this, religion and culture are deeply and inextricably intertwined and family law is an essential part of Islamic culture and identity. This does not mean that the behaviour and choices of individuals or the lifestyles of families either in Muslim countries or the West necessarily follow Islamic norms all the time. Of course pre-marital sex, cohabitation without marriage, and homosexual relationships exist among Muslim communities but no one would attempt to claim that these are valid alternatives to lawful marriage. Muslim society is inherently conservative: even among those who choose to live alternative lifestyles there is little desire to promote an open agenda of change, as most will attempt to protect their families and communities from shame and ostracism and potentially from real harm.

What we also have to remember is that while we may discuss aspects of social and professional interaction as they affect Muslims in Western countries such as Britain, for the majority of the world's Muslims in Muslim countries, where religion and society are virtually inseparable, this is simply not an issue. Dan's reference to Vardy's definitions of good religion are interesting, and academics may debate what the correct application of Islamic principles should be. In the end, however, Islam is whatever several hundred million Muslims say it is and what they establish by their actions. Unlike Judaism and Christianity in Europe and the West, Islam has not gone through the Enlightenment. This does not mean that Islamic law is not capable of reform or change; the *Shari'a* offers tools and resources for adaptation to meet the needs of a changing society, but the impetus for reform has to come from within, not from outside.

CHAPTER 12

WEALTH

Jews acquired the reputation for being rich. Jesus taught that riches were a barrier to entering the kingdom of heaven. Muhammad taught care for the poor. These are sweeping overgeneralizations, of course, but they raise the question of how one should legitimately acquire wealth. What do the three religions teach about work and earning a living? Is it wrong to be wealthy? Do the religions teach about ways of sharing one's wealth? How do we reconcile wealth creation with care for the environment, fair trade, and standards of integrity? Jews and Christians allow investments to attract unearned financial reward, whereas the Qur'an prohibits usury. Are there any means of wealth acquisition that should be avoided?

12(A) GEORGE:

Roughly a third of Jesus' teachings involve wealth or business transactions. The Gospels tell a story of a rich young ruler who came to Jesus and asked him how to gain eternal life. Jesus urged him to give away all his wealth to the poor, whereupon he went away disappointed, unwilling to give up his possessions. Jesus' comment was, "It is easier for a camel to go through the eye of a needle than for someone who is rich to enter the kingdom of God" (Luke 18:25). Jesus' negative comments on the rich and his concern for the poor might seem to suggest that Christians should adopt a life of poverty. Some do, such as those in monastic orders, but most affluent Christians hold on to their wealth, while making contributions to good causes.

The church has always been concerned about extremes of poverty, and teaches that we should share our wealth and not exploit the poor. Christians have therefore endeavoured to assist the poor – locally, nationally, and globally. Some organizations committed to this task are distinctively Christian, such as Christian Aid, CAFOD (Catholic Agency for Overseas Development), and Tearfund, although of course Christians are happy to support other organizations such as Oxfam. Christians have been at the forefront of the fair trade movement, and many churches are keen to be designated as "fair trade" congregations – bodies that are committed to using and selling fair trade goods whenever possible. Traidcraft, a trading company and development charity that is Christian in origin, is committed to the promotion of goods whose producers – mainly in Asia and Africa – receive a fair proportion of the profits.

Debt is a significant cause of poverty, and a matter for Christian concern. Christians have no inherent objection to lending money; indeed, Jesus said, "Give to the one who asks you, and do not turn away from the one who wants to borrow from you" (Matthew 5:42). Lending is one thing, but demanding interest on a loan is another, and the Bible condemns usury – excessive interest on the amount borrowed. But how much interest is excessive? In 325 CE the Council of Nicaea ruled that clergy should not lend money at more than 1 per cent interest per month, and later councils extended this rule to the laity. One per cent a month is quite a lot, and – depending on prevailing economic conditions – might now be regarded as excessive.

Christians are aware of the problems of unscrupulous lending and irresponsible borrowing, although they see no objection to depositing their money in banks, which should be expected to lend money responsibly (although one might question whether they always do so). One particular matter of recent concern involves the "payday loan" companies. In 2009, 1.2 million people took out such loans – usually involving relatively small sums, repayable at the end of the month with an added 25 per cent interest. Many borrowers, however, do not realize that the compound rate of interest for such loans can be as high as 2,250 per cent per annum, or more. In July 2013, Justin Welby, the Archbishop of Canterbury, openly criticized such loans, and went so far as to meet Errol Damelin, the director of Wonga – the most criticized payday loan company – informing him that the Church of England would actively compete by encouraging credit unions (small financial co-operatives run democratically by their members). Many churches, of course, offer debt advice and counselling – face-to-face, through publications, and on websites.

Investments present different problems. They differ from loans in that the investor and the entrepreneur jointly share the financial risks, and – unlike the debtor – the business organization does not have to repay losses to the shareholder. The problem for many Christians, congregations, and denominations is therefore the type of business enterprise one's money supports. Many Christians are concerned about ethical investments, and the Church of England, for example, has an Ethical Investment Advisory Group, avoiding investment in any firm with substantial involvement in armaments, alcohol, tobacco, human embryonic cloning, and lending at excessive interest rates. (Of course it is impossible to have absolutely clean investments in today's financial markets, hence the Church of England defines what substantial involvement means in these areas.)

Whatever our attitude to material wealth, Jesus taught that "spiritual wealth" was more important: "Do not store up for yourselves treasures on earth, where moths and vermin destroy, and where thieves break in and steal. But store up for yourselves treasures in heaven" (Matthew 6:19–20). Wealth can be conducive either to spiritual harm or well-being: it can give rise either to greed or to magnanimity. Jesus also taught that generosity is not dependent on riches. On one occasion he saw a poor widow putting two "mites" (very small coins) into the Temple's treasury box, and remarked that she had done more than all the rich people, who had only contributed a small proportion of their wealth (Mark 12:41–44).

12(B) DAWOUD:

Islam takes a very practical approach to money and property, wealth and poverty. Islam does not disapprove of the accumulation of wealth and people are encouraged to work to support their families, but it is essential that it should be by legitimate work or trade. Money that is earned through dealing in prohibited commodities – such as alcohol and pork, stolen goods or the sex industry – is unlawful. Honesty and trustworthiness in business are important. The Prophet was a trader and it was his reputation for trustworthiness in business that first brought him to the attention of his first wife Khadija, for whom he worked as an agent before they were married.

Islam is concerned with the poor and one of its Five Pillars is *zakat*, sometimes referred to as "alms tax". Muslims are required to give one-fortieth (2.5 per cent) of their wealth as *zakat* every year. This includes gold, silver, and money in banks and investments, but it does not include the value of a person's home and personal possessions such as clothes and furniture. Observant Muslims will calculate this carefully according to a prescribed formula. Today, in most countries it is paid through mosques and voluntary organizations. In some countries, including Saudi Arabia, it is obligatory and collected formally by the government, while in others it is voluntary but regulated by the government. Money collected is used for relief of the poor and destitute. Today there are websites that help with the calculation and for Muslims in non-Muslim countries who want to fulfil their obligation there are charities such as Islamic Relief and Muslim Hands which accept donations through their websites and which provide aid and education mostly in poor or troubled Muslim countries.

In addition to the specific requirement of *zakat*, Muslims may give *sadaqa* or voluntary charity at any time and are encouraged to do so if they are able. It is also normal to offer charity at the time of the major festivals, *Eid ul-Fitr* and *Eid ul-Adha*.

If a person is unable to fast during Ramadan due to health issues, he or she may make up for this by feeding the poor.

Gambling is prohibited in Islam and this means all forms of betting and games of chance. The rulings that apply to gambling also apply to certain forms of investment and insurances where there is an element of chance. The lending of money is not forbidden, but usury or the charging of interest is. It is notable that the prohibition of interest extends also to receipt of interest by customers. It has, of course, always been necessary for individuals and businesses to borrow money, and so Islamic law developed ways and devices for overcoming this difficulty from very early on. Money lent to a business may be in the form of a profit share, whereas for individuals there may be an administration charge. Many Islamic countries are trying to make their financial and banking systems more *Shari'a* compliant, and the Islamic banks worldwide are producing savings and investment products to meet the demand. In the West it is possible to take out an Islamic mortgage, even through some of the main high street banks. These mortgages usually take the form of a joint-ownership scheme where the loan is repaid interest-free and rent is paid on the amount of the equity that is owned by the bank. When all capital and rent is repaid, ownership transfers to the purchaser. This may appear in reality to be exactly the same as a normal mortgage, but it meets the formal requirements set by the *Shari'a*. Islamic economics is a rapidly growing field as individuals, financial organizations, and businesses seek a way to live, work, and compete in the modern world and in international markets without compromising the principles of the *Shari'a*.

12(C) DAN:

As George has pointed out, in Christianity the accumulation of wealth is perceived as a moral danger. For this reason Jesus said it is easier for a camel to go through the eye of a needle than for a rich man to enter the kingdom of heaven. Such a claim is consonant with the biblical prophets' denunciation of those who oppressed the poor. Yet it does not reflect the general Jewish attitude towards wealth. What is critical is that the poor are not allowed to suffer. Poverty itself is not extolled as a virtue; rather the tradition stresses the importance of charity (*tzedakah* in Hebrew). Islam and Judaism (and Christianity too) thus share the same concern for aiding the destitute.

The most well-known formula for charitable giving was formulated by the twelfth-century Jewish philosopher Moses Maimonides. According to Maimonides, the lowest degree of all is where the donor does give but is glum and appears to be reluctant. Next is when he gives cheerfully, but not as much as he can afford. Next is when he gives cheerfully and as much as he can afford, but only when his donation is solicited. Next in degree is when he gives without having to be asked. Higher still is when the donor does not know which of the poor he benefits. Higher still is when the poor do not know the identity of their benefactor. Higher still is when the money is given to the charity collectors. Here the donor is not aware whom he benefits and the poor do not know to whom they are indebted. Highest of all is when a person is prevented from becoming poor by being given a job or a loan without interest so that he can adequately support himself and have no need to be the recipient of charity.

As far as making a loan is concerned, there are strict rules about usury, or the payment on a loan by a borrower to a lender. Two biblical passages forbid the taking of money on interest. The first is: "If you lend money to one of my people among you who is needy, do not treat it like a business deal; charge no interest" (Exodus 22:25). The second biblical verse is: "Do not charge a fellow Israelite interest, whether on money or food or anything else that may earn interest. You may charge a foreigner interest, but not a fellow Israelite, so that the Lord your God may bless you in everything you put your hand to in the land you are entering to possess" (Deuteronomy 23:19–20).

The meaning of these verses is clear. In an agrarian society, a loan to a poor man to tide him over was a basic act of human kindness which should be done freely without demanding any return. For the lender to take interest on the loan would be further to impoverish the borrower. But a foreigner – a person who is on a visit to the land of Israel – is not bound by this law. He may take interest on any loans he makes to Israelites so that there can be no obligation for the Israelite not to reciprocate and take interest when lending to him. The Christian church in the Middle Ages adapted the Law as it stands in the Pentateuch but understood "thy brother" as referring to other Christians. This meant that Christians were not allowed to lend money on interest to one another. But the "foreigner" was interpreted as referring to non-Christians. Hence Jews were allowed to become money lenders. Shakespeare's *Merchant of Venice* indicates the terrible circumstances of this practice for the Jewish community. Throughout the Middle Ages Jews became the victims of anti-Semitic outbursts unleashed by those to whom they had lent vast sums, and frequently they were expelled from the countries where they resided and the loans they made were cancelled.

According to rabbinic law, the prohibition against usury applies to the borrower as well as to the lender; that is, it is not only forbidden to lend on interest but also to borrow on interest. These laws against usury are treated in detail in the Talmud. The general principle is that "any reward for waiting is forbidden", meaning that it is forbidden for a lender to be rewarded by the borrower for "waiting" for the return of his money. In modern times, however, the spirit of the law against usury in biblical and rabbinic sources is not viewed as violated when money is invested in business in an advanced economy. In such cases the money is being used to increase profits for a business rather than serving as a loan to a specific individual.

12(D) GEORGE:

Christianity teaches that everything we have comes from God, and hence we should not regard it as our own and waste it in a profligate manner. The theme of stewardship is prevalent in the Bible's teaching, but Christians are more inclined to exercise responsible judgment about how to do this, rather than slavishly follow rules that are set in stone.

Christianity has no inherent objection to wealth, and I think Dan is wrong to suggest that we see poverty as a virtue. A life of poverty is only a virtue if it is chosen, like the monastic life. For most of the world's population, poverty is involuntary and a serious problem for each of our religions to address. The rich man who refused to give up his wealth to follow Jesus was not simply being asked to pursue a life of poverty: Jesus specifically instructed him to give his money to the poor (Luke 18:22). The Bible does not say that "money is the root of all evil". This is a popular misquotation: the correct reading is, "the love of money is the root of all evil" (1 Timothy 6:10, KJV).

Christians are encouraged to enter into business dealings, to make a profit, and to accumulate wealth. In his parables Jesus commends worldly wisdom and financial astuteness. One rather curious parable that Jesus told is about an unjust steward ("shrewd manager" in modern translations) (Luke 16:1–12). This manager is about to be dismissed for mismanaging his rich employer's funds. To make provision for his imminent dismissal he goes round to his employer's debtors, and without authorization tells them that their debts are reduced, hoping that they might help him out after his sacking. Much to the manager's surprise, his employer actually commends his shrewd practice. (We are left to wonder whether or not his employment was terminated.) At one level, Jesus is commending business acumen, although not dishonesty. At another level, the parable is about God's kingdom: wealth should not be one's ultimate concern. The parable ends with Jesus saying, "No one can serve two masters… You cannot serve both God and money" (Luke 16:13). Money should be one's servant, not one's master.

As Dan points out, we are now living in an advanced economy, and this should certainly make a difference to the way we view financial transactions. Dan discusses taking interest from foreigners, but not one's compatriots. I guess the modern parallel might be the difference between transactions with individuals and financial dealings with larger organizations. I don't demand interest if I lend to a friend, but I ought to expect it if my money has worked for the benefit of a larger company.

As times change, the challenge facing religious believers is how to apply their faith to a changing world, without abandoning its fundamental principles. Here I have to take issue with Dawoud. Schemes like interest-free banking are interesting ideas, but surely calling interest an "administrative charge" on borrowing, or having exemption from bank charges in place of interest on a current account surely comes to much the same thing as I experience when I deposit or borrow money at a bank. I understand that such casuistic devices are sometimes called *hiyal* ("ruses") in Islam – ways of getting around obligations and prohibitions but, as Dawoud puts it, "without compromising the principles of *Shari'a*". Would it not be more straightforward to take the view that, as society changes, religions should adapt, and that – as Dan suggests – the spirit of a religion's ethic is the important thing, rather than sticking to a literalistic interpretation, while finding ways around it?

Dawoud mentions the Islamic prohibition on gambling. A few Christians are very strict about avoiding games of chance. In my childhood we once stayed at a Christian guest house which prominently displayed a notice in its lounge reading "No card games". Clearly those Christians feared that, once a pack of cards was produced, placing bets might follow! However, today's societal conditions enable moderate gambling to serve worthwhile causes. Churches often have raffles to raise funds, and many worthwhile causes, including churches, have benefited from schemes like the National Lottery.

I cannot deny that gambling can create serious problems. It can become an addiction, and it can have serious repercussions when large sums of money are involved, for example when people use their credit cards to gamble in places like Las Vegas. The *Catechism of the Catholic Church* states that games of chance only become unacceptable when they deprive people of their basic necessities, when gambling becomes an addiction, or when a gambler cheats in order to win (*Catechism* 2413). However, if we can enjoy ourselves responsibly, and help good causes into the bargain, why have an absolute prohibition?

12(E) DAWOUD:

George makes a valid point about Islamic banking and some of the *hiyal* or devices used to avoid interest in accordance with the technical terms elaborated in Islamic jurisprudence. Essentially commercial lending would not exist unless there was profit for the lender, whatever they may choose to call it. The movement to Islamize banking and finance in the Muslim world is relatively new. Throughout most of the twentieth century, in most of the Muslim world banks and businesses operated on Western models, and many continue to do so, but with the Islamic revival there has been increasing pressure to conform to the complex regulations of Islamic jurisprudence, and much of this pressure is from private banking customers who are concerned that their own affairs should comply with their faith. The nature of traditional jurisprudence means that solutions have to be sought from the primary texts and the opinions of the classical jurists using specific tools of reasoning which allow certain flexibility. What is not permitted, however, is "innovation", or *bid'a*, which means that new rulings cannot be derived without textual foundation. It is not possible, then, for Islam simply to adapt by sweeping away accepted norms.

Likewise, I understand George's point about gambling when this is at a level that does not affect people's lives and raises money for charity. The Qur'an says, "They ask you about wine and gambling. Say, 'In them is great sin and [yet, some] benefit for people. But their sin is greater than their benefit'" (2:219). The reasoning to the interpretation of this and similar verses is that gambling may lead people into believing in luck rather than believing in God and expecting to gain something by chance rather than by their own lawful effort. The problem is that it can become difficult to determine the point at which something harmless turns into something harmful. Addiction to gambling can destroy lives and families. The current intensive marketing of Internet gambling is particularly alarming in that it appears to be targeting those who can least afford it with TV adverts in between those of the compensation claims lawyers and the payday lenders. They have made it much too easy for anyone to be lured into gambling in the comfort of their own homes where previously they would have had to have acted much more positively and publicly to become involved in gambling and therefore to acknowledge and evaluate their actions more openly. Islam does, however, allow one form of gambling based on the *Sunna* of the Prophet. Wagers are permitted on archery competitions and horse racing and the like, but only by those actually participating in the competition, such that their reward is the product of their own skill, not merely a matter of luck. Third-party wagers are not allowed.

Islam is concerned with the protection of the money and property of the weak and vulnerable and the Qur'an specifically prohibits the squandering of the property of orphans by those who have responsibility for their welfare. Custodians of an orphan's property must not take payment for this and must give full account and transfer control to the orphan, with witnesses, when they come of age. Women have full rights to their own property, and their husbands have no right to take it from them unless it is freely given.

Islam is also deeply concerned with propriety in business and financial transactions. There are strict rules concerning trading and business ethics, including the giving of true measure, honest description of goods, monopolies, and unfair competition. There are *hadith* of the Prophet that indicate that the hoarding and withholding of foodstuffs in order to push up prices is forbidden. From the early years of Islam, traders were forbidden to ride out to meet trading caravans before they entered the cities in order to gain unfair advantage buying from merchants who were not aware of the market prices in the city and then controlling the supply and therefore the price to the consumer. In the medieval period a public official known as the *muhtasib* was responsible (among many other functions) for monitoring and controlling the operation of the markets and the practices of merchants. This corpus of rules and ethics for business has a great deal in common with the norms of business practice and consumer protection that apply in modern developed economies.

12(F) DAN:

I want to return to George's comments about poverty. He writes: "A life of poverty is only a virtue if it is chosen like the monastic life." This has not been my understanding of the Christian view, and I have always been under the impression that Jews and Christians basically are at odds over this issue. In the Hebrew Bible there are frequent references to God's concern for the poor and God's determination to rescue them out of their humiliation. Wealth is unashamedly regarded as a good thing; the wealthy are not called to give up their riches, but treat the poor and especially their own kith and kin with kindness and justice. Attempts were made in biblical times to build anti-poverty measures into the social system. Thus every fifty years at the time of Jubilee, the poor were to be given back their freedom if they had fallen into slavery and their debts were cancelled.

Some of these themes can be found in the New Testament. Thus Luke 1:46–55 echoes Hannah's song in 1 Samuel 2 and reflects the continuing hopes of the poor in God's promise to reverse their fortune. Jesus' inaugural sermon in Nazareth in Luke 4:18f is almost entirely focused on bringing good news to the poor. One of Paul's main concerns was to make a collection for the poor of Jerusalem (2 Corinthians 9). Nonetheless the New Testament strikes a different note. First, it is much more cautious about wealth. It is seen as potentially occupying too much of a preoccupation and can replace

God in one's concerns. Second, material poverty is not simply justified in certain circumstances, but actively advocated. Voluntary poverty is understood as a way of discipleship following the example of Jesus himself. Jesus had no place of his own to lay his head, but that for him was a matter of choice. Throughout his ministry he had little concern for material possessions.

These biblical themes of wealth and poverty set the agenda for all the debates that followed. Wealth became an issue even in the early church. The monastic movement, dating from the third century, exchanged a worldly life for the desert and the austere disciplines of poverty, chastity, and obedience. In the thirteenth century, Francis of Assisi, along with his followers and their sisters, the Poor Clares, gave away everything they had. Today, radical renunciation like his is still practised.

Such views are far removed from the Jewish view. Yet, I do recognize that there are many Christians today who do not follow this earlier teaching. There are rich and powerful Christians who see no need to apologize for their good fortune. Indeed, wealth has been accepted as the due reward of a Christian way of life, whether characterized by hard work (sometimes known as the Protestant work ethic) or frugal spending and careful saving (commended by John Wesley). Arguably Western culture has lost the knack of being challenged by prophetic teaching about riches and poverty. Yet, whatever the cause, there is a serious difference in emphasis about wealth and poverty in our two traditions. For the Christian, Jesus' teaching is paramount and has guided the faithful through the centuries. For the Jew, the biblical and rabbinic tradition takes a different course, stressing the evils of poverty and the importance of rescuing the poor from their plight.

PART IV

SOCIETAL ISSUES

CHAPTER 13

LAW CODES

Islam attracts the reputation for imposing unduly severe penalties for crimes such as theft and adultery, and when we hear that some Muslims want to introduce *Shari'a* law in the West, people fear that Western societies might also sanction such penalties. Jews are often thought of as legalists – nit-pickers over seeming minutiae of the Law. As for Christians, have they abandoned biblical laws altogether, teaching that faith supersedes the Torah?

13(A) DAN:

Judaism has always been a religion of law. According to tradition, God revealed 613 commandments to Moses on Mount Sinai. These laws, which are to be observed as part of God's covenant with Israel, are classified in two major categories: (1) statutes concerned with ritual performances characterized as obligations between human beings and God; (2) judgments consisting of ritual laws that would have been adopted by society even if they had not been decreed by God (such as laws regarding murder and theft). These 613 commandments consist of 365 negative (prohibited) and 248 positive (duties to be performed) prescriptions.

Traditional Judaism maintains that Moses received the oral Torah in addition to the written law. This was passed down from generation to generation and was the subject of rabbinic debate. The first authoritative compilation of the oral law was the Mishnah, composed by Judah Ha-Nasi in the second century CE. This work is the most important book of law after the Bible; its purpose was to supply teachers and judges with an authoritative guide to the Jewish legal tradition.

In subsequent centuries sages continued to discuss the content of Jewish law – their deliberations are recorded in the Palestinian and Babylonian Talmuds. Both Talmuds incorporate the Mishnah and later rabbinic discussions known as the Gemara. The Gemara text preserves the proceedings of the academies in both Palestine and Babylonia, where scholars assembled to study the Mishnah. The central purpose of these deliberations was to elucidate the Mishnah text.

After the compilation of the Talmuds (sixth century CE), outstanding rabbinic authorities continued the development of Jewish law by issuing answers to specific questions. These responses (known as "*responsa*") touched on all aspects of Jewish law and ensured a standardization of practice. In time, various scholars felt the need to produce codes of Jewish law so that all members of the community would have access to the legal tradition. In the eleventh century, Isaac Alfasi produced a work that became the standard code for Sephardic Jewry. Two centuries later, Asher ben Jehiel wrote a code that became the code for Ashkenazi Jews. Moses Maimonides in the twelfth century also wrote an important code that had a wide influence, as did the code by Jacob ben Asher (thirteenth to fourteenth centuries), the son of Asher ben Jehiel. In the sixteenth century Joseph Caro published the *Shulchan Aruch* (Code of Jewish Law), which together with glosses by Moses Isserles has served as the standard code of Jewish law for Orthodox Jewry until the present day. The *Shulchan Aruch* is divided into four divisions: (1) *Orah Hayyim*, dealing with everyday conduct, prayer, and festivals; (2) *Yoreh Deah*, concerning dietary and ritual laws; (3) *Even Ha-Ezer*, which deals with matters of personal status; and (4) *Hoshen Mishpat*, dealing with courts, civil law, and torts.

Today Orthodoxy is one of the largest movements worldwide. Yet the majority of those who profess allegiance to it do not always live by the Code of Jewish Law. This is also so within the other branches of Judaism. For most Jews the legal tradition has lost its hold on Jewish consciousness – the bulk of rituals and observances appear anachronistic and burdensome. In previous centuries this was not the case; despite the divisions within the Jewish world all Jews accepted the abiding authority of the Law contained in the Torah. The 613 commandments were universally viewed as given by God to Moses on Mount Sinai and understood as binding for all time. Thus food regulations, stipulations regarding ritual purity, the moral code as well as other *mitzvot* served as the framework for an authentic Jewish way of life.

Throughout Jewish history the validity of the written Torah was never questioned. In contemporary society, however, most Jews of all religious positions have ceased to regard the legal heritage in this light. Instead, individual Jews feel at liberty to choose which *mitzvot* (commandments) have a personal spiritual significance. Such an anarchic approach to the legal tradition highlights the fact that Jewish law no longer serves as a cohesive force for contemporary Jewry. In short, many modern Jews no longer believe in the doctrine of Torah from Sinai, which previously served as a cardinal principle of the Jewish faith. Instead they subscribe only to a limited number of legal precepts which for one reason or another they find meaningful. Such a lack of uniformity of Jewish practice means that there is a vast gulf between the requirements of legal observance and the actual lifestyle of the majority of Jews, both in Israel and the diaspora.

13(B) GEORGE:

Christians often get the impression that the Jews were nit-picking legalists, but I think Dan shows that this is an unfair characterization. The Jews have had to move on from the time of Moses and the Israelites' wanderings in the wilderness, and circumstances necessitate change. I can also understand Jews observing special laws as a means of asserting their identity and keeping up a tradition, even if its original justification is unclear. Dan also rightly draws attention to the point that we are not all perfect, or even good practitioners of each of our faiths. In a city in which I used to live it was common practice for some members of the Jewish congregation to drive to the city centre, park a block or two away from the synagogue, and walk the rest of the distance as if they were observing the traditional Sabbath day's journey. I don't blame them: there are times when I have tried to look as if I am a better Christian than I really am!

Christians, of course, have learned much from their Jewish origins. We cannot disagree with the Ten Commandments, even if our score out of ten is not as high as it should be, and we would certainly acknowledge Moses as one of the world's great lawgivers. In a previous chapter (chapter 8) we mentioned the Noahide Covenant – the part of the Jewish law that is binding on all people, not just Jews, and I have no problem with that. Christians have tended, however, to find problems with the notion of "the Law". Jesus taught that love of God and love of one's neighbour were the supreme ideals by which all other laws should be judged, and that unduly meticulous observance of detailed rules was unnecessary, especially where human compassion should take precedence. Paul taught that salvation was not obtained through detailed observance of the Law, but rather through God's grace: "We... know that a person is not justified by the works of the law, but by faith in Jesus Christ" (Galatians 2:16).

Christians have been at pains to avoid legalism. Although the Roman Catholic Church has formulated guidance on moral matters in its canon law, there is not the kind of detail or apparent pointlessness that one seems to find in much Jewish moral and ritual instruction. It is hard to see why one should not wear garments of mixed fabric, or mix meat and milk. Some of the ancient laws governing society seem unduly harsh – for example the recommendation to put homosexuals to death (Leviticus 20:13) or subject a suspected adulteress to a kind of trial by ordeal (Numbers 5:11–31).

Dan indicates that attitudes to Jewish law have moved on in the course of time, although this brings the obvious danger of compromising one's tradition. I wonder, though, if such change can occur within Islam, and I hope that Dawoud can clarify matters. Muslims still appear to believe in the inerrancy of the book that recommends the amputation of hands as a penalty for theft (5:38), the flogging of adulterers (24:2), the permission for a husband to beat his wife (4:34), and the right of male children to inherit twice as much as their female siblings (4:11). To what extent do Muslims implement these laws, and what scope has there been for change in Islamic attitudes? Such penalties are still in force, and one hears about them in the media from time to time.

Both Judaism and Islam have operated as political systems as well as religions, but of course things changed when the Jews were driven out of their homeland, and Islam is no longer one single political state. There have been times and places where church and state have been interconnected, for example in the Holy Roman empire, and in John Calvin's theocratic state in Geneva. However, most Christians today prefer a separation of church and state and, particularly in multicultural societies like Britain and the United States, it seems inappropriate to coerce their populations into obeying the laws of any one particular religion.

The Christian faith teaches obedience to civil authorities, however. Paul said, "Let everyone be subject to the governing authorities... The authorities that exist have been established by God" (Romans 13:1). There are limits to compliance with the law, however. Where there have been corrupt and repressive political regimes, Christians have resorted to civil disobedience, and can claim biblical authority for doing so. When the early disciples were forbidden to preach about Christ, Peter declared, "We must obey God rather than human beings!" (Acts 5:29). Unfortunately, insufficient numbers of Christians took a stance against Adolf Hitler, although, as previously mentioned (see 7e), some were prepared to forfeit their lives, such as Bonhoeffer.

I think we are agreed about the obvious need to maintain order in civil society by means of law codes. But we disagree about what should be in these codes, and the extent to which they should be subject to review as time progresses.

13(C) DAWOUD:

For Muslims the *Shari'a* is central to Islam. In our discussions in preceding chapters we have touched on various aspects of *Shari'a* as it has a bearing on every part of life and every field of law – constitutional, international, criminal, civil, commercial, and family law, as well as doctrine and worship.

The *Shari'a* is derived from two main sources. The first and most important of these is the Qur'an, which Muslims believe to be the literal and infallible word of God revealed to the Prophet Muhammad through Jibril (the angel Gabriel) over a period of approximately twenty-three years from 610 CE. The Qur'an is not a book of law and does not offer a codified body of legislation in any way comparable with the Jewish law described by Dan. In fact it contains relatively few detailed legislative provisions. For the greater part it consists of narratives and injunctions to belief and right behaviour framed in terms that are often general and rhetorical and sometimes vague and open to interpretation. They are by no means comprehensive, however, and so from earliest times the Muslim community looked to the Prophet to interpret and explain the Qur'an and to provide guidance and leadership. During his lifetime and within the limited terms of reference of the early Muslim community this would have been relatively straightforward. After his death they sought guidance initially from the examples in the memory of the community of his *Sunna* or practice, being his words, deeds, and tacit acceptance of certain actions. These were later collected, collated, assessed for authenticity, and categorized by *hadith* scholars in the eighth and ninth centuries CE, resulting in six main authoritative collections of *hadith* (individual reports) which refer to all aspects of human activity, both public and private. This is the second main source of the *Shari'a*.

With the rapid spread of Islam and the need to provide for the infinitely varied needs of an expanding civilization it was necessary to establish methods of regulation and adjudication. The religious scholars developed tools and methods for deriving rulings in specific cases using a set of principles of jurisprudence: *ijtihad* (independent reasoning); *ijma'* (consensus); *qiyas* (analogy); *istihsan* (choosing the most preferable); *masalih mursalah* (the public benefit), and *'urf* (custom or practice). The division of the jurists into various "schools" began during the Umayyad Caliphate (661–750 CE) and developed further during the Abbasid Caliphate that succeeded it. Sunni Islam recognizes the mutual orthodoxy of its four main schools – the Hanafi, Maliki, Shafi'i, and Hanbali schools named after their most important scholars. Other schools arose but did not attain the same prominence, although the Zahiri school produced many important opinions.

The Shi'a are divided into two main denominations and numerous smaller groupings. The Shi'a accept a more limited range of *hadith* as a basis for rulings (they recognize only those that can be traced to the Prophet and his immediate family) and a more limited range of tools of jurisprudence.

In the ideal Muslim society there should be no division between religion and state and the incentive to obey the *Shari'a* should be faith and the desire to obey God's will, not the fear of punishment by the state. There is, of course, no such thing as an ideal society or ideal individuals and, as George points out, none of us are perfect in the practice of our faith. There are elements of the *Shari'a* that are difficult to reconcile with the modern world. George mentions a number of these, notably the *hudud*, or specified penalties for certain offences against God. While I cannot in this brief space present the range of scholarly thought with regard to each of these, there is, for example, an opinion that the ruling authorities are not justified in imposing the penalty of amputation for the offence of theft unless they have created a perfect society in which there is prosperity and full employment, and need and poverty have been eliminated. These are issues that Muslims and Muslim communities and countries are wrestling with and there is a divide between those who would like to see a more rigid and traditional interpretation of the *Shari'a* and others who believe that it is possible to view the *Shari'a* in the light of centuries of progress, in environments completely different from the one in which Islam arose, and to find answers within the faith for the questions of the present.

13(D) DAN:

Both George and Dawoud have so far focused on the status of law within their religious traditions. As I stressed previously, there is a deep gulf fixed between observant Orthodox Jews (known as Haredim) and the rest of the Jewish community. As we have seen, strictly Orthodox Jews observe the entire corpus of Jewish law, believing that both the written and oral Torah were given by God to Moses on Mount Sinai. This doctrine – *Torah mi Sinai* – has been central to Judaism from the earliest rabbinic period until today. Over the centuries various codes of Jewish law were formulated to guide the faithful. Today the *Shulchan*

Aruch (Code of Jewish Law) guides the lives of believers throughout the Jewish world.

Yet the vast majority of Jews today do not regard biblical and rabbinic law as binding. This has inevitably led to considerable disagreement, and has raised the question whether contemporary Jews need a modern code of Jewish law based on the Jewish heritage. Seeking to guide the faithful, various non-Orthodox movements (such as Conservative, Reconstructionist, and Reform Judaism) have formulated guidelines to determine which laws should be followed in contemporary society. One frequently mentioned principle is that Jews must observe God's will. Yet inevitably there are difficulties with this approach. Where is God's revelation to be found? In the Pentateuch or in the prophetic books? Or the rest of scripture? Is God really concerned if Jews eat lobster? Does He care whether they wear fringes, or seethe the kid in its mother's milk? Is He annoyed if they go out to work, drive a car to synagogue, or smoke on the Sabbath? Is He angry if they commit adultery or steal? Perhaps He does concern himself with such things, but if so, does He care about all these matters equally? In the past non-Orthodox rabbinic authorities have been anxious to distinguish between ritual and moral law, but is this distinction valid as far as God is concerned? These are, I believe, unanswerable questions for one reason: there is no basis for knowing what God's intention is. Some modern non-Orthodox rabbis have stated categorically that they have some sort of knowledge of God's revelation, but any examination of the wide diversity of opinion among these rabbis illustrates that such claims are nothing more than subjective beliefs based on personal disposition and judgment.

If there is disagreement as to what constitutes revelation, then what can be said about following the claims of conscience? This is another approach frequently advocated by non-Orthodox rabbinic authorities, but it too is beset with difficulties. No doubt many Jews do follow their consciences, but how can they be sure that what they are doing is right? The dictates of one person's conscience often differ from those of someone else's. The same applies to such standards as ethical propriety, justice, and aesthetic value which have been recommended as well. From everyday experience it is clear that what is offensive to one person is totally acceptable to another.

Contemporary non-Orthodox Judaism is thus in considerable confusion about the legal tradition. Modern rabbis lack clear principles for distinguishing between traditional observances which should be retained and those which should be eliminated. Given such difficulties, it appears impossible to evolve a modern code of law for the Jewish community. Rather than seeking to create a new legal framework for contemporary Jews, modern non-Orthodox Judaism should encourage all individuals to exercise freedom in selecting those observances which they find meaningful. This is not an innovation – it has always been a tenet of non-Orthodox Judaism that individuals have the right to select elements from the Jewish heritage which are personally significant. But this principle should be carried to its logical conclusion. All Jews should feel free to make up their minds in all spheres. No one – no rabbi, nor rabbinic body – should legislate what practices are acceptable for the community as a whole. In other words, there should be no law nor legislators in the modern Jewish world. What is needed instead is a declaration of personal liberty and freedom. Possibly George will agree that the same applies to modern Christians, but I imagine Dawoud would not be sympathetic to such an approach in the Muslim world.

13(E) GEORGE:

There are three stances we can take regarding ancient law codes: we can regard them as superseded, and abandon them; we can try to reinterpret them, finding new meanings for a modern world; or we can stand firm with them, refusing to allow prevailing social attitudes to alter them. Dan seems to want to do the first, while Dawoud seems to opt for the second.

While I am aware that there are different interpretations of *Shari'a* law, Dawoud's suggestion that the severe punishments only apply in a perfect society seems very strange to me. Why would the Qur'an prescribe penalties for a society that does not and cannot exist? In any case, we are surely aware that in numerous Islamic countries such penalties are actually handed out in law courts, as news reports confirm. In 2013 in the Maldives, a fifteen-year-old girl was sentenced to

100 lashes for pre-marital sex, despite being a rape victim; in Somalia, four youths were each sentenced to have their right arm and left leg amputated in public for stealing cell-phones; in Saudi Arabia a woman was condemned to ten lashes for defying a law forbidding women to drive cars. Surely such penalties are barbaric in this day and age?

Dan seems to opt for the other extreme, and his suggestion of freedom to choose which laws to accept sounds somewhat anarchic. Can the Jewish faith really survive without rabbis and law codes? This sounds much more problematic than using one's conscience, which I don't think reduces us to moral relativism, as he suggests. Conscience always involves some uncertainty: we are all used to agonizing in hindsight about decisions we have made. Christians of any tradition, when faced with moral uncertainty, can always seek guidance from those in authority within the church, especially its clergy. I am therefore worried about Dan's suggestion that there should be no laws and no rabbis: this seems to leave the believer adrift, in a state of moral anarchy.

Dan's commendation of religious liberty and freedom opens a further dimension to our discussion of religious law. So far, the three of us, coming from different religions, have talked as if we subscribe to different law codes. However, since we all live in the same Western country, each of us is required to obey the law of the land, and this raises questions about the relationships between our religion and the law. How can we protect our religious identities within it, and how can the law give support to these identities? I am sure we would all approve of recent British legislation banning discrimination on the grounds of religion, and outlawing incitement to religious hatred. I think all three of us agree on the need to practise our religions freely, at least within the law of the land.

What is more controversial is the question of whether religions should be entitled to set up their own systems of law within a Western society. On 7 February 2008, Dr Rowan Williams – then Archbishop of Canterbury – gave a lecture in London on Civil and Religious Law. The Archbishop argued the case for "supplementary jurisdiction", which would allow British Muslims to give legal judgments in *Shari'a* courts which could run side-by-side with British civil ones. Predictably, the lecture was controversial, and many non-Muslim British citizens may have had visions of such courts curtailing the rights of widows to inheritance, sanctioning forced marriages, and authorizing lashings for adultery and limb amputations for theft. Unfortunately this kind of Islamophobia is fuelled by the news reports I have mentioned above. I should be interested to hear Dawoud's observations on this issue.

Christianity has traditionally taught that the Christian is a dual citizen, belonging to an earthly and the heavenly kingdom, and subject to the laws of both. Churches have produced their own codes of canon law, with their own ecclesiastical courts, and with their own ways of disciplining members, even if such sanctions are only rarely invoked. Such laws do not apply to those outside the religion, and similarly the pronouncements of an organization like the Islamic Shari'a Council are in no way binding on non-Muslims. Is it not reasonable to allow Muslims their own courts to settle certain disputes, just as the Jews have their own *beth din*, at which they can resolve their own civil disputes?

Clearly there are difficulties when a religion and the law come into conflict. What concessions should society make to accommodate one's religious convictions? Should a flight attendant be banned from wearing a necklace displaying a cross? Should a Muslim supermarket check-out assistant be entitled to refuse to sell alcohol to customers? In a multi-faith and multicultural society, it is often difficult to assert one's faith, while respecting that of others.

13(F) DAWOUD:

Naturally, the way that laws are interpreted and enforced depends on the nature of the society and the government in power. Many Muslim countries such as Egypt have had more than a century of civil society and legal reform and have constitutions, codified legislation including penal codes, and strong judiciaries. On the whole in these countries, punishments for crimes including those that would fall under the *hadd* categories are dealt with through ordinary civil penalties including fines and custodial sentences.

George and Dan are correct in mentioning the severe penalties that do take place in some countries and societies. Many cases are reported from the two great Islamic theocracies, Saudi Arabia and Iran, the homelands of Sunni and Shi'i Islam, respectively. These have unique positions in their respective traditions. Saudi Arabia has only existed as a state for some eighty years, and society is still dominated by tribal politics and the role of custodianship of the holy cities of Islam. The rapid influx of wealth in the mid-twentieth century into a previously relatively poor and undeveloped country brought changes that society has not yet managed to catch up with. The law is still *Shari'a*-based and its interpretation and enforcement is in the hands and essentially at the personal discretion of religious scholars who derive their opinions directly from the applicable school of jurisprudence. In contrast Iran has codified legislation including a penal code based on the *Shari'a* and formally incorporating the *hadd* penalties. This is the legacy of the Islamic revolution of 1979 that overthrew the Shah who was perceived to be a Western puppet.

Beyond these, *Shari'a* punishments occur largely where tribal justice prevails outside state law as has been the case in Afghanistan, or in areas of conflict, political turbulence, and revolution where there are no statutory bodies or checks and balances and "justice" falls into the hands of self-appointed and unregulated cadres.

The majority of moderate Muslims would agree that while living in non-Muslim countries such as the UK they are obliged to live by the law of the land. Where it is important to them, they may find ways to comply with the *Shari'a* within the boundaries of the law, for instance by using Islamic banks or making Islamic marriage contracts. The discussion of the introduction of *Shari'a* courts in the UK is somewhat misleading. There has never been any real suggestion of a separate or parallel legal system that could be legally imposed on any community, and it is unthinkable that there could be anything other than one law for everybody. Under the 1996 Arbitration Act, a number of *Shari'a* arbitration tribunals have been established, and it is possible for them to provide binding arbitration decisions in certain matters such as business affairs and disputes between neighbours. In order to do so, however, they must comply with the legal requirements for the constitution and operation of tribunals in the same way as any other arbitration organization, and the participants must be fully informed of their legal position and agree freely to the arbitration and to be bound by its decisions. They are not permitted, however, to issue decisions in personal status or criminal matters. At the same time, a number of *Shari'a* councils in the UK offer a dispute resolution service in family matters. Their decisions have no legal standing but some people may choose freely to seek advice in this manner. Concerns have been raised, however, that people may be misled into believing that the decisions of these councils are legally binding or that they may be pressured directly or indirectly by their families and communities into resorting to their services. There is evidence that they may be acting in ways that are discriminatory towards women and children in matters such as marriage, divorce, custody, and inheritance, and parties may not receive proper advice or be advised of their legal rights. There have been reports, for instance, of abusive husbands being required to attend anger management counselling and their wives being told they must accept this without involvement of the police, and of rulings being given on the distribution of estates in ways that are detrimental to wives and daughters. Women who live in closed communities with little or no English are particularly vulnerable. UK law, as is the case with most Western countries, applies equally to all irrespective of gender, religion, or ethnicity and it would be a retrograde step to permit anything that undermines this.

CHAPTER 14

SOCIAL JUSTICE

The Abrahamic religions all teach the need to care for the poor and protect the weak. Is this a topic on which we can all agree, or are there important differences? Just over half of the world's population subscribes to one or the other of our three faiths, so why have we not managed to achieve social justice? What are the barriers to a just society – and what do we mean by social justice, anyway?

14(A) DAN:

Judaism does not separate religion from life – instead Jews are called to action, to turn humankind away from violence, wickedness, and falsehood. It is not the hope of bliss in a future life but the establishment of the kingdom of justice and peace that is central to the Jewish faith. Morality is at the heart of the religious tradition. The people of Israel as a light to the nations reflect the moral nature of God. Each Jew is to be like the creator, mirroring the divine qualities revealed to Moses: "The Lord, the Lord, the compassionate and gracious God, slow to anger, abounding in love and faithfulness, maintaining love to thousands, and forgiving wickedness, rebellion and sin" (Exodus 34:6–7).

God as a moral being demands moral living, as the psalms declare: "The Lord is righteous; he loves justice" (11:7). "Righteousness and justice are the foundation of his throne" (97:2). "You have established equity; in Jacob you have done what is just and right" (99:4).

Given this theological framework, Jews are directed to obey the revealed will of God, which is the basis of the covenantal relationship between God and the Jewish nation. Orthopraxis, rather than conceptual reflection, serves as the foundation of the religion of Israel.

It is pre-eminently in the legal codes of the Torah that we encounter moral guidelines formulated in specific rules. The Decalogue in particular illustrates the centrality of moral praxis in the life of the Jew. The first four commandments are theological in character, but the last deal with relationships between human beings. The first commandment describes God as the one who redeemed the Jews from Egypt; the one who forbade the worship of other deities and demands respect for the Sabbath and the divine name. These commandments are expressions of the love and fear of God. The remaining injunctions provide a means of expressing love of other human beings. The Decalogue makes it clear that moral rules are fundamental to the Jewish faith.

Such ethical standards are repeated in the prophetic books. The teachings of the prophets were rooted in the Torah of Moses. The prophets saw themselves as messengers of the divine word. Their special task was to denounce the people for their transgressions and call them to repentance. In all this they pointed to concrete action as the only means of sustaining the covenantal relationship with God. The essential theme of their message is that God demands righteousness and justice.

Rabbinic literature continues this emphasis on moral action. Convinced they were the authentic expositors of scripture, the rabbis amplified biblical law. In their expansion of the commandments, rabbinic exegetes differentiated between the laws governing human relationships to God and those that concern human relationships to others. As in the biblical period, rabbinic teachings reflect the same sense of the primacy of morality.

By choosing the moral path, the Jew can help to complete God's work of creation. To accomplish this task the rabbis formulated an elaborate system of traditions, which were written down in the Mishnah, subsequently expanded in the Talmud and eventually codified in the Code of Jewish Law. For the Jew, the moral law is absolute and binding. In all cases the Law is precise and specific; it is God's word made concrete in the daily life of the Jew. The commandments to love one's neighbours embrace all people. In the Code of Jewish Law the virtues of justice, honesty, and humane concern are regarded as central principles of community life. Hatred, vengeance, deceit, cruelty, and anger are condemned as antisocial. The Jew is instructed to exercise loving-kindness towards all, to clothe the naked, to feed the hungry, to care for the sick, and to comfort the mourner. By fulfilling these ethical demands, the Jewish people can help to bring about God's kingdom on earth, in which exploitation, oppression, and injustice will be eliminated.

14(B) GEORGE:

Well! What Dan has just written could almost equally have been said by me as the Christian contributor! As Christians, we also accept the Hebrew scriptures as a source of authority – the Torah with its Decalogue, the prophets who called the people to repentance and to social justice, and the psalms which extol God's justice, His sovereignty over the earth, and our duty to care for it. Dan mentions the notion of covenant: Christians hold that they are also in a covenant relationship with God, being "grafted in" to the covenant that was first offered to the Jews (Romans 11:24).

Amos is frequently read in Christian churches, with his stern warnings to the Jewish people to repent and to pursue the virtues which Dan mentions: justice towards the poor, honesty, integrity, and the rejection of wickedness and falsehood.

Dan also mentions the ideal of being like the creator. That too is a Christian aspiration: the Eastern Orthodox tradition in particular lays great emphasis on *theosis* – becoming godlike – and, as with the Jew, this entails the rejection of all other gods, including material commodities that can become our "gods", if we value them more highly than spiritual matters. Jesus said, "No one can serve two masters... You cannot serve both God and money" (Matthew 6:24). Jesus also taught that one should not seek revenge, and that being angry was a violation of Moses' commandment against murder (Matthew 5:22).

Obviously I can't endorse the authority of the Mishnah or the Talmud, both of which were written considerably after Jews and Christians parted company. However, Christians have their own tradition of ethical and social teachers who have elaborated on biblical teachings about society, and the Roman Catholic Church in particular is renowned for its codification of moral as well as theological teachings.

So why can't we get along, then? I guess a number of reasons have led to the conflicts that have occurred between our three different faiths. If only we all practised our respective faiths as we should! Unfortunately most, if not all, religious believers – including me – are bad practitioners of our faiths, and it is precisely because we *don't* practise our religions properly that we cause injustice, neglect of the poor, ecological damage to our planet, and the many wrongs that have plagued society from its beginning.

Perhaps too we are unduly sensitive to differences between us. People from different cultural backgrounds often look different from us, and this has happened both with Jewish and Muslim communities in Britain. Particularly if the economy is experiencing a downturn, and jobs are scarce, people sometimes resent minority communities, which they are quick to assume have secured jobs at the expense of the indigenous population. There can be problems too when we have not got to know those who come from these different backgrounds. Understandably, we all like to mix with our own communities with which we have most in common, and hence the presence of other religions creates an "other", which can readily become the target of racism and xenophobia. As Britain becomes more multicultural and multi-faith, and different communities now readily meet in colleges and in the workplace, perhaps some of these prejudices might be dispelled.

There are historical differences, too, that have given rise to age-old resentments between different faiths. Unfortunately, from its early years, Christians blamed the Jews for the death of their messiah, describing them as "Christ-killers" and being blind to the truth. Since we regard Jesus as God's final revelation, Christians tend to resent the Islamic conviction that a greater prophet has come in the form of Muhammad. Since Christians and Muslims in particular have tended to regard their faiths as exclusive means to salvation, religious zeal has often been the motivator for violent conflict. In fact, theological differences between members of the same religion have often proved sufficient to cause conflict, and armed conflict leaves in its wake injury, injustice, poverty, and ongoing resentments.

We should also remember some of the basic underlying causes of injustice: human greed, and desire for power or self-aggrandizement. We prefer to hold on to our wealth rather than give it away to relieve world poverty, and we want to enjoy our material comforts and advanced technological lifestyle, even though we know that it contributes to phenomena such as global warming and the depletion of dwindling planetary resources. Political leaders often prefer to hang on to office rather than do what is in the interests of their citizens.

Christianity teaches the doctrine of "original sin": when Adam and Eve disobeyed God in the Garden of Eden, their sin affected the whole of humankind. We may not necessarily take the story literally, but it illustrates the obvious fact that we have innate sinful tendencies: humans don't have to learn how to be selfish and greedy. We need to draw on our various faiths to find ways to counter these inclinations and to make a start at addressing problems of deprivation and injustice. But how do we go about it?

14(C) DAWOUD:

The era before the advent of Islam is referred to as *Al-Jahiliyya*, the "age of ignorance", and the received view of this period depicts it as a time of injustice, cruelty, and oppression. Although historical research challenges the accuracy of some of the detail of the description of pre-Islamic Arabian society that is propounded rhetorically, it is central to the belief of most Muslims that Islam came to sweep away this era of oppression and to establish a new order of peace, justice, and compassion.

All of our faiths teach us that we have a responsibility for the welfare of others. There is a well-known *Hadith Qudsi* (one of a specific genre of *hadith* deemed to be divinely inspired):

O son of Adam, I fell ill and you visited Me not. He will say: O Lord, and how should I visit You when You are the Lord of the worlds? He will say: Did you not know that My servant So-and-so had fallen ill and you visited him not? Did you not know that had you visited him you would have found Me with him? O son of Adam, I asked you for food and you fed Me not. He will say: O Lord, and how should I feed You when You are the Lord of the worlds? He will say: Did you not know that My servant So-and-so asked you for food and you fed him not? Did you not know that had you fed him you would surely have found that (the reward for doing so) with Me? O son of Adam, I asked you to give Me to drink and you gave Me not to drink. He will say: O Lord, how should I give You to drink when You are the Lord of the worlds? He will say: My servant So-and-so asked you to give him to drink and you gave him not to drink. Had you given him to drink you would have surely found that with Me.

This is of course very close to Matthew 25:31–46. Both the *hadith* and the Gospel are explicit that it is God's expectation of us that we must not ignore those in need and that it is on our treatment of others that we will ultimately be judged. The Qur'an states clearly: "Whoever comes with a good deed will have ten times the like thereof, and whoever comes with an evil deed will not be recompensed except the like thereof; and they will not be wronged" (6:160).

Responsibility for the weak and vulnerable is a frequently repeated theme in the Qur'an:

And do not approach the orphan's property except in a way that is best until he reaches maturity. And give full measure and weight in justice. We do not charge any soul except [with that within] its capacity. And when you testify, be just, even if [it concerns] a near relative. (6:152)

The importance of honesty and bearing true witness without fear or favour is also emphasized: "O you who believe, stand firmly for justice as witnesses to Allah, even if it be against yourselves, your parents and your relatives, or whether it is against the rich or the poor" (4:135).

The message of all of our faiths is clear and there is much that we can agree upon with regard to establishing social justice. George makes a valid point, however, that most of us do not live up to the ideals. Performing personal acts of worship is easy and may make us feel that we are doing our religious duty, but the harder part and undoubtedly the more important has to be to try to live by the true principles of our faith in our treatment of others. The essence of this is contained in the "Golden Rule", the ethic of reciprocity which is found in one form or another in most religions and cultures – the injunction to "do as we would be done by". This was proclaimed as a universal principle in the Declaration Toward a Global Ethic of the World Parliament of Religions held in 1993. The Qur'an points to this: "Woe to those... who, when they have to receive by measure from men, they demand exact full measure, but when they have to give by measure or weight to men, give less than due" (83:1–4).

It is summed up, however, in the *hadith*: "None of you [truly] believes until he wishes for his brother what he wishes for himself."

14(D) DAN:

Given the importance of social justice in our three faiths, why have Jews, Muslims, and Christians hated each other through the centuries? In contemporary society, the Arab world continually vilifies the Jewish community for its Zionist aspirations. Soon we will discuss the Israeli– Palestinian conflict. But at this juncture, it is important to note our communities have not always lived up to the social ideals they espouse. If we are to explore social justice honestly, we must look beyond the lofty sentiments of our theological traditions and face the evils that we have perpetuated against one another.

I want first briefly to survey relations between Jews and Christians. Some years ago I wrote a book entitled *The Crucified Jew: Twenty Centuries of Christian Antisemitism*, in which I focused on the Christian roots of anti-Semitism. The aim of this volume was to answer the question of why Jews have been so bitterly hated for nearly four millennia. At the outset, the New Testament served as a basis for the early church's denunciation of the Jews. Drawing on this tradition, the Church Fathers regarded the Jewish people as lawless and dissolute. Because of their rejection of Christ, the Jewish nation was viewed as excluded from God's grace and subject to His wrath. This *Adversos Judaeos* teaching of the early church continued into the medieval period. During the Crusades Christian mobs massacred Jewish communities: Jews were charged with killing Christian children to use their blood for ritual purposes, blaspheming Christ and Christianity in their sacred literature, and causing the Black

Death by poisoning wells. Throughout the Middle Ages Jews were detested, and the image of the satanic Jew became a central feature of Western iconography. Repeatedly Jews were accused of demonic activities and regarded as a sub-species of the human race.

In the post-medieval world such negative stereotypes of the Jew became a central feature of Western European culture. In France Jews were depicted in the most terrible fashion. In England Jews were detested, as they were in Germany. Such Christian anti-Semitism was most forcefully expressed in Martin Luther's diatribes against German Jews. Elsewhere Jewish converts to Christianity became subject to the Inquisition. Jews living in Poland were also subject to assault. In the mid-seventeenth century, a Cossack pogrom led to the death of thousands of Jews. Such attitudes continued into the modern period, where traditional Christian prejudice was coupled with commercial interests. In Germany merchants alleged that Jewish trade would pollute the nation and undermine the economic vitality of the country, while in France the French bourgeoisie resisted Jewish settlement as did the British. This legacy of Christian hostility to the Jew paved the way for the racial doctrines of the Nazis and the Holocaust, and Hitler was careful to site his extermination camps in countries with strong histories of anti-Semitism among their supposedly Christian population.

As far as relations between Jews and Muslims are concerned, the ongoing struggle between Israel and the Palestinians has intensified Arab anti-Semitism and has led to the destruction of Jewish communities in Arab lands. Throughout the Arab world, Jews are continually denounced – as a consequence, the Zionist aspiration to solve the problem of anti-Semitism by creating a Jewish state in the Middle East has proved an illusion. In modern times the Arab community has become the greatest proponent of anti-Jewish attitudes, and has transformed the demonic image of the Jew to suit its own purposes. During the last fifty years a vast quantity of anti-Semitic literature has been published in Muslim countries utilizing religious as well as racial motifs. Some of this literature, such as Hitler's *Mein Kampf*, Henry Ford's *International Jew*, and the poisonous tract *Protocols of the Elders of Zion*, has been translated into Arabic and is widely available. Other writings have exploited stereotypical images of the Jew inherited from the past. In all cases, these negative depictions of Jewry have been reinterpreted to express Arab antipathy towards Jews: repeatedly the Jew is portrayed as an evil force determined to corrupt and exploit the society in which he lives.

14(E) GEORGE:

I said that I agreed almost entirely with Dan's previous contribution, but there is much to take issue with in what he says now. We can agree that Christianity has a fairly appalling track record in its attitude to Jews and its treatment of them. However, I think it is unfortunate that Dan should catalogue the persecution of Jews, rather than to deplore persecution of any faith or to identify instances in which a religion is the perpetrator rather than the victim.

Christians too have been victims of persecution, from the first century to the present day. After Jesus' death, the Jewish authorities commissioned Saul of Tarsus to hunt down the early Christians, and in the so-called "Great Persecution" of the third and fourth centuries CE Christians were thrown to the lions in the reigns of Roman emperors Diocletian and Galerius. Christians have suffered persecution in the former Soviet countries, in North Korea, in Pakistan, and in Saudi Arabia. A recent survey claims that in the period 2008–2010, 75 per cent of all persecution was against Christians. (I'm not sure how one measures persecution statistically, however, and of course some of this persecution may well have been by Christians against other Christians.) Islam too has been persecuted and persecutor, suffering at the hands of the Christians during the Crusades, and subsequently engaging in active physical hostility towards the Bahá'í, the Ahmadiyya and the Alevis.

Many Christians' problems regarding the Jewish faith are often due to ignorance and bad education, but the church has attempted at various points throughout the centuries to correct misconceptions. There have been papal pronouncements from the thirteenth century against blood libel, and the Vatican II *Declaration on the Relation of the Church to Non-Christian Religions* (*Nostra Aetate*) states:

True, the Jewish authorities and those who followed their lead pressed for the death of Christ; still, what happened in His passion cannot be charged against all the Jews, without distinction, then alive, nor against the Jews of today. Although the Church is the new people of God, the Jews should not be presented as rejected or accursed by God, as if this followed from the Holy Scriptures. (Pope Paul VI, 28 October 1965)

I think only a minority of Christians would see their faith as superseding Judaism. Paul asks rhetorically, "Did God reject his people?", and answers that "God's gifts and his call are irrevocable" (Romans 11:1, 29), arguing that Jews remain in a covenant relationship, into which non-Jews may be grafted, and that God's relationship with the Jews through their history has been necessary for the world's salvation. The New Testament never refers to the church as the "new Israel" or the "second Israel": the word "Israel" is always used to refer to the Jews or their land. Such expressions are subsequent inventions of a minority of Christians who contend that the gospel supersedes the Jewish faith and its laws.

Inevitably, and understandably, Dan mentions the Holocaust. There can be no doubt that it was one of the most horrendous atrocities in the whole of human history, and that most of its propagators in Nazi Germany were (at least nominally) Christians. I realize how offensive it can be to make comparisons with the wilful extermination of 5 million Jews, or to attempt to belittle or deny the magnitude and the appalling nature of this genocide. However, the theme of this part of our dialogue is social justice, and we also need to recognize that millions of people in the twenty-first century continue to die, not as a result of genocide, but from human greed, selfishness, and cruelty. According to the World Hunger Education Service, some 5 million children die annually through malnutrition worldwide. Just over half the population in sub-Saharan Africa continue to find themselves in one-dollar-a-day poverty, and just over half that number can read and write. The United States' population owns 50 per cent of the world's wealth, despite having only 6.3 per cent of its population. There is enough food in the world for the average person to consume 2,720 kcal per day (the average man's recommended intake is 2,500), yet Western farmers destroy crops in order to boost their prices. Malnutrition is related to a cluster of international problems: harmful economic systems with unfair trade conditions and resultant debt, lack of education, armed conflict, and unfavourable climatic conditions.

Social justice is about more than religious prejudice and discrimination. Perhaps the topics I have outlined don't make good debating material, either because we agree that they need to be tackled, or perhaps because we don't have easy remedies for them. Is there any way that we can all work together to bring about change and end injustice?

14(F) DAWOUD:

We seem to have taken two distinct lines of discussion here in our understanding of social justice, and I think both are important and interconnected. I agree we have to acknowledge the wrongs of the past and learn from them, and I think that we have to be vigilant to avoid them in the future. I also think that we have to move forward; not forgetting of course, but taking steps towards trusting each other. Persecution happens when people lose sight of each other as fellow human beings just like themselves. George mentions that in our multi-faith society we come together in colleges and universities and in the workplace and this is of course wonderful and enriching. I do have concerns, however, that we are allowing the segregation of children at a much earlier and more critical age. Children have little awareness of racial or religious difference and even less of its significance. Left together without adult interference they will form childhood friendships irrespective of each other's backgrounds. If we educate our children in the closed communities of faith schools, as some Muslims and even those of other denominations are wont to do, their knowledge of each other, and more importantly their experience of interacting with each other, will be limited and they will, therefore, be more susceptible to prejudice and preconception.

I entirely agree, however, that social justice is about more than prejudice and discrimination, and the problems that George mentions are of enormous significance on a global scale. Poverty, oppression, lack of opportunity, and competition for scarce resources, appalling as they are in their own right, are also all factors that can feed into civil conflict, terrorism, and the kinds of atrocities that we have discussed.

We are also witnessing problems of poverty, deprivation, and lack of opportunity on our own doorstep. In the UK and throughout Europe and the US, many people are trapped in debt or on low wages, while those responsible for the economic crisis live comfortably and will never feel the misery and humiliation of those who cannot pay their fuel bills or put food on the table. How did we come in the second decade of the twenty-first century to a point where there are people who are homeless on our streets, elderly people are dying or hospitalized because they cannot heat their homes, and where people, including many who are working, are forced to resort to food banks to be able to feed their children? Who would have predicted that we would see rickets and other forms of malnutrition re-emerge in our times?

This is not restricted to any one community, and there are many organizations – both faith and non-faith based – that are working to help those who are suffering the most. The Salvation Army has been supporting the poor and vulnerable for almost 150 years. The Trussell Trust, a Christian-based organization, runs food banks throughout the UK and indicates that it fed almost 350,000 people in the year 2012–13 on a basis of need and without discrimination. There are also many that are run by Jewish and Muslim charities, and there is cooperation between these and with other local and national agencies and charities. All of our faiths tell us that this is our duty, and George is right in suggesting both that we agree and that we do not have easy remedies.

There are increasing tensions in our society, including Islamophobia on the one hand and the activities of some of the right-wing groups, such as the BNP (British National Party) and EDL (English Defence League), but also a poisoning of the minds of young Muslims by radicals with destructive agendas. These tensions are fed on all sides by poverty, unemployment, social exclusion, and lack of opportunity. The best chance we have of living together in peace and cooperation is to see and know each other as people and not as "the other" and to find ways to work together.

CHAPTER 15

BLASPHEMY

The publication of Salman Rushdie's *The Satanic Verses* in 1988 brought accusations of blasphemy on the part of Muslims, as did the *Jyllands-Posten* Muhammad cartoons in 2005. Why do Muslims seem to be so sensitive about the way Muhammad and the Qur'an are treated? Must we be so serious about our religion that we cannot take a bit of ridicule? Jews are renowned for their humour, and many Christians make jokes about God and Jesus. Blasphemy laws were still in force in Britain at the time of these incidents, but they only protected the Christian faith. However, the media in the UK were unwilling to publish the Danish cartoons. Could this be justified in a multi-faith society? Some time before these incidents, Mary Whitehouse successfully instigated blasphemy proceedings against *Gay News* for printing a "blasphemous" poem.

15(A) DAWOUD:

People of faith may feel deeply hurt and offended by what they perceive to be an insult towards God, their beliefs, or their prophets, but in a society where freedom of expression is a fundamental right, to what extent can we restrict this?

Blasphemy refers to the act of insulting or showing contempt for God or sacred things by words or actions, whether deliberately or accidentally, as distinguished from heresy (the holding or expressing of a belief that deviates from an official or orthodox creed), or apostasy (the leaving or renunciation of one's religion). Naturally, however, there are grey areas in between these, and in Islam they are not always clearly distinguished.

Many Muslims do feel very strongly about insults, real or imagined, to Islam and in particular anything deemed to be denigrating to the Prophet Muhammad and his family, who are held in deep love and reverence. There have been numerous prominent cases in the media in recent years. The first really to make the headlines was Salman Rushdie's *The Satanic Verses* in 1988. The response to *The Satanic Verses* was phenomenal worldwide, but the number of Muslims who ever read the book is infinitesimally small compared with the number who rallied to the cry of blasphemy. Most, therefore, did not know what they were objecting to but followed popular opinion in calling for Rushdie's punishment or even death. In 1989 Ayatollah Khomeini issued a *fatwa* or formal judicial opinion (the word itself does not mean death sentence) enjoining the killing of Salman Rushdie and anyone complicit in the publication of the book, which led to Rushdie going into hiding under police protection for several years.

It is difficult to understand how a man of Rushdie's background and education would not have anticipated the reaction to his novel, even if not its extent. While not wishing to condone censorship or the notion that freedom of expression should be restricted by terror, it seems almost reckless.

There is, however, no death penalty, or indeed any other worldly punishment for blasphemy prescribed in the Qur'an, which says: "When you hear the verses of Allah [recited], they are denied [by them] and ridiculed; so do not sit with them until they enter into another conversation" (4:140). Emphasis is on repentance and forgiveness, or punishment in the hereafter: "Hold to forgiveness, command what is right; but turn away from the ignorant" (7:199).

The extreme penalties for blasphemy were only extrapolated later on by the jurists. Few Muslim countries have the death penalty for blasphemy in their legislation. Most prescribe prison sentences and fines. Pakistan includes the death penalty explicitly in its Islamized penal code for insults to the Prophet, but while there have been several sentences passed by the courts there have to date been no executions.

Laws on blasphemy in all faiths have a long and often shameful history. The notion that a person could be punished for expressing, either intentionally or unintentionally, an opinion deemed offensive to the beliefs of others is difficult in a free society. The perception of insult is by its nature subjective and the possibility that one group might have the power to punish another, or even its own, on such an arbitrary basis opens the door for abuse of power, malicious prosecution, and the persecution of religious minorities.

The last execution for blasphemy in England was in the seventeenth century, and the last custodial sentence was in 1922. Other prosecutions, mostly private, have taken place, and some have been upheld, up to the point where the blasphemy law was revoked in 2008. The law only gave protection to Christianity and therefore had become untenable in a multicultural society. The function of the law has now been taken over in part by the Racial and Religious Hatred Act of 2006, where the emphasis is on preventing hatred and the incitement of violence between religious groups.

Most of us would not want to give offence to people of other religions and would be mortified if we felt we had done so. The greatest problem is perhaps ignorance about religion and of each other's beliefs and sensitivities. It may be more important than ever for social cohesion for schools to promote religious education and mutual understanding of religion and culture to enable us to live together in peace and mutual respect.

15(B) GEORGE:

Most of the taxi drivers in Walsall, where I live, are Muslims, and I often get into interesting conversations with them. On one occasion we discussed blasphemy, and the driver said that insulting Allah or Muhammad was equivalent to someone insulting one's wife or husband. Dawoud mentions deep love and respect for the Prophet Muhammad, and the followers of all three Abrahamic faiths give God and their founder-leaders the kind of love and respect that equals or surpasses the esteem one holds for one's spouse and family.

As Dawoud says, few Muslims had read *The Satanic Verses*, and the same goes for the rest of the public, many of whom seemed to think that Muslims were being unduly touchy, or that Salman Rushdie simply misjudged the scale of the offence he was likely to cause. However, if

Rushdie did not know that Muslims would be outraged by Muhammad being portrayed as getting drunk, and the angel Jibril (Gabriel) eating pork, then he would have been very ignorant indeed. Likewise it should have been obvious to the editors of the Danish newspaper *Jyllands-Posten* that – to put it mildly – it was quite unacceptable to publish a cartoon of the Prophet Muhammad with a bomb in his turban, only four years after the 9/11 bombing of the World Trade Center.

The British public has a low level of religious literacy, and the fact that religion is progressively less understood can easily cause people to minimize the impact of such attacks on people's faiths. On several occasions I have heard people voice the opinion that religious believers ought to be able to take a joke, that Rushdie and the cartoonists were contributing to public debate on religious matters (although they don't explain how), or that we surely have the right to criticize another religion. Those who offer such defences might well take my taxi driver's advice to heart and consider how they would feel if someone wrote a novel about their husband frequenting a brothel, or some such scenario.

Of course, I am aware that my own faith was founded by someone who was accused of being a blasphemer. What is blasphemy to one person can be a deep-seated conviction to another, and Christians view Jesus as someone who appropriately challenged the religious status quo of his time. There are times when prevailing religious beliefs and practices need to be called into question, and one of the worries about redefining the blasphemy law to include all faiths was that it might preclude the kind of forceful dialogue in which the present authors are engaged. It is vital in a free society, with its spirit of enquiry and discussion, that people are able to voice criticisms and disagreements, without their targeted recipients feeling threatened, slandered, or blasphemed against.

Dawoud rightly points out that in the past blasphemy laws have protected the Christian faith, and not others, which can also be the recipients of hatred and disparaging comments, perhaps more so than Christians. In a multi-faith society it is only right that all faiths should be treated on an equal footing, and I believe it was a right decision in 2008 to abolish the common-law offences of blasphemy and blasphemous libel in England and Wales. The Racial and Religious Hatred Act (2006) seems a much more promising way of dealing with hate-provoking comments against someone's religion, since it uses the criterion of their likely effects on society, rather than arcane opinions about what kinds of remarks are likely to offend the deity.

One worry that was expressed at the time of these changes in British law related to religious humour. A number of professional actors such as Rowan Atkinson – renowned for his religious comedy – expressed concerns that they might be subject to prosecution for some of their sketches. The question of religious humour is a difficult one. When *The Life of Brian* was released in 1979 I was living in Plymouth where the City Council was conservative enough to ban the film. In some venues where it was shown, it was picketed by evangelical Christians. In order to see it I had to wait until I was next in London, and it remains one of my favourite films.

Is the film blasphemous? And does it matter whether or not it is? It's hard to tell whether or not God approves of it. The Bible does talk about laughter in heaven (Psalm 2:4), and there can be dangers in regarding one's faith as deadly serious. But religious humour has its boundaries: I think the publication of the Danish cartoons was certainly an editorial misjudgment. Perhaps the test of religious humour is the extent to which members of that faith are able to join in the laughter.

15(C) DAN:

In the modern Jewish world blasphemy is not an issue. Living in a secularized and assimilated community, most Jews have largely ignored traditional teachings about defiling God's name or abusing their religious heritage. It is unknown for Jews to share the kind of outrage expressed in Islamic countries about the vilification of the faith. On the contrary, most Jews are relaxed about criticisms of any aspect of their heritage. For the vast majority of Jews, Muslim reactions about cartoons satirizing Muhammad are incomprehensible.

This does not mean, however, that Judaism lacks specific teaching about blasphemy. On the contrary, within Jewish sources blasphemy is referred to as *birkat ha-shem*, which is understood as reviling God. One guilty of this offence is called a blasphemer. In two main passages in the Bible (Leviticus 24:10–23; 1 Kings 21:8–13), the penalty for this crime is stoning to death. Yet, it is not entirely clear what is involved. It could mean either to insult God, or to curse God. According to the Gospels of Matthew and Mark (Matthew 26:63–66; Mark 14:53–64), Jesus was tried by the Sanhedrin on a charge of blasphemy. New Testament scholars have puzzled over the historicity of this event as well as the nature of the offence – thus it is not entirely clear how blasphemy was understood in New Testament times.

In the Mishnah (Sanhedrin 7:5), the penalty of stoning applies only when the blasphemer used the sacred name of God (the *Tetragrammaton*) with which to curse God. The *Tetragrammaton* was not to be pronounced except by the high priest once a year in the Holy of Holies in the Temple on *Yom Kippur*. The curse would thus be: Let God (the *Tetragrammaton*) curse God (the *Tetragrammaton*). As the Jewish scholar Louis Jacobs in *The Jewish Religion* points out, this would make the whole offence impossible in practice, since the blasphemer would ask God to curse Himself. In any event, Judaism holds that it is a severe offence to revile God. In medieval times, courts placed a ban on anyone guilty of this crime. Yet, as far as the full offence of blasphemy is concerned, it remained purely theoretical, and it appears that trials for blasphemy hardly ever took place in post-biblical times. There is one additional point I should note: to insult the Torah, Moses, the prophets, or the sages was also held to be a serious offence. This was an extension of the blasphemy law, but was not covered by the death penalty even in theory.

Despite these historical precedents concerning blasphemy, it is not surprising that most Jews are not disturbed by criticisms of their tradition. Judaism itself has undergone a revolutionary development in modern times with the emergence of a wide range of interpretations of the Jewish past. Beginning in the early nineteenth century with the rise of Reform Judaism, Jews themselves criticized their own traditions and called for substantial revisions to the faith. The development of biblical criticism questioned assumptions about Mosaic authorship of the Torah. In addition, rabbinic interpretation of the Law was similarly challenged, and modern Jewish movements have espoused revision and change.

No longer do Jews live in ghettos or *shtetls* (Jewish villages) in closed, isolated communities. In essence, Judaism has liberated itself from the fetters of the past. This is the result of internal self-criticism, and such changes heralded the creation of modern movements based on continuing reinterpretation. To the Jewish mind, Christians and Muslims who denounce critics of their traditions as heretics and blasphemers are living in the past. They are viewed as backward and unenlightened. Throughout our discussion, I have myself expressed such a view. To my mind, Christian and Muslim traditionalists should allow the light of modern knowledge and discovery to shine on their faiths, and they should seek to make their religions relevant to modern believers.

15(D) GEORGE:

I agree with Dan that the Gospel account of Jesus' trial is confusing. It was not necessarily blasphemous to claim to be the messiah and, according to Mark, Jesus volunteers the evidence that the high priest needs, despite the absence of witnesses (Mark 14:53–64). In Matthew, Jesus is more equivocal, and in both accounts it seems to be Jesus' reference to the Son of Man sitting at God's right hand – an allusion to Daniel 7:13 – that causes the outrage (Matthew 26:64–65). Perhaps the Gospel writers hesitated to portray Jesus as a blasphemer. John's Gospel is more explicit: in a separate incident, some Jews threatened to stone Jesus "for blasphemy, because you, a mere man, claim to be God" (John 10:33). However, Jesus does not receive the Jewish penalty for blasphemy – stoning, as Dan mentions – but the Roman penalty of crucifixion.

In the Leviticus passage to which Dan refers, God instructs Moses to "take the blasphemer outside the camp" (Leviticus 24:14). This instruction is significant. While neither of us would recommend the stoning that ensued, anyone who speaks contemptuously against their faith has by that very act declared themselves to be outside that faith community. We cannot belong to an organization that we treat with contempt.

Religious bodies have a right to determine who is inside and who is outside and, although modern-day heresy trials are rare, a religious community has a right, as well as a duty, to ensure that its leaders are providing sound doctrine and practice, and that its sacred space is being duly respected. When the Russian punk rock group Pussy Riot staged their demonstration inside Moscow's Cathedral of Christ the Saviour in February 2012, the church's security officials justifiably took action. The state-imposed penalties that ensued – two years' imprisonment – were less acceptable, and raise the question of when civil law should step in, for what reasons, and what sanctions are appropriate.

When Mary Whitehouse, the founder of the National Viewers and Listeners Association, instigated legal proceedings in December 1976 against *Gay News* for publishing James Kirkup's poem "The Love that Dares to Speak Its Name", different issues were involved. The poem led to a successful prosecution under blasphemy laws that most of us thought belonged to the history books. Few people were able to read the poem, and even media reports did not describe its contents in any detail. The poem remains banned in Britain, although it can easily be accessed on the Internet. It portrays the centurion at Jesus' crucifixion taking his body down from the cross and proceeding to have a sexual relationship with his corpse. Denis Lemon, then editor of *Gay News*, claimed that Kirkup's purpose was "to celebrate the absolute universality of God's love", although this interpretation was no doubt lost on most readers.

There is an important difference between the Pussy Riot case and the Kirkup poem. Anyone who enters a cathedral has a right to expect an atmosphere of quiet and reverence. By contrast, readers of *Gay News* might expect provocative contributions on gay and lesbian issues that challenge the status quo. Those who do not wish to read such material would be well advised to find alternative literature. If the poem had been displayed on a hoarding, or nailed to the door of Canterbury Cathedral, it would have been a different matter – although more modern laws such as the various Obscene Publications Acts would be more relevant. Dan is right in suggesting that traditionalists need to move into the twenty-first century on such matters. Invoking age-old blasphemy laws suggests that it is the role of the state to maintain religious discipline. The state's role is rather to ensure public safety and the protection of human rights.

Dan comments on the Muslim reaction to blasphemy. While *The Satanic Verses* caused grave offence to Muslims, I think those who organized demonstrations and book burnings were misguided. Their actions only gave further publicity to Salman Rushdie, leading to greatly increased sales. A much better strategy would surely have been quietly to ignore the book, which might have disappeared into oblivion.

As religious believers, we need to come to terms with the fact that there will always be those who ridicule and insult our various faiths. Jesus himself experienced such opposition. His own teaching on blasphemy is found in a rather cryptic saying: "People can be forgiven all their sins... but whoever blasphemes against the Holy Spirit will never be forgiven" (Mark 3:28–29). The context of this remark was an accusation that Jesus was possessed by Satan. He may have meant that it is much more serious to conflate truth and falsehood, and good and evil, than to make impious remarks about religion. Whatever he meant, he left God to impose the sanctions, rather than invoke the law or organize public demonstrations.

15(E) DAWOUD:

I understand Dan's point about a modern religion for a modern world but it has to be borne in mind that the majority of Muslims in the world do not live in modern Western democracies but in countries where, even if they are not theocracies as such, religious scholars and authorities are able to exert considerable influence, and where people expect to live and be governed in accordance with Islamic law. For Muslims the attachment to a heritage, continuity of tradition, and the unchanging nature of the core of the faith are fundamental. The narrative of the life of the Prophet and the early years of Islam is an essential part of the faith that unites them all. Regardless of their ethnicity or nationality, it is a shared history that they experience as an immediate reality. They live with the received history as if it were the lives of their own immediate family, and when they discuss the example of the Prophet it is as if it were something that had happened in their own lifetimes. The Prophet and the family of the Prophet are intensely real to Muslims and any slight is deeply felt. George recounts the explanation of a Muslim driver who describes an insult to the Prophet as being comparable to an insult to one's spouse and I would agree that for many people this is how it would feel. Another way to try to describe the offence felt would be to ask people of faith to imagine the revulsion they would feel at the desecration of their place of worship.

I am not proposing that Muslims should receive special treatment in this or that their feelings and sensitivities are any more important or should be given greater consideration than those of others, nor would I suggest that anyone should be above criticism. All I would suggest is that out of simple politeness and consideration and desire to live harmoniously we should try to avoid offending each other or hurting each other's feelings. As George emphasizes, the best way to do this is through understanding and by knowing more about each other, which is what we are trying to do here.

At the same time, I think we should also make an effort not to be offended where no offence is intended. In 2007 in a story that made international headlines, an English schoolteacher working in Sudan was arrested and charged with blasphemy after allowing her class to name the class teddy bear Muhammad. This was done in complete innocence and with no idea that this would cause such offence, leading to protests in the street calling for her execution. Many Muslim organizations including the Muslim Council of Britain spoke out against the charge of blasphemy, describing it as a disgraceful decision defying common sense. Although it was initially thought that it was oversensitive parents who had initiated the complaint, it later transpired that it was a school secretary, and the parents and children all testified in favour of the teacher. Eventually, through mediation by two British Muslim peers, she was pardoned and released. In subsequent interviews she expressed her respect for Islam and Muslims and how mortified she felt at the thought that she could have caused such offence. This might easily have been avoided by some basic knowledge and cultural awareness, but equally it was clear that many Muslim organizations and the governments of other Muslim countries found it unacceptable that a person should be persecuted in this manner when there was no intention to offend.

If our faith is sound, then it cannot be threatened by the words of others, particularly where this is unintended. George argues that ultimately judgment should be left to God in this, and the Qur'an agrees.

> *And do not insult those they invoke other than Allah, lest they insult Allah without knowledge. Thus We have made pleasing to every community their deeds. Then to their Lord is their return, and He will inform them about what they used to do. (6:108)*

15(F) DAN:

The discussion about blasphemy opens up a significant area of difference between our three faiths. Both Christianity and Islam are primarily religious in character. Although there are ethnic characteristics of both faiths, they are so large and all-embracing, it is difficult to perceive them as ethnic communities. It makes no sense to regard oneself as a Christian or Muslim if one is a non-believer (even if one is born into the tradition). In addition, there are so many ethnic groups included within both religions that it is impossible to define any form of ethnic identification. What binds the faithful is an allegiance to the beliefs and practices of Christianity and Islam.

The Jewish community is different. According to tradition, a person is Jewish if he or she has a Jewish mother regardless of an adherence to the belief system of Judaism or its multifarious practices. Today in Israel and the diaspora there are millions of Jews who have no desire to affiliate with the Jewish religion. Instead, they view themselves as Jewish by birth and therefore ethnically related to all other Jews. That means that *Klal Ysirael* (the body of Israel) includes the strictly Orthodox, modern Orthodox, Conservative, Reform, Reconstructionist, and Humanistic Jews, as well as individuals who are secular and uncommitted. Judaism is thus incredibly variegated, lacking a unifying religious structure. In previous centuries, of course, this was not the case. Prior to the Enlightenment in the late eighteenth century, the vast majority of Jews lived their lives in accordance with Jewish law.

What this means in practice is that the concept of blasphemy has lost its significance in Jewish life. As I indicated, the Torah and rabbinic sources define blasphemy in precise terms. Not only was it a sin to vilify God, but one was forbidden to denigrate historical personages such as Moses. It was also sinful to disparage the great rabbinic sages of the past. Today some traditionalists continue to subscribe to these prohibitions, taking the notion of blasphemy seriously. However, on the whole most Jews are quite relaxed about criticisms of the faith as well as its leaders.

As I mentioned previously, most Jews find it incomprehensible that Muslims feel such outrage about caricatures of Muhammad. It is simply incomprehensible that Jews could ever have such strong feelings about cartoons of Moses, the prophets, or rabbinic sages. Indeed, Jews are renowned for telling jokes about and against themselves. Jewish humour is filled with self-depreciation. In other words, Jews do not take themselves seriously in the way that Muslims and some Christians do. In modern society there could never be the equivalent of a Jewish *fatwa* against those who ridicule the faith.

This does not mean, however, that Jews are relaxed about anti-Semitism or anti-Zionism. On the contrary, there are a variety of pro-Jewish and pro-Zionist lobbies that function in many ways. The Anti-Defamation League in the United States, for example, is constantly on the alert for manifestations of anti-Semitic opinion and activity. In Britain the Jewish Board of Deputies undertakes to safeguard the welfare of the community and is alert to any form of attack on Jews or Jewish institutions. Such bodies, however, do not press charges of blasphemy against individuals or organizations. Instead, they undertake to safeguard the interests of Jews, and actively resist any form of attack against the Jewish community.

Perhaps I should mention that in the last few years I have acted as an expert witness for the Counter-Terror Agency of the Crown Prosecution Service. Two British anti-Semites had vilified Jews on the Web, and they were charged with inciting hatred under the Race Relations Act. After a lengthy trial, they were charged and imprisoned. Here British law enabled the community to defend itself. I heartily endorse such an approach to hate crime, but this is far removed from the charge of blasphemy that both of you have been discussing within your respective traditions.

CHAPTER 16

THE MIDDLE EAST PROBLEM

The Israel–Palestinian conflict is one that bitterly divides Jews and Muslims. Is Israel the Jews' homeland, given to them by God? Or have the Arabs firmly established their right to live in Palestine? Where do Christians stand in this situation? Is the Jews' return to Zion a part of God's plan, or is Christian Zionism a dangerous movement that fuels the controversy? The land has important significance for all three faiths. Is there any hope of a solution?

16(A) DAN:

Of all topics that divide Jews from Muslims in the modern world, the key area of dispute is the Holy Land. Jews claim it as their rightful homeland. Palestinians contend they are the indigenous population whose land has been stolen by Jewish colonialists. But there is a Christian background to this conflict. As I have mentioned previously, the Jewish people have been subjected to twenty centuries of hatred and murder at the hands of Christians wherever they have lived. The church stands guilty of two millennia of such contempt. This poisonous attitude is rooted in the Gospels, Paul's epistles, and the writings of the Church Fathers. Whatever positive Jewish–Christian encounter exists in contemporary society, this legacy of Judeophobia cannot be ignored. It is the constant stain with which both communities have to live.

Secular Zionism is the direct outcome of this terrible history. At the end of the nineteenth century the Austrian journalist Theodor Herzl witnessed the Dreyfus trial in Paris of an innocent Jewish soldier. The crowds cried for his blood. Watching this outburst of antipathy, Herzl was convinced that Jews would never be secure in the lands where they lived as a minority. They would always be regarded as aliens, he believed. Always detested. Always persecuted. In Herzl's view, and in the eyes of other leading Zionists, there was only one way out of this problem: Jewish nationhood. In *The Jewish State*, Herzl called upon his co-religionists to join together in creating a place of refuge. Jews, he wrote, must bind together in this quest. It is their only salvation.

In 1897, a small number of fellow Zionists gathered together in Basle at the first Zionist Congress. Subsequently they met every year. As their leader, Herzl sought to obtain approval for their plan in Palestine from the Sultan and later from the British. In 1917 Arthur Balfour, representing the British government, issued a declaration to Lord Rothschild, who was viewed as the head of the Jewish community in Britain, expressing the British government's intention to create a homeland for the Jewish people while at the same time protecting the rights of the Arab population. Throughout the Jewish world Jews were elated by this commitment. Arabs in Palestine, however, were deeply dismayed.

From the outset Jewish settlers purchased land from Arabs, in some cases absent Arab landlords. Yet, the native Arab population was horrified. In a series of violent attacks on the Jewish population, they expressed their anger and dismay. The leader of the Arab revolt, the Grand Mufti of Jerusalem, sought to drive the Jews out of Palestine. This notorious figure, who later met Hitler in Germany to gain his support against the Jews, was a relative of Dawoud's.

Once the United Nations agreed to the partition in 1947 and the State of Israel was declared the following year, the Arabs launched a major attack on the new Jewish nation. For Jews this was the War of Independence. For Arabs, it was the *Nakba* (catastrophe). This was the beginning of a series of wars between Israel and its neighbours, and the conflict has consumed Jewish consciousness ever since. In its wake established Jewish communities in Arab lands have fled from their countries of residence. Jew against Palestinian. Jew against Arab. Today there is a new kind of anti-Semitism, as vicious and as corrosive as any form of previous religious or racial hatred. In summary, it was the Christians who inaugurated this terrible chain of events. It has been the Muslims who have kept alive such animosity. If you ask why Jews and Muslims, and for that matter why Jews and Arabs, do not get along, the answer is clear.

16(B) DAWOUD:

We do not have the space here to do much more than scratch the surface of the issues of the Middle East, about which so much has been said and written over the course of the last century. The risk is that we will just repeat the simplistic and selective mantras of our respective sides of the argument. The Middle East is, however, infinitely more complex than the received narratives of the two sides suggest.

There are episodes in the history of the Middle East that have left lasting marks on the relationships between our faiths, not least the Crusades of the eleventh and twelfth centuries when Christian armies from all over Europe attempted and ultimately failed to capture and hold Jerusalem and the Holy Land. Jerusalem is important to all of our faiths, and at the beginning of the first Crusade it had been under Muslim rule for more than 400 years.

Overall, however, Jews, Christians, and Muslims lived alongside each other in peace for centuries. There are ancient Christian communities in many parts of the Arab world, and there have been strong and prosperous Jewish communities throughout the region. Jewish life and Jewish scholarship flourished there until the middle of the twentieth century. The Cairo Geniza documents found in the storeroom of the Ben Ezra Synagogue in Old Cairo in the late nineteenth century give a picture of Jewish life in Egypt, North Africa, and the Eastern Mediterranean and beyond over a period of a thousand years and include a range of religious scholarship, court documents, and business records. The Ottoman empire provided a refuge for Jews from the Inquisition in Spain in the late fifteenth century and some Jews emigrated to Egypt and other parts of the Arab world in the nineteenth century to escape persecution in Europe, going on to establish some of the most successful businesses in the region.

It would be wrong to suggest that relationships between the communities were always ideal, and different Muslim dynasties and regimes took different approaches, but for the greater part there was a coexistence in which all communities were able to follow their own faiths and to thrive.

The reasons that caused the Jews of Europe to seek a safe haven are entirely understandable. The early Jewish settlers in the first *Aliyah* to Palestine in the late nineteenth century came to build a life and formed peaceful, idealistic, mostly agricultural communities. The land could have accommodated many immigrants, who could have contributed to the development of the country alongside its inhabitants. Some land was, indeed, purchased, but this was insignificant compared with that which was later occupied and taken by force.

The indigenous population was afraid of the Zionist ambition in Palestine, but the turning point was the Balfour Declaration. At this point Palestine was still part of the Ottoman empire in its final years and Britain was making contradictory promises, with regard to a land that it did not possess, to the Zionists and to Sherif Hussein of Mecca in its desire to seek his support against the Ottomans. The Declaration talks about the creation of a national home for the Jewish people, but the people, Muslims and Christians, whose home Palestine was at that time are simply dismissed as "existing non-Jewish communities", not the many and diverse peoples that they actually were and whose opinion in the matter was not sought.

Naturally the indigenous population resisted the usurpation of their land – but Dan has not mentioned the terrorist activities of the Irgun, which is considered responsible for the bombing of the King David Hotel in Jerusalem, and the Deir Yassin massacre, which was used to terrorize the inhabitants of other villages to flee their homes, and the Stern Gang, whose stated aim was forcibly to evict the British and allow unrestricted immigration. The so-called War of Independence and the creation of the State of Israel was a *Nakba*, a catastrophe for the Palestinians, leaving more than 400 villages destroyed and almost a million people as refugees. Sixty-five years on they remain refugees, stateless and dispossessed. It was also a catastrophe for the ancient Jewish communities of the Middle East, a majority of whom had no desire to leave their settled lives to emigrate to Israel but were forced to do so by the anger stirred up in the Arab world by the Zionist project in Palestine.

There is no room here for a complete and balanced discussion of this issue. We could go over and over the old arguments but until we move beyond the history we will not move one step forward. Israel exists, and the Palestinians exist. How many more generations do we have to sacrifice? There are, however, numerous Israeli-Palestinian cooperative projects working for peace. This week I heard a talk by the founders of the Parents Circle, an organization of bereaved Israelis and Palestinians working together for dialogue and understanding. The message was "Do not be pro-Palestinian or pro-Israeli, be pro-Solution, otherwise all you will do is import our conflict into your countries."

15(C) GEORGE:

Although some prominent Christian leaders in the course of their church's history have been vehemently anti-Semitic, I think Dan has grossly exaggerated Christian anti-Semitism, and I think his readings of Paul and the Gospels can certainly be challenged. Paul never denies that the Jews continue to fall under God's covenant, and have not been cast off from Him (Romans 11:1).

Today a substantial proportion of Christians have great sympathy for the Jewish people. In my childhood we used to sing a hymn, which ran:

Let Zion's time of favour come;
O bring the tribes of Israel, home;
And let our wondering eyes behold
Gentiles and Jews in Jesus' fold.

Not all Christians aim to convert Jews, of course, but a good number, particularly in the Protestant tradition, view the gathering of Jews in their homeland as necessary in order for Christ to return, and for the programme of end-time events to be completed.

Christian Zionism – known as Restorationism until 1890 – began with the Protestant Reformation, and the Puritans brought such ideas to America. They gained further momentum with "dispensationalist" theology, frequently attributed to John Nelson Darby (1800–82), and made popular by Cyrus Scofield (1843–1921), who published a version of the Bible with an introduction that set out a number of "ages" in human history.

The various dispensations are defined differently by different proponents of the theory, but in essence the idea is that for a number of centuries (the Jewish Age) the Jews had their own country, but since the Babylonian exile, the Jews have spent many centuries without their own homeland, and that the years from the exile to the present day are the "Times of the Gentiles". A particular way of reading the Bible suggests to dispensationalists that the Gentile times are due to end or – according to some – have already ended. These conclusions are arrived at by means of examining biblical prophecy – principally the books of Daniel and Revelation – and performing various calculations on the times and dates to which they refer. Such ideas were particularly popular among Adventists, and continue to be held by groups such as the Jehovah's Witnesses. These Christians have seen modern-day events such as the 1917 Balfour Declaration and the establishment of the State of Israel in 1948 as predicted in biblical prophecy.

Although most Christians are wary of biblical numerology, many Christian fundamentalists have appropriated the idea of the Gentile Age, which is ending, heralding a Jewish Age, in which the Jewish people will return to their homeland. Prominent American fundamentalist preachers, such as Jerry Falwell and Pat Robinson, subscribe to these ideas, and they have been made popular by Tim LaHaye and Jerry B. Jenkins in their series of end-time novels, *Left Behind*.

Some Christian Zionists have held that the return of the Jews will be accompanied by their conversion to Christianity, while others are content to believe that the Jewish people have a special relationship with God, which might exempt them from this expectation. The Hebrew professor George Bush (1796–1859) – a distant relative of the former US presidents of the same name – wrote a book entitled *The Valley of Vision: or, The Dry Bones of Israel Revived* (1844). The book deplored the lawful oppression of Jews, and made a plea that they should have "a rank of honorable repute among the nations of the earth" by restoring the Jews to the land of Israel where the bulk would be converted to Christianity.

Religion and politics inevitably intertwine on the Middle East issue. If one adds to these considerations the US Jewish population, one can readily see why the US is typically pro-Israeli. The US has the largest number of Jews outside Israel, practically level pegging in number with the Israeli population. Proportionally 1.7 per cent of the US population are Jewish, compared with 0.6 per cent Muslim. Winning the Jewish vote is therefore an important consideration for American politicians. All this adds up to strong reason for the US to champion the Jewish cause.

However, while there exist a number of Christian Zionist organizations, such as Christians United for Israel (CUFI), and the Messianic Jewish Bible Institute (MJBI), not all Christians by any means endorse such ideas. On 22 August 2006, a number of Christian denominations endorsed a Jerusalem Declaration on Christian Zionism, and dissociated themselves from the movement, claiming that Zionism emphasized political and military activities in place of the gospel of Christ. In 2007 in the US, the National Council of Churches took an anti-Zionist stance, claiming that Zionism was not only harmful to peace in the Middle East, but treated Jews as pawns in a series of eschatological events, and Muslims as subordinate to Jews. Zionism, they claimed, was harmful to Middle East Christian relationships, as well as to interfaith dialogue.

So, many Christians would have much sympathy with Dawoud's arguments in favour of the Palestinians. Arguments based on the Jews' historical rights to a homeland, or on questionable interpretations of biblical prophecy, are to my mind extremely dangerous, and can only fuel Arab-Israel conflict. As Dawoud says, we must be pro-Solution, rather than pro-Arab or pro-Israeli.

16(D) DAN:

George seeks to exonerate Christians from the terrible legacy of Jew-hatred. But to do so would blind oneself to the horrors the Christian community has inflicted on the Jews for two millennia. As I pointed out, the New Testament served as the basis for the church's vilification of the Jews. According to the Church Fathers, the Jewish people are lawless and dissolute. Because of their rejection of Christ, the Jewish nation has been excluded from God's grace. This *Adversos Judaeos* teaching of the early Church Fathers continued into the medieval period. During the Crusades Christian mobs massacred Jewish communities. Throughout the Middle Ages Jews were detested. In the post-medieval period Jews continued to be regarded with contempt as exemplified by Martin Luther's diatribe against the Jews. In later centuries such animosity continued in Europe and elsewhere. It is this history of Christian Jew-hatred that has paved the way for the Holocaust.

What George overlooks in his account of Christian Zionism is the fact that these believers, while encouraging the restoration of the Jewish people in the Holy Land, in fact foresee the end of Judaism and the Jewish nation. Hal Lindsey, for example, in *The Late Great Planet Earth* asserts that biblical prophecy demands the national restoration of the Jews. However, in his view many Israelis will die in the final days of Armageddon. Jerusalem will become the spiritual centre of the entire world where Christ will rule supreme: all people will come to worship Jesus in this holy place. And – most significantly – the Jewish nation will vanish in this cataclysmic event. Judaism will be replaced by the true knowledge of Christ's redemptive power.

For Christian Zionists this is the goal of history in which the Jews will be swallowed up despite their return to Zion. Indeed, this is the theme of the short hymn that George refers to:

Let Zion's time of favour come;
O bring the tribes of Israel, home;
And let our wondering eyes behold
Gentiles and Jews in Jesus' fold.

In Jesus' fold! There is no difference between this aspiration and the ancient aim of the church to convert the Jewish people to the one true faith. It might appear that Christian Zionists are friends of the Jews. But their real aspiration is that the restoration of the Jews in Israel should serve as a prelude to the second coming of Christ. For Christian

Zionism there is no future for the Jews, nor a future for the Jewish faith. George cites the Christian Zionist movement as an example of a positive Christian response to the plight of the Jewish nation and their aspirations for a homeland. What he fails to acknowledge fully is the real goal of Christian Zionism: the fulfilment of the Christian longing for redemption which would result in the disappearance of the Jewish people and their religious heritage.

So I say to George as we near the end of this book that for positive Jewish–Christian encounter to take place, there must be a conscious recognition of the terrible history that has divided Christians from Jews over the centuries. In the past Jews and Christians have been bitter enemies. For Jews the cross has been the symbol of persecution and murder. The church has cast a dark shadow over the synagogue. And the Jewish quest to create a safe haven in Zion is the consequence of this terrible past. The Jewish community is united in its determination to survive. We are committed to a Jewish future, not one in which the nation will be consumed in a holocaust of destruction prior to Christ's coming.

In his response about the Middle East Dawoud has briefly outlined the relationship between Christians, Jews, and Muslims through the centuries. He is right to stress that there has been considerable positive encounter. The tragedy is that the modern conflict between Israelis and Palestinians has created mistrust and hatred between our two communities. I agree that the disappearance of Jewish communities in Arab lands is a terrible loss for both Jews and Muslims. Dawoud points out that violence has been the hallmark of the conflict between our two peoples for over a century. In my view the only way out of this deadlock is for a Palestinian state to emerge through negotiations between both sides. A two-state solution is the only way.

15(E) GEORGE:

Jews are not accurately described either as a religion, a race, an ethnic group, or a nation. Some 42 per cent of Israeli Jews describe themselves as "secular". The concept of race is problematic, and there is a prevalent view that there is no such thing. Jews come from a variety of countries and ethnic backgrounds, and may not necessarily have Moses as an ancestor. And of course only a minority of Jews live in Israel. However, the concepts of race, ethnicity, nation, and religious community are easily conflated, enabling Christian Zionists to regard Jews as having a special status. Another hymn in the Christian tradition has a line, "Ye seed of Israel's chosen race", which associates Jewish identity simultaneously with religious, national, and racial identity.

The hymn goes on to recommend, "Hail him who saves you by his grace", giving expression again to the view that the Jews must finally be saved through accepting Christ. But I think Dan possibly misconstrues my comments on Christian Zionism. I was certainly not endorsing them: I don't think I have a single Christian acquaintance who has any sympathy for authors like Hal Lindsey or LaHaye and Jenkins, whose millennialist dispensationalist writings are at best ridiculous, and at worst frightening. What is frightening about them is that a number of influential American religious figures, as well as some politicians, have bought into these ideas and allowed them to influence policies on the Middle East.

Of course Dan is right to home in on the phrase "in Jesus' fold" in the hymn I quoted. It was in the hymn book used in my childhood, over fifty years ago, and I doubt whether it is found in any currently used Christian hymnary. Although there are still organizations around like Jews for Jesus, more liberal Christians would not try to convert Jews to Christianity.

By reading their Bibles, many Christians share with Jews the perception that they are God's chosen people who were brought to the Promised Land, surrounded by enemies who displaced them at several points in their history, notably Babylonians, Greeks, and Romans. It is easy to think therefore that the Jews are people who have been deprived of "their land", and to have been persecuted and pilloried ever since, culminating in the Holocaust.

However, if one goes back into earlier history, the Jewish people acquired the Promised Land through invading Jericho and, as the Bible states, they "destroyed with the sword every living thing in it – men and women, young and old, cattle, sheep and donkeys" (Joshua 6:21). Perhaps if there were identifiable descendants of Canaanites still around today, they could also stake a claim to owning territory in the area!

The argument that Jews needed a safe haven where they would be free from persecution has some force. However, as Dawoud has ably argued in *The Palestine-Israeli Conflict* (co-authored with Dan), it is difficult to see what authority the British had to produce the Balfour Declaration, and one might cynically think that the British had commercial and strategic interests and not merely concern for the Jews. The Balfour Declaration clearly stated "that nothing shall be done which may prejudice the civil and religious rights of existing non-Jewish communities in Palestine". This is not what has happened, however. While Dan is right to point out that the present-day land of Israel did not come into existence through usurpation, but by Jews purchasing land from Arabs, not all their land has been acquired through legitimate commercial transaction. Consider, for example, the Jewish occupation of the West Bank, where the Jews have built opulent homes at the expense of making many of the Palestinians become refugees.

I recently spoke to a number of people from my own church who had returned from a Holy Land pilgrimage. They shared two principal impressions: the building on the West Bank, and the ubiquity of the Israeli soldiers, whom they found officious, particularly at the country's numerous checkpoints. It is ironic that an ethnic/religious group who claims to have been victimized throughout the ages now becomes the aggressor. In the same book Dawoud aptly quotes Edward Said: "So long as there is a military occupation of Palestine by Israel, there can never be peace."

I don't profess to have a solution to the Middle East conflict, and I don't know who has. It is hard to shake off centuries of persecution, conflict, and mistrust, often coupled with vested religious interests and justifications for our respective interests in the land. The Holy Land has particular significance for all three faiths, and somehow we must all learn to co-exist.

16(F) DAWOUD:

I think our discussion here shows how it is almost impossible to tease out the arguments of religion, ethnicity, economics, and politics in this area. At its heart this is a dispute about territory, not about religion, but religion has been brought into it by both sides as part of the rallying call. The Holy Land is important to all of us and is part of the heritage of all of our faiths and of the Old and New Worlds. I believe that the arguments of religion on both sides regarding rights to land are untenable and only distract us from the real arguments of ownership, possession, occupation, economics, resources, security, equality, and civil and human rights. We have barely even mentioned the Palestinian Christians who have suffered at the hands of Israel as badly as Muslim Palestinians with whom they stood shoulder to shoulder for decades, but whose lives are now becoming intolerable under the rule of Hamas. Nothing is simple or straightforward in the discussion of the Middle East. There is much that I can agree with in the points made by both Dan and George. There is indeed a great deal of scurrilous material about Jews and Israel in the Arab press and I would make no excuse for it, but at the same time one does not have to look far to find pernicious stereotypes of Arabs and Muslims throughout the Western media. Many cartoons of Arabs and Muslims in the US and Western media present the kind of stereotypes that would no longer be acceptable with regard to any other racial or religious group. In his *Reel Bad Arabs – How Hollywood vilifies a people*, Jack Shaheen catalogues and analyses 100 years of stereotyped images of bandits, wealthy oil shaykhs, lechers, greedy and evil villains, terrorists, and abusers of women in some 900 films. He quotes the author Sam Keen, who says: "You can hit an Arab free; they're free enemies, free villains – where you couldn't do it to a Jew or you can't do it to a black anymore." How often do we see Arabs or Muslims in films or on television as ordinary people who work, study, live, and love like everyone else? This kind of preconception has found its way into the racial profiling that takes place in our security systems and which has led to hate crimes not only against Arabs and Muslims but against people who look like them, including Hindus, Sikhs, and even Jews and

Arab Christians. In the words of Aldous Huxley, "The propagandist's purpose is to make one set of people forget that certain other sets of people are human."

There are many people both inside and outside the Israeli–Palestinian situation working for peaceful solutions. People want to live, they want to send their children to school, to work and build a life, a home, and a country, but at the same time there are those on both sides who, it seems, do not want peace but victory at any price, which in reality is impossible for either side. There is also the sense that both sides are condemned forever to carry the burden of other people's agendas. The rest of the Muslim world has adopted the Palestinian cause, thereby tying their hands and preventing them from finding a peaceful way forwards; at the same time the Israeli people are charged with a responsibility for the Zionist ambition and the Jewish community worldwide. Neither can lose face, but in the process, the anger, hatred, and misery are perpetuated; both sides have lost generations and no one even knows what it is like or might be like to live an ordinary life in peace. Dan mentions the proposed two-state solution, and I agree that this could be ideal, but Israeli "facts on the ground" in the form of settlements, militarily protected roads that only Israelis are allowed to use that criss-cross Palestinian lands, and the concrete scar of the Wall or "separation fence" make this increasingly difficult. Dan and I have debated this many times and we have discussed the possibility of a "Truth and Reconciliation" process along the lines of the South African post-apartheid model. This would require a genuine will for peace and coexistence, however, and some painful acknowledgment on each side of the wrongs that have been done. It would also require Israelis and Palestinians to treat each other as absolute equals. This is an ideal, but sadly I do not think we are there yet.

CHAPTER 17

CONCLUSIONS

How can we get along? Have our exchanges helped to clarify the issues that divide us, and are we any nearer to finding solutions for our differences? In this final section the authors offer their reflections on the discussion.

17(A) DAN:

We are now at the end of a long journey. Along the way we have surveyed a wide variety of topics, ranging from theology, to practice, to ethics. What has emerged is that, despite the many similarities between our three traditions, there is much that separates us. Perhaps that is unexpected given that Judaism, Christianity, and Islam emerged from the same source. We are all monotheists. Yet for over fifteen centuries our three faiths have been in conflict. This has been particularly true of Judaism and Christianity. Accused of killing Christ, Jews have been continually persecuted and massacred in Christian lands. We have lived in the shadow of the cross, fearing attempts to convert us. This terrible legacy of hatred continues to haunt the Jewish community, particularly given the Nazi quest to exterminate us. The Third Reich was motivated by racial rather than religious concerns, yet the stereotypical images of Jews fostered in previous centuries profoundly shaped the Nazis' perception of Jewry. It is not surprising that this history of horror continues to haunt Jewish–Christian relations in the modern world.

With regard to Jewish–Muslim encounter, the story is different. Jews and Muslims have much in common. For both faiths Abraham is central. He is our father, and we are bound together in belief about God's nature and activity. Both communities reject doctrines about the incarnation and the Trinity. Although Islam regards Jesus as a prophet, it is Muhammad who is central. For the Jew it is Moses. Yet despite the positive links between Jews and Muslims, Arab anti-Semitism has in modern times consumed the positive connections between our two faiths. For over a century, the conflict between Israel and the Palestinians has turned us into bitter enemies. Across the Islamic world, Jews are vilified. In Arab countries vicious anti-Semitic literature is continually disseminated, fostering deep hostility towards Israel and Jews in general.

This, then, is the past and current context of this book. The starting point is Jewish–Christian–Muslim suspicion and misunderstanding. But in our trialogue I think we have been able to surmount these barriers to fruitful encounter and have been able to reflect dispassionately on what unites and separates our three traditions. Most significantly it is the theological assumptions that divide us. For the Christian it is Jesus' life and message that is critical. He is messiah and Lord. Here is the fundamental parting of the ways. For Jews and Muslims such notions are impossible. This is, however, only the starting point of difference. In our survey of belief and practice we have uncovered a wide range of topics that separate us, from personal issues to more general concerns.

Nevertheless, I believe what is remarkable about this trialogue is the respect we have been able to show each other. It is reassuring that adherents of three faith traditions can speak candidly and critically. Even at crucial points of disagreement, we were prepared to listen and learn. If nothing else, our conversation highlights the possibility of fruitful discussion. Currently there exist a wide range of interfaith organizations that seek to foster global harmony. But all too often the adherents of faith traditions are reluctant to explore explosive issues. Their aim is reconciliation rather than understanding. This project is different. From the beginning we resolved to speak openly and honestly. It has been our aim to uncover discontinuities as well as points of similarity. It is our hope that this trialogue will serve as a model of what can be achieved in interfaith encounter, if members of different religions speak openly to one another. In a world torn by religious conflict, this task is more urgent than ever.

17(B) GEORGE:

A supporter of interfaith dialogue recently advocated the idea of "holy envy". By that he meant that we should do more than acknowledge points of agreement, but rather attempt to see features in other people's traditions that we lack, and would positively like to have. If I were to identify points that I envied in Judaism and Islam, I think it would be the sense of identity that one has as a Jew or Muslim, and the fact that they appear to practise their faith in an overtly religious rather than a merely cultural way.

There is much too on which we can agree. We share the same roots, worship the same God, and have the same concern for injustice and suffering. However, while we have found much in common among our three faiths, there remain some very serious points of divergence. In particular, I think Dan has overemphasized Christian anti-Semitism and the role of the Jew as the oppressed victim, although clearly I would not want to play down the indelible mark which the Holocaust has left. Dan is right to point out that some of the church's most prominent theologians, such as Chrysostom, Augustine, and Luther, have expressed anti-Jewish sentiments that Christians today can only deplore. However, I don't think the New Testament itself is anti-Semitic. With the possible exception of Luke, all its authors were Jewish, as were the earliest Christians. Paul (Saul) of Tarsus was a Jew, and he presents Christ's followers as being "grafted on" to God's chosen people, the Jews. It is hardly anti-Semitic to present the gospel as the fulfilment of the Jewish faith, or to deplore the Jews' rejection of Jesus as the messiah. This is no more than forceful expression of one's convictions. In more recent times Christians have explicitly stated that the Jews are not to be held responsible for Christ's death, and the Christian creeds explicitly state that Jesus "suffered under Pontius Pilate", not "was put to death by the Jewish Sanhedrin".

I think that many Christian preachers could afford to reappraise the portrait of the Pharisees as nitpicking legalists, and do more to portray

Conclusions

Jesus as a rabbi who interpreted the Torah. Paul's idea of being "grafted on" to God's covenant with the Jews indicates that without the Jewish faith there could be no salvation through Christ (Romans 11:1, 11–24). We owe our very existence to the Jews, and we understand our faith better when we try to understand Judaism.

Turning to Dawoud, I think that Islam presents a faith that is embedded in daily life, and is concerned with social justice and the welfare of the poor. However, I still think that Islam needs to move into the modern world. Muhammad himself did much to improve the status of women, but I think they have become left behind in much of the Muslim world. Women need to have equal rights in Islamic law, and they should not be prevented from engaging in basic activities such as driving cars, as they are in Saudi Arabia. I think they should be trusted to socialize with men, recognizing that friendship is possible without sexual attraction being involved.

I believe that Islam has still to engage with the European Enlightenment, as Dawoud himself acknowledges at one point (11F), and needs to ask critical questions about itself. Penalties such as amputation and lashing, for example, have no place in the twenty-first-century world, and I think that numerous Islamic states could afford to take aboard Western considerations about human rights. I am not satisfied with Dawoud's explanation that harsh penalties belong to local native religion. They are clearly prescribed in the Qur'an, but if Dawoud were right, then he would have embarked on source criticism of the Qur'an, acknowledging that Muhammad may have been influenced by the various surrounding religions of his locality. This is precisely what he wants to avoid, if he wants to maintain the Qur'an's status as direct revelation from Allah.

At a personal level, all three authors have got along really well. This is no doubt because our own personal fortunes are secure, and we have not felt ourselves to be victims of each other's prejudice and hatred, and do not have an agenda with each other about rights to land or property. When these issues impinge on one's own fortunes, however, getting along becomes much more problematic. We have not attempted to provide solutions to the serious political and social problems involving our three faiths. However, we hope that we have shown that it is possible to engage in frank discussion that goes beyond the cordiality of many interfaith gatherings. While recognizing points in common is an appropriate starting point for interfaith encounter, it is by acknowledging differences that we truly come to accept one another more fully.

17(C) DAWOUD:

Over the years all three of us have been involved in interfaith dialogue in one way or another. The interfaith movements have the highest of objectives in bringing together like-minded people of different faiths in positive interaction and cooperation. By their very nature, however, interfaith groups are self-selecting and open to understanding and accepting each other, and very often they avoid getting to grips with some of the difficult issues that concern all of our faiths.

In our discussions that have taken place over the greater part of a year we have touched on subjects ranging from doctrine and religious law to lifestyle and social attitudes and even politics. We have discovered that there is much that unites us, but there are issues that divide us perhaps irreconcilably and forever. What I think we have seen most clearly, however, is that we have only just scratched the surface of what there is to talk about. What we have done is to start to ask questions, and to answer them as honestly as we can, but then we have had to constrain our discussion to the scale of this book. We can only hope that this may offer food for thought for others to continue and expand the discussion. We are, I think, three fairly reasonable people, academics, men of a certain age and with a certain perspective on life; we have lived and worked in similar environments, and this probably gives us things in common that counterbalance any differences in religious outlook that we may have. Moreover, none of our faiths is monolithic. Within each there is enormous diversity of nationality, ethnicity, culture, and religious denomination and doctrine, and so none of us can really claim to speak for all of our co-religionists or to have presented all of their opinions. What I hope we have done is to explain some of the most important differences and similarities and offer some of the key topics for further discussion.

Conclusions

On a personal level, I feel that this has been a valuable experience and that I have learned a great deal. I think that we have demonstrated that it is quite possible for us to explain our differences to each other and to seek to understand each other in a civilized and amicable manner, trying to avoid either apologetics or proselytizing. We have not tried to gloss over the areas where our faiths disagree but have tried to be as frank as possible.

All of us believe in the same God, although we may worship Him in different ways. The God that I believe in says: "O mankind, indeed We have created you from male and female and made you peoples and tribes that you may know one another" (49:13). This verse is clear. If we accept that we are all God's creation, then we have a duty to find ways to accept and learn from each other, and I hope that this is what we have done here.

Our three faiths have come together in conflict, cooperation, and coexistence over many centuries. Our cultures have touched, interacted with, and influenced each other in more ways than most of us are aware of. We can recognize our differences and agree to disagree on points of theology, we can examine our histories and acknowledge the wrongdoings and injustices on both sides, but we must then seek ways to promote peaceful, equitable, and productive coexistence.

GLOSSARY

The following are quick definitions of specialized terms used in the text. The aim is to help understanding, rather than to give detailed explanations of what are sometimes complex, and at times contested, concepts. Readers who require fuller explanations should consult more comprehensive reference works.

Adventism: A Protestant movement originating in nineteenth-century America, expecting Christ's imminent return. Seventh-day Adventists observe Saturday rather than Sunday as their holy day.

Ahmadiyya: A movement founded in 1889, originally a reform movement within Sunni Islam.

Alevis: An Islamic movement, found mainly in Turkey, combining folk elements from the Sunni tradition with Sufism.

Apocrypha: Scriptures written in Greek during the inter-testamental period.

Ashkenazi: Jews of Western descent, particularly from Central and Eastern Europe.

Bahá'í: Originating as an Islamic group in late nineteenth-century Persia, followers declare their prophet Bahá'u'lláh as God's final messenger, beyond Muhammad, and not recognized by Muslims.

canon: Authoritative body of scripture.

Christian Zionism: Protestant movement attaching importance to the modern State of Israel as a prelude to Christ's return.

Christology: Branch of theology concerned with the nature of Jesus Christ.

Conservative Judaism: A progressive movement within Judaism.

covenant: A binding agreement between God and His people, with mutual obligations.

Deobandis: Conservative Islamic reform movement, founded in 1867.

dhikr: Remembrance or invocation of God as an act of devotion.

dispensationalism: Protestant Christian movement originating in the nineteenth century, which asserts a number of "ages" in history in which God's plan operates.

Glossary

Eid ul-Adha: Feast of sacrifice at end of *hajj*.

Eid ul-Fitr: Muslim celebration at the end of Ramadan.

Enlightenment: Western intellectual movement asserting the importance of reason rather than faith, spanning a variety of disciplines, arising around the eighteenth century.

eschatology: Doctrine relating to the end of time.

evangelical: Concerned with preaching the gospel. The word generally describes a conservative Protestant Christian who wants others to convert to the faith.

exile: Period of Jewish captivity in Babylon (587–528 BCE).

fundamentalism: A Protestant movement that originated in the late nineteenth century, affirming the inerrancy of the Bible.

Gemara: Commentary on the Mishnah, incorporated in the Talmud.

hadd (pl. hudud): Prescribed penalties for contraventions of acceptable behaviour.

hadith: Report, or body of reports, of the deeds, words, and things tacitly accepted by the Prophet Muhammad. *Hadith* may be described as "sound", "weak", or "fabricated", according to the reliability of tracing them back to Muhammad.

hajj: Pilgrimage to Mecca.

halal: Literally, "permitted"; foodstuffs that are lawful or prepared in the prescribed manner.

Hanbali: One of four main Sunni Islamic schools of jurisprudence, the other three being Hanafi, Shafi'i, and Maliki.

Hanif: Seeker of the one true God.

Hanukkah / Chanukkah: Jewish "festival of lights", occurring around December.

hypostasis / hypostatic union: Literally, "substance".

imam: Leader of Muslim worship.

jinn: Supernatural beings created by Allah, in addition to humans and angels.

Ka'aba: Sacred shrine at Mecca.

Kabbalah: Jewish mystical system, symbolically portrayed by the Tree of Life, depicting humanity's relationship with God.

Kaddish: Jewish prayer in Aramaic, used in the synagogue and at times of mourning.

kosher: (Jewish) food certified as conforming to Jewish dietary law.

Levites: Ancient Jewish Temple officials.

Maimonides: Twelfth-century Jewish philosopher.

Midrash: Rabbinical interpretation of Jewish scripture.

mikvah: Ritual bath for cleansing.

millennialism: Belief in an imminent end of human history.

Mishnah: The original written version of the "oral Torah" – commandments believed to have been given verbally to Moses in addition to the "written Torah".

mu'adhdhin **(muezzin):** One who calls Muslims to prayer.

Nag Hammadi: Place in Upper Egypt where ancient scrolls (mainly Gnostic writings) were discovered in 1945, and which include the Gospel of Thomas.

Noahide Covenant/Laws: Seven laws, believed to have been given to Noah after the flood, and which are prescribed for Gentiles as well as Jews.

Orthodox Christianity: Eastern churches, which separated from the West in 1054.

Orthodox Judaism: Traditional Judaism, which accepts the written and oral Torah as binding in their entirety.

Pentateuch: The first five books of the Jewish-Christian Bible, called the "Torah" in Judaism.

Pentecostalism: Protestant Christian movement originating in the early twentieth century, emphasizing "speaking in tongues".

progressive Judaism: Jewish movement, originating in the nineteenth century, which seeks to reconcile the Jewish faith with modernity.

Pseudepigrapha: Writings that are falsely attributed to another, usually famed, author.

rak'a(t): Sequence of prostration accompanied by recitation, with specified numbers of repetitions in formal prayers.

Reconstructionism: Twentieth-century progressive movement within Judaism.

Reform Judaism: Jewish movement, originating in Germany in the early parts of the nineteenth century, seeking to adapt the Jewish faith to modern society.

sacraments: Rituals that are outward signs of inner grace.

Salafi: Conservative traditionalist movement within Islam, arising in the second half of the nineteenth century, opposing Sufism and modernism.

Sanhedrin: Ancient Jewish religious court.

Sephardi: Spanish Jews, originating from the Mediterranean and Middle East.

seven deadly sins: Pride, covetousness, lust, envy, gluttony, anger, sloth.

shahada: Islamic confession of faith.

Shari'a: System of Islamic law.

Shema: Literally, "Hear!" (Deuteronomy 6:4) – Jewish assertion of monotheism.

Shi'a: Shortened form of *Shi'at Ali*, the Party of Ali. Resulting from the first major division in Islam, the Shi'a believe in the succession of Muhammad through his descendants, rather than the Caliphate.

Shi'i: Adjective from "Shi'a".

shirk: The ascription of partners to God; the claiming of divinity of any entity other than God.

Sunna: The custom or habit of the Prophet Muhammad, recorded in the *hadith*; also shortened form for *Ahl al-Sunna*, the People of the Sunna, often referred to as Sunni Muslims.

Sunni: Adjective from "Sunna". Sunni Muslims are the largest broad denomination in Islam, accepting the first four "Rightly Guided Caliphs" as the lawful successors to Muhammad.

sura: Chapter of the Qur'an.

Talmud: Containing the Mishnah and the Gemara, the Talmud is the compilation of rabbinical debates on theology and ethics, and is the principal source of Jewish law.

Tetragrammaton: Four-character Hebrew word for God (YHWH).

Torah: Jewish law books – Genesis, Exodus, Leviticus, Numbers, and Deuteronomy.

United Reformed Church: UK Protestant denomination founded in 1972 from the merger of the English Presbyterian and Congregationalist churches.

Vedas: Ancient Indian scriptures.

Wahabis: Ultra-conservative movement within Islam, opposed to Sufism, and seeking to return to the fundamentals, as found in the Qur'an and *hadith*.

wudu: Ritual ablution before prayer.

Zionism: *See Christian Zionism.*

BIBLIOGRAPHY

RECOMMENDED FURTHER READING

JUDAISM

Blech, Benjamin (2003). *The Complete Idiot's Guide to Judaism*. London: Alpha.

Cohn-Sherbok, Dan (2003). *Judaism: History, Belief and Practice*. London: Routledge.

Cohn-Sherbok, Dan (2010). *Judaism Today*. London: Continuum.

de Lange, Nicholas (2010). *An Introduction to Judaism*. Cambridge: Cambridge University Press.

Lehman, Oliver (2011). *Judaism: An Introduction*. London: I. B. Tauris.

Hoffman, C. M. (2008). *Teach Yourself Judaism*. London: Hodder.

Solomon, Norman (2000). *Judaism: A Very Short Introduction*. Oxford: Oxford University Press.

CHRISTIANITY

Chryssides, George D. (2010). *Christianity Today*. London: Continuum.

Chryssides, George D. and Wilkins, Margaret Z. *Christians in the Twenty-first Century*. Sheffield, UK: Equinox.

Hill, Jonathan (1996). *The History of Christianity*. Oxford: Lion Hudson.

Kim, Sebastian and Kim, Kirsteen (2008). *Christianity as a World Religion*. London: Continuum.

Woodhead, Linda (2004). *Christianity: A Very Short Introduction*. Oxford: Oxford University Press.

ISLAM

Esposito, John (2011). *What Everyone Needs to Know About Islam*. New York: Oxford University Press.

Geaves, Ron (2011). *Islam Today*. London: Continuum.

Gilliat-Ray, Sophie (2010). *Muslims in Britain*. Cambridge: Cambridge University Press.

Hourani, Albert (1991). *Islam in European Thought*. Cambridge: Cambridge University Press.

Lings, Martin (1983). *Muhammad, His Life Based on the Earliest Sources*. Cambridge: Islamic Texts Society.

Rahman, Fazlur (1979). *Islam* (2nd ed.). Chicago: University of Chicago Press.

Ruthven, Malise (2012). *Islam – A Very Short Introduction*. Oxford: Oxford University Press.

INTERFAITH DIALOGUE

Braybrooke, Marcus (1992). *Pilgrimage of Hope: One Hundred Years of Global Interfaith Dialogue*. London: SCM.

Braybrooke, Marcus (1996). *A Wider Vision: A History of the World Congress of Faiths 1936–1996*. Oxford: Oneworld.

Cohn-Sherbok, Dan, Chryssides, George D., and El-Alami, Dawoud Sudqi (2013). *Love, Sex and Marriage*. London: SCM.

Küng, Hans, and Kuschel, Karl-Josef (eds) (1993). *A Global Ethic: The Declaration of the Parliament of the World's Religions*. London: SCM and New York: Continuum.

Smock, David (2002). *Interfaith Dialogue and Peacebuilding*. Washington DC: United States Institute of Peace Press.

WORKS CITED IN THE TEXT

Augustine (1957). *The City of God*. John Healey (transl.) 2 vols. London: Dent.

British Council of Churches (1983). *Can We Pray Together?: Guidelines on Worship in a Multi-Faith Society*. London: British Council of Churches.

Bultmann, Rudolf (1926/1958). *Jesus and the Word*. London and Glasgow: Collins.

Bush, George (1844). *The Valley of Vision; or, The Dry Bones of Israel Revived, an attempted proof, from Ezekiel, chap. xxxvii, 1–14, of the restoration and conversion of the Jews*. New York: Saxton and Miles.

Church of England (1662/1968). *Thirty-Nine Articles (Articles of Religion)*. In *The Book of Common Prayer*. Glasgow: Collins: 388–396.

Clark, Stephen (1993). *How to Think about the Earth*. London: Mowbray.

Cohn-Sherbok, Dan (1997). *The Crucified Jew: Twenty Centuries of Christian Antisemitism*. Grand Rapids, MI.: Eerdmans.

Cohn-Sherbok, Dan and El-Alami, Dawoud (2001). *The Palestine-Israeli Conflict*. Oxford: Oneworld.

Farquhar, J. N. (1913/1930). *The Crown of Hinduism*. Oxford: Oxford University Press.

Fox, Matthew (1991). *Creation Spirituality: Liberating Gifts for the Peoples of the Earth*. San Francisco: HarperSanFrancisco.

Gerth, H. H. and Mills, C. Wright (transl. & ed.) (1947). *Max Weber: Essays in Sociology*. London: Kegan Paul.

Ibrahim, Ezzedin (transl.) and Davies-Johnson, Denys (transl.) (1997). *Al-Nawawi's Forty Hadith Qudsi* (new ed.). Cambridge: Islamic Texts Society.

Jacobs, Louis (1999). *A Concise Companion to the Jewish Religion*. Oxford: Oxford University Press.

Khalidi, Tarif (ed. and transl.) (1991). *The Muslim Jesus: Sayings and Stories in Islamic Literature*. Cambridge, MA: Harvard University Press.

LaHaye, Tim and Jenkins, Jerry B. (1995). *Left Behind: A Novel of the Earth's Last Days*. Wheaton, IL: Tyndale House.

Maimonides, Moses (1968). *Commentary to the Mishnah Aboth*. New York: Bloch.

Pope Paul VI (1965). *Nostra Aetate* ("For our time"). Declaration on the Relation of the Church to Non-Christian Religions. 28 October 1965. Accessible online at URL: www.vatican.va/archive/hist_councils/ii_vatican_council/documents/vat-ii_decl_19651028_nostra-aetate_en.html. Accessed 3 December 2013.

Shorter Catechism (1649/1969). In *The Confession of Faith; Agreed upon by The Assembly of Divines at Westminster*. Edinburgh: William Blackwood and Sons: 113–132.

Vardy, Peter (2010). *Good and Bad Religion*. London: SCM.

Vatican (1994). *Catechism of the Catholic Church*. London: Geoffrey Chapman.

Wansbrough, John (1977). *Quranic Studies: Sources and Methods of Scriptural Interpretation*. Oxford: Oxford University Press.

INDEX

Index

Kook, Abraham Isaac   141
Küng, Hans   109

lesbianism   147, 149, 150, 154, 156, 206
Luther, Martin   194, 218

Maimonides, Moses   32, 39, 40, 55, 164, 175
marriage   27, 71, 74–75, 146–152, 154–58, 184, 185, 186
Mary/Maryam, mother of Jesus   30, 33, 38, 47, 52, 98
Mendelssohn, Moses   62, 113
miracles   53, 60, 139
Mishnah   16, 95, 174, 175, 188, 189, 204
mission   52, 61, 108–110, 111, 113–16, 119
monasticism   152, 160, 166, 170, 171
Moses/Musa   21, 23, 42, 43, 48, 55, 56, 59, 79, 83, 130, 174, 177, 180, 187, 189, 204, 205, 210, 220, 225
myth   23, 25, 26, 57, 66

Nahmanides   77
Nakba   212, 214
Noah/Nuh   48, 61, 113, 115, 136, 142
Noahide Covenant   61, 113, 115–16, 118, 138, 177

Orthodoxy, Christian   33, 73, 87, 98, 133, 147, 148, 189
Orthodoxy, Jewish   18, 24, 55, 57, 62, 65, 71, 77, 124–25, 128, 130, 131, 134, 138, 149, 155, 158, 175, 180, 209

Palestine   11, 24, 40, 97, 155, 175, 211, 212, 214–15, 221
Paul of Tarsus   19, 44, 50, 58, 59, 72, 74, 79, 88, 27, 138, 139–140, 149, 170, 177, 178, 196, 211, 215, 226–27
persecution   78, 80, 99, 103, 105, 115,

133, 195, 197, 201, 208, 212, 213, 219, 220, 221, 224
Pharisees   19, 42, 43, 51, 59, 142, 226
politics   45, 48, 123, 130, 133, 178, 185, 191, 217, 220, 222, 227, 228
polygamy/polygyny   147, 151–52
poverty   19, 28, 153, 160–61, 162, 164, 166, 170–71, 180, 190–91, 196, 198
prayer   16, 27, 28, 36, 39, 60, 72, 75, 76, 81, 83–87, 89–91, 99, 100, 124, 135, 175
prophets   21, 26, 30, 31, 36, 42, 46, 47–48, 51–54, 59–61, 66–67, 83, 93, 104, 113, 130, 164, 188, 199, 204, 210
proselytism   76, 79, 82, 108, 111–12, 229
Protestantism   19, 23, 33, 73, 84, 87, 88, 98, 105, 109, 133, 147, 171, 215
psychology   17, 23, 25
punishment   21, 22, 26, 60, 79, 82, 114, 151, 180, 182, 184, 185, 200

Rahner, Karl   109
Ramadan   28, 76, 87, 95, 100, 106, 145, 163
reconciliation   16, 26, 50, 96–99, 105, 116, 223, 225
redemption   18, 24, 25, 41, 45, 59, 66, 188, 219
Reform Judaism   24, 70, 115, 124, 131, 140, 142, 150, 155, 181, 204, 209
repentance   16–18, 21, 27, 81, 96, 98–99, 188, 189, 200
resurrection   18, 20, 21, 44, 45, 58, 97, 152
revelation   21, 24, 25, 29, 30, 42, 55–64, 67, 111, 113, 181, 190, 227
ritual   27, 32, 43, 50, 62, 71, 79, 83, 85–87, 91, 92, 94, 99, 104, 107, 113, 118, 137, 141, 155, 158, 174–77, 181, 193